United Nations Peace-Keeping Operations: A Military and Political Appraisal

PRAEGER SPECIAL STUDIES IN
INTERNATIONAL POLITICS AND PUBLIC AFFAIRS

United Nations Peace-Keeping Operations: A Military and Political Appraisal

James M. Boyd

Foreword by
Leland M. Goodrich

PRAEGER PUBLISHERS
New York • Washington • London

PRAEGER PUBLISHERS
111 Fourth Avenue, New York, N.Y. 10003, U.S.A.
5, Cromwell Place, London S.W.7, England

Published in the United States of America in 1971
by Praeger Publishers, Inc.

Library of Congress Catalog Card Number: 72-143966

Printed in the United States of America

FOREWORD

The major success of the United Nations in the
maintenance of international peace and security--
according to the Charter, its primary purpose--has
been its peace-keeping operations. Because they
have been so regarded, and have stood out in pleasant
contrast to some of the more modest accomplishments,
and even failures, of the Organization in the peace
and security field, it is only natural that they have
received a great deal of attention not only from
serious students but also from commentators and
others writing for a larger public. As a consequence,
the literature on the topic is very extensive and, on
the whole, of good quality. What, then, can another
book contribute?

James Boyd brings to his contribution to the
subject a rather unusual combination of experiences.
When he first came to Columbia University for a
year's academic experience, he was an officer in the
U.S. Air Force who had been posted in Egypt at the
time of the invasion of that country by Israeli and
then British and French military forces. In my
seminar at Columbia, he became interested in the
analysis of United Nations peace-keeping operations
against the background of his own extensive and
varied military experience. Subsequent to his period
of residence at Columbia, he was appointed to the
U.S. Delegation to the United Nations Military Staff
Committee. He also participated actively in the
work of the Special Committee on Peace-Keeping
Operations (Committee of 33) as adviser to the U.S.
representative on the Committee.

Writing with the advantages of this varied
experience, Colonel Boyd is able to analyze and
evaluate United Nations peace-keeping operations not
only from the point of view of the serious student
of international affairs, but also from the angle
of the military man who is aware of the practical
requirements of successful military operations and
the difficulties in the way of combining military

units from different countries with diverse operational methods and traditions. Add to these the
special frustrations that military men must face
when called upon to use the restraints peace-keeping
forces must exercise when faced with the uncertainties
and provocations encountered in performing the varied
missions of peace-keeping forces.

This study provides anyone interested in United
Nations peace-keeping operations with an analysis
that is firmly grounded in an understanding of the
organizational, political, and military aspects of
the problem. At the same time, it is forward-looking,
as the author does not share the view so commonly
held today that peace-keeping is a thing of the past.
He believes that it has a future, and that one way
to assure this future is to do now what is necessary
to make future peace-keeping operations more efficient
and effective.

Leland M. Goodrich

University of Toronto

ACKNOWLEDGMENTS

Few works of this nature are solely the product of one individual's efforts. The present study is no exception.

The research was begun while a Research Associate with the Institute for War and Peace Studies, Columbia University, during the academic year 1964-65 and continued in connection with the completion of Ph.D. studies at Columbia through 1968. I am particularly indebted for the advice and assistance of two individuals, both of whom I greatly admire and respect--Professor Leland M. Goodrich, who spent many long hours going over the manuscript and providing invaluable suggestions, and Professor William T. R. Fox, the Director of the Institute of War and Peace Studies, who similarly shared his wisdom so generously.

I also owe a debt of gratitude to the other members of the Institute of War and Peace Studies who freely offered comments on the initial drafts as well as to the many persons, too numerous to list, more directly involved in peace-keeping whom I had the privilege to interview during the course of the study. The fact that this work was completed while serving as an active member of the U.S. Air Force does not imply Department of Defense endorsement of the opinions expressed. The ideas set forth are my sole responsibility.

My appreciation must also be expressed to the publishers of International Organization for their kind permission to reprint certain passages originally contained in an article published in that journal (Vol. XX, No 1, 1966).

Finally, I must acknowledge the assistance and encouragement of my wife, Vicki, who served as proof-reader, non-expert critic, and counsellor--with great understanding and forbearance.

CONTENTS

Page

PART I: THE DECISION TO USE A UNITED
        NATIONS PEACE-KEEPING FORCE

Chapter

LIST OF FIGURES

LIST OF ABBREVIATIONS

ONUC   Operation des Nations Unies au Congo
              (United Nations Force in the Congo)

UNCIP   United Nations Commission India Pakistan
              (Kashmir)

UNEF   United Nations Emergency Force (Middle East)

UNFICYP   United Nations Peace-Keeping Force in Cyprus

UNIPOM   United Nations India-Pakistan Observer
              Mission

UNMOGIP   United Nations Military Observer Group in
              India and Pakistan

UNOGIL   United Nations Observer Group in Lebanon

UNSCOB   United Nations Special Committee on the
              Balkans

UNTEA   United Nations Temporary Executive Authority
              (West New Guinea)

UNTSO   United Nations Truce Supervision Organization
              (Palestine)

UNYOM   United Nations Yemen Observation Mission

PART I

THE DECISION TO USE A UNITED NATIONS
PEACE-KEEPING FORCE

CHAPTER 1 INTRODUCTION

On March 16, 1964, a contingent of Canadian troops landed in Cyprus and, along with the British forces already located there, assumed the role of international peace-keepers. Within the next few days, additional troops from other countries arrived and, on March 27, the United Nations Peace-Keeping Force in Cyprus (UNFICYP) became fully operational. This force was created at the direction of the Security Council which, after due consideration of the troubles in Cyprus, recommended the dispatch of a peace force to help ease the tensions. With this action, the United Nations launched another in a series of international peace-keeping operations.

"Peace-keeping" as a general concept in international relations has a long history. Taken literally, this hyphenated term can have a rather inclusive meaning.* As such, it has been applied loosely on different occasions to describe a wide range of measures, actions, or proposals of varying degrees of comprehensiveness that have generally been intended or designed to maintain peace. Proposals advanced by the early Greeks as well as those suggested by Dante, Henry IV, the Abbe St. Pierre, Rousseau, Kant, and other hopefuls were thus "peace-keeping" in nature. These and similar suggestions reflected man's continuing common concern to maintain the peace.[1] This concern was given new expression in the League of Nations scheme and, once again,

---

*Just as there is no neat and generally agreed definition of "peace-keeping," there is no agreement as to whether the term should be hyphenated or written as one word. The usage varies. However, the initial and still prevalent practice appears to favor the hyphenated version. For this reason, this form will be used throughout this study.

3

several decades later in the Charter of the United
Nations. However, in the actual experience of the
United Nations, the term "peace-keeping" has come
to have a more precise and specialized meaning, and
the United Nations operation in Cyprus falls within
this narrower definition.

The pattern of peace-keeping initiated in Cyprus
in 1964 was not new. The United Nations had previously undertaken similar operations. The first
instance was in the Middle East in 1956 when the
United Nations Emergency Force (UNEF) was created;
a second occurred in 1960 with the creation of a
United Nations Force in the Congo as part of the
Operation des Nations Unies au Congo (ONUC). These
three major peace-keeping efforts by the United
Nations involved the use of fairly sizable military
forces and reflected a new and distinct pattern of
operations designed to assist in reducing or containing a threat or potential threat to the peace.
However, they drew upon the experiences from earlier
less comprehensive peace-keeping undertakings and
each, in turn, created precedents for the future.

The present study proposes to analyze, compare,
and contrast these three principal United Nations
peace-keeping efforts. It will investigate the
pattern of activity in each of these three operations
to see how it developed in each instance and against
what particular background. An attempt will be made
to answer certain key questions. What were the
conditions that gave rise to the particular peace-
keeping operation? What were the alternatives to
United Nations action? What was the constitutional
basis for United Nations action when these alternative courses were not appropriate or practicable?
What were the problems--legal, political, technical,
and administrative--surrounding the force creation,
composition, and operation?

At the outset it must be acknowledged that
peace-keeping, in the form that it has developed
within the United Nations scheme, has served a useful
but not unlimited role in the efforts to preserve
peace. In general, it has been limited to the
extent that political agreement or consensus has
been possible. Given the difficulties in reaching
such agreement in many instances, it is not surprising that this form of endeavor does not provide
a universal formula applicable to all situations.
This is perhaps too much to hope for within the
present political realities. However, within those

limitations, there exist possibilities for strengthening the United Nations' capabilities. Accordingly,
a central question is to be answered: How can peace-
keeping procedures be improved and institutionalized
to make them more effective?* Important also is a
second and related question: What are the prospects
for implementing these procedures in the future?[2]
In short, what are the prospects for the future of
peace-keeping as it has evolved and as it may be
enhanced in its further evolution? Before attempting
to answer these questions, however, it will be useful
to look briefly at how this pattern of activity
evolved and to formulate a working definition of
peace-keeping.

EVOLUTION OF A PATTERN

     Although the concern for maintaining interna-
tional peace in a broad sense has ancient roots, it
is interesting and significant to observe that the
shape, dimensions, and characteristics of the effort
launched in Cyprus reveals a relatively new pattern
for giving form to this concern. This pattern first
became clearly recognizable in the United Nations
operation following the Suez crisis in 1956,** and

----

     *In general, two ways to enhance the United
Nations' capacity to initiate peace-keeping operations
more rapidly and effectively may be readily identified: (1) improving the institutional procedures in
advance of an operation to enhance the readiness
posture of the forces that may become engaged, or
make them more effective when committed; and (2)
devising procedures to anticipate and identify more
quickly situations appropriate for the use of peace-
keeping forces. The second suggestion would require
political judgments which neither the Secretariat
nor the political organs of the United Nations are
able to render on a regular basis. The possibilities
suggested under the first heading appear to offer
more immediate promise. Accordingly, this study
will concentrate on proposals within this general
category.

     **The word "Suez" when not otherwise qualified
will be used throughout this study as a shorthand
reference to the situation that developed leading
to the establishment of the United Nations Emergency
Force (UNEF) in the Middle East in 1956.

was manifested again, with certain variations, in
the Congo operation. It built upon the precedents
established in earlier United Nations operations
undertaken in Greece, in Indonesia, and in Kashmir
and continued in Lebanon, in Yemen, in West Irian,
and elsewhere. It bears little resemblance to the
form of military action taken in Korea, and it
differs markedly from the pattern of collective
action originally envisaged in both the Charter of
the United Nations and the Covenant of the League
of Nations. Yet, this is not intended to imply that
the present activities of the United Nations in
Cyprus are inconsistent with the provisions of the
Charter or that they are not a normal and worthwhile
development in the evolution of peace-keeping procedures.

The Provisions of the Charter

The first and most important task given to the
United Nations concerns the maintenance and preservation of international peace. The scheme envisaged
in the Charter to fulfill this responsibility
embodies both a sequence of actions designed to
achieve peaceful settlement of disputes likely to
disrupt the peace and a plan for collective action
in the event that the procedures of pacific settlement fail. The concept of collective action that
entrusted a major share of the responsibility to the
Great Powers is familiar.[3] The Great Powers were
charged with safeguarding the peace during the
transitional period pending the coming into force
of the more lasting arrangements envisaged in the
Charter of the United Nations. These latter responsibilities were specifically granted to the Security
Council and spelled out in the provisions of Chapter
VII of the Charter which sets forth the enforcement
powers to be exercised for the benefit of the organization as a whole by the Security Council. The
Charter provisions leave little doubt that enforcement action is the primary responsibility of the
Security Council, or that within that organ the
permanent members were to have the determining
influence. This is in essence the collective
security system for maintaining peace originally
envisaged within the United Nations.[4]

The Charter provisions marked an attempt to improve on the League of Nations system for peace preservation, which was based on a universal responsibility for collective security. The League system had failed, among other reasons, because it was not attuned to the political realities of the inter-war period. The League was neither a truly universal organization nor did it enjoy the wholehearted support, especially in its "peace-keeping" efforts, of all of its members. In addition, its potential usefulness in this all-important area was further impaired by organizational defects.[5] The effectiveness of the Charter system was likewise undermined when the initial concept of the United Nations peace enforcement scheme based on Great Power cooperation failed to materialize. With this failure, community action to maintain the peace through the use of enforcement measures was not possible.[6] Yet at this juncture of history, immediately following a devastating world war and in a precarious international environment that could be disrupted with limited or little advance notice by nuclear war, preserving the peace was, more than ever before, an imperative for man's most profound consideration.

The "Uniting for Peace" Resolution

The one real effort to follow at least a modified Charter concept and to mount an "enforcement of peace" effort was exemplified in the Korean action.[7] However, even in this instance, action by the United Nations was made possible only by the existence of a particular set of circumstances which was not likely to be repeated. The set of circumstances that made possible the circumvention of a Soviet veto is well known, as is the subsequent attempt to provide a basis for future action in the "Uniting for Peace" Resolution.[8]

With the adoption of the "Uniting for Peace" Resolution, a new avenue for safeguarding the peace was opened. In recognition of the difficulties in securing Great Power agreement within the Security Council, the peace-maintaining function was to be given a broader base. This was to be achieved by recognizing the residual responsibility of the

General Assembly. When the Great Powers were unable
to agree, the General Assembly could, theoretically,
initiate positive action. Although the General
Assembly could under the provisions of the resolution
move quickly to consider a potential threat to the
peace in the event that the Security Council was
unable to act, it could only recommend collective
sanctions against an aggressor; it could not initiate
actions binding on member states. Hopefully, it was
anticipated that these new procedures would permit
action in a wide variety of cases including those
to which one of the permanent members might be
opposed. Again, this hope was not completely in
harmony with the political facts of life.

Subsequent history has continued to demonstrate
the need for Great Power agreement, or at least their
acquiescence, if effective collective measures are
to be initiated. Otherwise, one of the Great Powers
could devise roadblocks to place in the way, frustrating the United Nations attempts to preserve or
restore peace. The very fact that the procedures
recommended by the General Assembly were to be
voluntary and not binding on the member states
against their will placed a formidable obstacle in
the way of achieving an effective system for enforcement action. Voluntary schemes have not provided
great promise for success in this respect in the
past; it is doubtful that they can offer a panacea
for the future. An inherent defect of such schemes
is the fact that voluntarism requires a community
of interest and places great reliance on the good
will of the individual members of the international
community. Unfortunately, it has often proved
difficult to transform good will into effective
action in practice.*

_____

*It should perhaps be noted that the alternative
to voluntary schemes would require either (1) a
binding legal obligation, assumed in advance, of
member states to use their national forces or a
portion thereof in response to a decision by the
community organ, or (2) the creation of a truly
international force subject to the control of the
central agency. Legal obligations alone, not supported by an element of good faith and a willingness
to cooperate in the common cause, are unlikely to
succeed. The answer would seem to lie somewhere in

Although the initial hopes for maintaining or
restoring international peace in accordance with the
scheme embodied in the Charter were not realized,
the "Uniting for Peace" Resolution provided a procedure for adopting a plan of action when the circumstances might be appropriate. The creation of UNEF
was the first major effort to set up a peace force
under this resolution. The general response of the
membership in support of this endeavor and its subsequent success in maintaining peace in the Middle
East for a period of ten years gave hope for a new
era in peace-keeping, one in which the General
Assembly could exert a positive influence when the
Security Council was unable to act.* With the
advantage of hindsight, it appears clear that the
creation of UNEF and the initial period of its
operation marked the high point in the prestige and
influence of the General Assembly and the Secretary-
General in the field of peace-keeping. This led
some enthusiasts to see a bright future for "preventive diplomacy," a term that came to be applied to
this form of activity,[9] and UNEF seemed to present
a useful pattern for the future.

To a certain extent, this optimism was justified.
The action taken to provide a United Nations Force
in the Congo marked a second attempt to apply this
pattern of operation to a peace-threatening situation
and, at a later date, the UNFICYP became the third.
Although the circumstances in these three cases were
not identical, there were many similarities. Each
operation was supported by a widespread consensus
of the international community which agreed with

---

between--reasonable and commonly accepted legal
commitments based on a community of interests plus
an element of good faith made possible by a recognition of that mutual interest. Until such a community
of interests exists and is recognized, neither of
the foregoing alternatives appears to be possible.

*Against this "success" in maintaining peace
in a potentially unstable situation must be balanced
the fact that the operation was abruptly terminated
in 1967 and to date the United Nations has been
unable to promote a permanent peace in the area.

the general idea that such an effort to maintain or
restore peace was proper and worthwile. This goal
was to be achieved by the use of limited force,
using measures short of enforcement. In each of
these operations, there was a degree of Great Power
agreement, or acquiescence, as well as the broad
support by the other member states. Furthermore, a
substantial number of nations indicated a willingness
to provide finances or forces, or both, to the enterprise.

A WORKING DEFINITION OF PEACE-KEEPING

Despite the emergence of a new pattern of
"peace-keeping," there is still no fully agreed-upon
definition of the term. This fact has been deplored
by many, including a Citizens' Commission charged
with preparing a report for a "White House conference"
on this subject. As noted by the Citizens' Commission, peace-keeping within the United Nations'
experience has encompassed "both political and
military missions, the defining factor being their
function as an adjunct to pacific-settlement endeavors."[10] The lack of an agreed definition has
led to some confusion and has made the task of
reviewing, discussing, and furthering the goals of
peace-keeping more difficult. However, there have
been efforts to overcome this deficiency. For
example, Paul Martin, the Canadian Secretary of State
for External Affairs, has outlined a four-part
definition as follows:

1. Peace-keeping involves the interposition of an international presence in
one form or another.

2. The object of peace-keeping is,
essentially, to prevent violence from
breaking out or to contain or curtail it
where it has already broken out. United
Nations forces are strictly debarred from
taking the initiative in the use of armed
force and, indeed may, use it only as a
last resort.

3. Peace-keeping is designed to
create or restore, as the case may be, an
environment in which a peaceful solution
to the problems at issue can at least be
contemplated.

          4. While peace-keeping is not itself
     a form of conciliation or mediation, it
     has been specifically coupled with
     mediation in some situations and has
     served to underpin the carrying out of
     mediatory solutions in others.11

With some slight modifications, this definition
will be accepted for the purpose of this study.

The basic elements of peace-keeping may then be
considered to include (1) an international military
or quasi-military presence in some form; (2) the
consent of the country or countries in which the
operation occurs and of the troop-contributing
states; (3) the objective of preventing or curtailing
violence; (4) strictly limited use of force to achieve
this objective; and (5) an attempt to create the conditions or environment in which pacific settlement
can occur.

It must be acknowledged that this "definition"
is still deficient. It provides no detailed guidance
regarding the size or nature of the international
presence. Furthermore, it lacks precision regarding
other particulars such as the extent to which force
may be used to achieve the objective, the relationship of peace-keeping to pacific settlement procedures, and the constitutional aspects governing
initiation. In the absence of full agreement on
such questions, it is considered that an effort to
be more specific would prove to be limiting and
could be counterproductive. Peace-keeping as it has
in fact evolved within the United Nations' experience
has resulted from the ability to reach agreement on
ad 'hoc arrangements--arrangements peculiarly suited
to the particular circumstances at hand. These
arrangements have varied considerably and make the
task of setting forth a precise, yet inclusive,
definition difficult. However, lacking such a
definition, it will be useful to delineate further
what is meant by peace-keeping through reference to
specific missions. As used herein, peace-keeping
will encompass the use of an international force
for the following: fact-finding; observation and
surveillance; monitoring a cease-fire, truce, or
armistice line or an international boundary; assisting in the maintenance of local law and order or in
the creation of peaceful conditions; aiding in the
resolution of differences likely to endanger the
peace; and other related purposes. In accordance

with this general concept, peace-keeping will not be
construed to encompass police actions on the order
of those undertaken in Korea in 1950 or other coercive actions.[12]

The pattern of peace-keeping that has evolved
does not approach the comprehensive system proposed
in the third and final stage of the current U.S.
disarmament proposals which envisage a permanent
international peace force. An international police
force having a monopoly on the use of force in a
disarmed world is clearly beyond the prospects for
the immediate future. Accordingly, this study will
not speculate on such a possibility.* Similarly,
it will not dwell on the possibilities of even a
more modest permanent peace force which would be
designed for enforcement action. The conclusion of
a general agreement to create a permanent peace
force of sufficient size and authority to impose
sanctions has obviously not been possible to date
and does not appear likely. Even if it were possible
to consummate such an agreement, it is doubtful
whether a permanent force could operate successfully
in the existing political environment. The first
crisis involving the national interests of the Great
Powers would very likely pose a challenge that would
be difficult to surmount.

Although this conception of peace-keeping is
sufficiently inclusive to cover a variety of United
Nations actions taken since 1945, this study will
concentrate primarily on the pattern of operations
reflected by the actions taken in the Middle East,
the Congo, and Cyprus. Those three operations have
been both highly praised and criticized. However,
the fact remains that they represent the most comprehensive type of peace maintenance effort the
United Nations community has been more or less
consistently willing to accept within the prevailing

---

*Likewise it must be acknowledged that many
other matters relating to the over-all problem of
peace, such as the causes of conflict, conflict
resolution, and the techniques for negotiating and
settling disputes, will be considered only inciden-
tally. These subjects, although deserving of continuing and urgent consideration, are clearly beyond
the scope of this study.

international environment. At the same time,
reference will be made to other, more modest peace-
keeping operations as appropriate.

NOTES

1. For a brief historical survey of the proposals for the use of international forces, see
Gabriella Rosner, The United Nations Emergency Force
(New York: Columbia University Press, 1963), pp.
207ff.

2. Although peace-keeping has become the
subject of increasing concern during the past few
years, these two aspects have not been given the
attention they warrant. There have been several
excellent case studies on specific operations,
particularly those conducted in the Middle East and
the Congo; see, for example, Rosner, op. cit., and
Ernest W. Lefever, Crisis in the Congo (Washington,
D.C.: The Brookings Institution, 1965). There has
been published by the Ohio State Unversity Press a
study on the Cyprus operation: James A. Stegenga,
The United Nations Force in Cyprus. Less has been
done in the way of comparative study of the various
operations, and as yet there has been no attempt to
produce a comprehensive comparison of these three
principal peace-keeping operations. With respect
to analyses of the operational method and procedures
of field operations, the International Information
Center on Peace-Keeping Operations of the World
Veterans Federation in Paris has published a very
useful series of monographs and papers on particular
aspects of peace-keeping. What is particularly
lacking, however, is an over-all comparative analysis
of the three major peace-keeping efforts. This study
attempts, at least in part, to fill this requirements.

3. For a discussion of this concept, see
Leland M. Goodrich, "The Maintenance of International
Peace and Security," International Organization, XIX
(Summer, 1965), 429ff.

4. For a discussion of whether this system of
action may properly be labeled "collective security,"
see Inis L. Claude, Jr., "The United Nations and the
Use of Force," International Conciliation, No. 532,
March, 1961, p.331.

5.   For a discussion of the League system for peace preservation, see, for example, T. P. Conwell-Evans, The League Council in Action (London: Oxford University Press, 1929), or F. P. Walters, A History of the League of Nations (2 vols.; London: Oxford University Press, 1952).

6.   See Ruth B. Russell, "Changing Patterns of Constitutional Development," International Organization, XIX (Summer, 1965), 413-16.

7.   See Leland M. Goodrich, Korea: A study of U.S. Policy in the United Nations (New York: Council on Foreign Relations, 1956), for a comprehensive analysis of the characteristics of the United Nations collective action in Korea.

8.   General Assembly Resolution 377 (V), November 3, 1950.

9.   See "Introduction to the Annual Report of the Secretary-General on the Work of the Organization, 16 June 1959-15 June 1960," U.N. General Assembly, Official Records, Fifteenth Session, Suppl. No.1A (A/4390/add 1).

10.   National Citizens Commission, Peacekeeping Operations, A Report to the White House Conference on International Cooperation, Washington, D.C., November 28 to December 1, 1965, p. 2.

11.   Paul Martin, Speech to McGill Conference on World Affairs, Montreal, November 21, 1964.

12.   Although it is difficult to arrive at a uniformly agreed-upon definition, there is fairly widespread agreement along the lines of the general conception outlined above. See, for example, D. W. Bowett, United Nations Forces: A Legal Study (New York: Frederick A. Praeger, 1964), pp. 267-74. David W. Wainhouse distinguishes between peace-keeping and peace-observation but notes that the latter may be included within the former. See David W. Wainhouse and Associates, International Peace Observation (Baltimore, Md.: The Johns Hopkins Press, 1966), p. 2. Arthur M. Cox describes peace-keeping as an "extraordinary military act because it calls for the use of soldiers not to fight and win, but to prevent fighting, to maintain cease-fires, and to provide order while negotiations are being conducted," in

Prospects for Peacekeeping (Washington, D.C.: The
Brookings Institution, 1967), p. 4. Lincoln P.
Bloomfield refers to the "contemporary invention of
a new form of military presence--the non- (or almost
non-) fighting U.N. force," in International Military
Forces (Boston, Mass.: Little, Brown and Co., 1964),
p. 1.

CHAPTER **2** THE BACKGROUND OF
SELECTED PEACE-
KEEPING EFFORTS

In the international environment that prevailed
following the end of World War II, the system for
providing collective security initially envisaged
failed to materialize.[1] The United Nations has,
however, been able to undertake a number of peace-
keeping measures of a less comprehensive nature.
This development has to a large extent been evolution-
ary. It has taken place in the context of, and been
compatible with, the prevailing system of international
relations. However, the peace-keeping efforts undertaken have been of a different character from those
originally foreseen.*

In looking forward to the question of how to
enhance the capacity of the United Nations to respond
to such situations in the future, it will be useful
to investigate the background of several of the
principal peace-keeping efforts launched to date and
to analyze these similarities and the differences.
What made the particular operation necessary? What
was the background against which it was initiated?
How did this situation develop? Can we identify
common elements, the recurrence of which might signal
other situations appropriate for United Nations action?

THE SUEZ CRISIS

The United Nations action in Suez in 1956 was
in direct response to an outbreak of hostilities in
the Middle East. Arab resentment and dissatisfaction
with the creation of the State of Israel coupled with

---

*See Chapter 5 for a discussion of the patterns
of peace-keeping operations.

the Israeli attempt to consolidate and safeguard its
newly achieved independence had produced a situation
of continuous friction which constituted a potential
threat to the peace of the entire area. The attempt
to resolve this matter once and for all in the Arab-
Israeli War of 1948 merely resulted in a temporary
armistice and delayed the final reckoning. Although
the United Nations Truce Supervision Organization
(UNTSO) and the Mixed Armistice Commissions, created
following the 1948 conflict, helped to keep the
tensions from erupting into open conflict, they did
not insure a final settlement. They did, however,
assist in reducing the total number of incidents and
in resolving those that did arise. Accordingly, in
the period from 1948 to 1956, these agencies played
a useful role in maintaining at least an uneasy peace.
The inability of the conflicting parties to reach a
permanent settlement and the continuance of border
incidents, accompanied on each occasion by charges
and countercharges, perpetuated this unstable condition. Against this background, certain events
stand out in the days preceding the Suez crisis.

     In February, 1955, the Israelis launched a
slightly larger than usual retaliatory raid in Gaza
in response to a series of Egyptian fedayeen raids.[2]
This particular incident reflected unfavorably on
Egypt which came out second best in the encounter to
the great embarrassment of President Nasser.   It
also provided an added stimulus, if one were needed,
for the Czech arms deal consummated in the fall of
1955 and the receipt of Soviet bloc arms by Egypt.
This development in turn tended to upset the already
precarious arms balance in the area. The subsequent
withdrawal of the Anglo-American offer to help
finance the construction of the Aswan Dam in July of
1956, immediately followed by Nasser's announcement
on July 26 of the nationalization of the Suez Canal,
further complicated an already complex situation.
This event led to an extended and unsuccessful series
of discussions. Finally, on October 29, 1956, the
situation boiled over when Israeli forces moved into
the Sinai. The following day the two original contestants, Israel and Egypt, were confronted with an
Anglo-French ultimatum which was the prelude to
French and British action. Initially, the Anglo-
French endeavor took the form of air strikes against
Egyptian territory which were shortly followed by
amphibious assaults in the Canal Zone. To further
confuse the international picture, the outbreak of

the Hungarian revolt occurred almost simultaneously.
Thus the world and the United Nations were faced
with two potential time bombs, one ticking in the
Middle East, the other in Eastern Europe. Either
could run its course and explode causing further
widespread and catastrophic consequences. In attempting to analyze these developments as the backdrop for
the subsequent United Nations peace-keeping action in
the Sinai, we return to this question: What were the
essential elements in this series of event?

     First, immediately preceding the United Nations
action, a state of armed hostilities existed between
sovereign states. At the outset, this was a relatively
simple two-party affair involving only Israel and
Egypt. The initial attack by Israel was in violation
of the armistice agreements and this was sufficient
in the eyes of some to identify the aggressor and the
victim. However, the issues underlying the conflict
were complex and were such as to create sympathies
or attachments for each of the two contestants by
other nations not directly involved. This created
a confusing situation and it was against this background that the member states were called upon to
consider and recommend United Nations action. The
area of engagement and the number of participants
were expanded with the entry of the British and the
French. The international character was broadened
and the hostilities took on the character of a three-
sided operation. Furthermore, with the entry of
these two new contestants, the emotional question of
colonialism was superimposed on the Arab-Israeli
regional issue. The action of the United Kingdom
and France also created a dilemma of major proportions
for the United States.

     Outside reaction was highly critical of the
Anglo-French intervention. World opinion crystal-
lized quickly in opposition to this joint intervention and served to inhibit the freedom of action
of the two intervening allies who, in addition to
having their area of choice limited, found themselves
in an embarrassing and exposed position.3 It is
difficult to disregard the force of world opinion,
especially when the two largest states, the United
States and the Soviet Union--one an ally, the other
an opponent of the newly committed contestants--were
both, for their own reasons, directly opposed to the
Anglo-French military action. In addition, particularly in the case of the United Kingdom, domestic

opinion imposed certain constraints.* This turn of
events created an immediate and urgent pressure for
the British and French to search for, or at least be
amenable to, a quick solution.

Egypt, greatly embarrassed by its military
defeats, by the poor showing of the Egyptian armed
forces, and by the resulting adverse political
situation, was likewise anxious to remedy this
situation. This clearly could not be accomplished
by reliance on her own resources. It could only be
achieved by securing outside assistance.** This
suggested that the Egyptians might be receptive to
alternatives that could provide a convenient face-
saving formula.

In this situation, we must consider the position
of the two super-powers. Here we note a certain
degree of converging interests. The United States
and the Soviet Union shared the belief that the crisis
should be tempered. The United States was prompted

----

*The pressure of these events eventually led to
the resignation of the Prime Minister, Sir Anthony
Eden. It is also worth noting that the United Kingdom
was subjected as well to great pressure from within
the Commonwealth.

**Subsequent to the nationalization of the Suez
Canal in July, 1956, speeches by President Nasser
and other Egyptian leaders and the propaganda ema-
nating from the Cairo radio and the Egyptian press
all contained frequent references to a willingness
to "fight to the last drop of our blood" in the
defense of Egyptian national interests. Such statements were loud, repetitious, and carried a great
emotional appeal. After the Israeli attack and the
Anglo-French intervention, similar statements continued, possibly with the same sincerity but in an
obviously more subdued and chastened tone. In
response to a direct question posed by this writer
shortly after the initial British-French bombings of
Cairo, a high-ranking Egyptian military officer
confirmed the Egyptian determination to continue to
fight. However, by this time the Egyptian forces
were completely disorganized and hardly in a position
to stage a comeback, and this particular statement
was not made with the determination displayed earlier.

by a desire to keep the hostilities from spreading[4] for a variety of reasons, humanitarian and others. Similarly, despite their missile-rattling statements, there is no indication that the Soviets wished to extend the crisis and risk a world conflict. Conversely, it appeared that Soviet interests would best be served first by denying the Israelis, the British, and the French any gains from this action; and second by demonstrating their support of their new-found friend and potential ally Nasser. This could be accomplished by forcing a withdrawal of forces or by promoting a "satisfactory" general settlement. The Soviet Union was also influenced by the simultaneous occurrence of the Hungarian revolution which proved embarrassing and necessarily diverted Soviet attention in part to Eastern Europe. The complications arising from the revolt in Hungary made it necessary for both super-powers to act with a greater measure of caution to avoid extending the risks of escalation than otherwise might have been required.

Finally, as a footnote to the foregoing, it should be recognized that the scene of action for this peace-keeping operation was a strategically important area. The Suez Canal forms an important axis of communication which, in the past, had been referred to as the lifeline of the British Empire and the crossroads of the world. Although these descriptions may have been modified, particularly in the light of the discovery and development of new oil reserves west of Suez, this waterway continues to be important to world maritime navigation. The control of the Canal and the surrounding area has long been an important factor in international politics. During the nineteenth century and the first half of the twentieth century the West had attempted to prevent Russian encroachment or penetration into this area. These efforts entered a new phase with the expansion of Soviet power after World War II, and, since 1955, Soviet influence had made significant inroads in the Middle East. The area thus became an active arena for the Cold War.

DEVELOPING CRISIS IN THE CONGO

The political events leading up to the entry of United Nations forces in the Congo are inextricably intertwined with complex questions of colonialism and rising nationalism. Both issues are highly charged with emotion and do not lend themselves readily to the achievement of rational, quick, or easy solutions. The Congo proved to be no exception in this respect.

In the period immediately following World War II, the Belgian Congo appeared to present a good case for paternalistic colonialism. Outwardly, the colony seemed stable and prosperous. On the surface, there did not appear to be any indication why the situation should not continue indefinitely. During the latter part of the 1950's, however, certain preliminary signs portended ill for the future. Up to this time, Belgian political and economic dominance had been complete. However, during the late 1950's the Belgian authorities permitted the beginnings of Congolese self-government, and this unleashed pressures for independence. Once initiated, these pressures were difficult to contain or suppress. As has been demonstrated in many former colonial areas, limited concessions open the door for additional demands leading sooner or later to the demand for complete independence. In response to the rising demands in the Congo, the Belgian Government bowed to the request, precipitously granted independence, and the Republic of the Congo was established on June 30, 1960.

It is necessary to consider briefly the principal elements that provided the background against which the United Nations was called into action. What were the ingredients in this situation?

First, a territory that had formerly been under the complete and absolute control of a colonial power was abruptly transformed into an independent sovereign nation. Because of the speed with which this transformation was accomplished, the base for the necessary transfer of power was not adequately prepared. The new government was not capable of assuming the reins of authority or of managing its own affairs. There were almost no trained leaders, administrators, or professional men available to assist in the process. To complicate the sudden transfer of governmental control, local factions representing different tribal groups vied with each other for dominance.

Second, the Congo comprises a strategic land
area in the heart of the African continent. Although
the new state contained great potential economic
promise, it also had certain inherent handicaps.   It
lacked natural frontiers and, with boundaries
inherited from the colonial period, it sprawled over
an area approximately one fourth the size of the
United States. Within this area, there were a
number of competing tribes, the most powerful of
which wanted either to dominate the new country or
to secede and establish their own political units.
There was no common language, no common cultural
ties, and a complete absence of historical feeling
of national unity. Because of the great distance
between regional centers and the difficulties of
moving across these distances, the internal lines of
communication were long and tenuous. In short, the
obstacles to national unity were numerous and
formidable. They served to accentuate the normal
difficulties any new state might be expected to
encounter in establishing its own independence.

Third, residual elements of colonialism remained
in the form of long-established foreign economic
interests, Belgian administrators in the Congo Civil
Service, and Belgian officers in the Congolese army.
These remaining vestiges of colonial rule provided
an easily identifiable and convenient whipping boy
for use by the various local factions in appealing
to the populace for support. Within this environment,
it was only natural that the competing groups would
attempt to outdo each other and further exacerbate
the existing relationships.

Finally, and not surprisingly, came the actual
outbreak of violence. Violence occurred first in
the form of tribal rioting and then as mutiny within
the army. After this, civil strife spread rapidly.
The new government was unable to exercise effective
control, and Belgian efforts to assist in restoring
order merely gave credence to the charge of external
interference.

PEACE-KEEPING IN CYPRUS

For the Cyprus United Nations peace-keeping
venture, the political background has been long and
complex. Likewise, the number of participants and
interested bystanders standing off-stage ready to

assume an active role has been large. Greece, Turkey,
the United Kingdom, and the two Cypriot communities
are directly involved. On the sidelines are a number
of other interested parties--the United States, the
Soviet Union, and the United Arab Republic, to mention
just a few. The cast of characters should be expanded
to include the countries that now have forces serving
as peace-keepers in Cyprus. Still another interested
actor of a somewhat different nature is the Communist
party in Cyprus which, because of its size and
cohesiveness, exerts great influence on the affairs
of Cyprus. One indication of that strength may be
seen in the fact that the Communists have accounted
for one third of the Greek Cypriot vote in national
elections.

What is the background for the conflicting
interests and claims of the primary participants?
The underlying difficulties that led to the outbreak
of violence in December, 1963, have a long history.
They stem basically from the friction between two
ethnic groups, the majority Greek Cypriot community
and the less populous Turkish Cypriot community. The
cultural ties of the Greek Cypriots date back to the
Hellenic period of the Golden Age of Greece; the
Turkish bonds may be traced from the sixteenth century
when Turkey took over rule of the island from the
Venetians. Turkey retained political control until
1878 when the British occupied the island as part of
a secret agreement with the Ottoman Porte. It is
interesting to note that concern for Russian expansion
toward the Mediterranean played a part in the drama
at that time. In return for taking over the administration of Cyprus, the British agreed to assist Turkey
in withstanding Russian pressure along the northern
borders of the Ottoman Empire.[5] Turkish sovereignty
was acknowledged by the British until 1914 when the
island was annexed, but it was not until 1923 that
Turkey, under the provisions of the Treaty of Lausanne,
formally ceded the island to the British. From 1925
until after World War II, Cyprus was governed as a
Crown Colony.[6]

An interesting sidelight to this history was the
offer of Cyprus to Greece as an inducement to secure
Greek entry into World War I in 1915. This inducement
was apparently not sufficient to motivate the Greeks
at that time and nothing came of this offer.[7] Cyprus
remained a British possession until 1960 and, during
the post World War II period, occupied a high place

in British strategic thought. It provided the
geographic setting for one of the main British base
complexes facing toward the East and, as such, became
increasingly important with the loss of possible
alternate locations in Palestine, Egypt, and Libya.
Cyprus still occupies a relatively important position
in British strategic thinking--but possibly less so
as the future of the base, despite the formal treaty
guarantees, becomes more questionable.

During the last years of British rule, Cyprus
became increasingly more restive. The Turkish
Cypriot community was generally satisfied, but the
movement for Enosis, or union with Greece, developed
among the Greek Cypriots. This movement took on
increased significance when open revolt broke out
in 1955. An underground terrorist organization
spurred this activity, and a Cypriot-born Greek army
officer, George Grivas, arrived on the scene to direct
the campaign of terror that followed. As this campaign gained momentum, the British began to look for
a way out that would still provide the British certain
continuing base rights. Simultaneously, the concern
of both the Turkish Government and the Turkish
community in Cyprus over the future became more acute.

The various pressures and counterpressures
finally culminated in a meeting of the parties
concerned in Zurich on February 14, 1959. During
this meeting, an interlocking set of agreements was
drafted and shortly thereafter accepted by the
governments of the United Kingdom, Greece, and
Turkey, and representatives of the Greek and Turkish
Cypriot communities. The Zurich agreements ruled out
both extremes, Enosis or partition, and instead set
forth a list of guarantees for the rights of the
two communities. These guarantees were embodied in
a new Cypriot Constitution. The complete package of
the Zurich agreements included, in addition to the
Constitution, a Treaty of Guarantee, a Treaty of
Alliance, and a Treaty of Establishment.[8]

Under the terms of the Treaty of Guarantee, the
United Kingdom, Greece, and Turkey assured "the
independence and territorial integrity and security"
of Cyprus and guaranteed the basic articles of the
Constitution. In the event of a breach of the
treaty provisions, Greece, Turkey, and the United
Kingdom agreed to consult together with a view to
securing agreement on a course of concerted action.
If agreement on concerted action proved impossible,

each party could then take action unilaterally to
restore the state of affairs existing at the time
of independence. The Cypriot Constitution, as well
as setting forth the fundamental law for the new
state, provided the Turkish minority with broad
rights in communal affairs and an absolute veto on
important government matters. The Treaty of
Alliance established a common defense arrangement
between the signatories, and the Treaty of Establishment granted the United Kingdom virtual sovereignity
over the two strategic base areas retained by the
British.

     The Zurich agreements were accepted reluctantly
by the Greek Cypriot leader, Archbishop Makarios,
after pressure from the British and Greek governments.[9]
Although certain articles appear in some respects to
be inconsistent with the principle of national
sovereignty, Archbishop Makarios obviously believed
that half a loaf was better than none. Perhaps he
believed that the agreements provided a sound basis
for the indefinite future. Perhaps, as others feel,
he was willing to accept what he could get at the
time, to move forward on that basis, and to regroup
and re-negotiate at a later, possibly more favorable,
time. It is unquestionably true that the Archbishop
at a later date (1963), as the head of an independent
state and with his own representative in the United
Nations, was in a better bargaining position than he
had been in 1960.

     In any event, by 1963 the Greek Cypriot leaders
had become increasingly concerned about the provisions
of the Constitution that gave a 20 per cent minority
an absolute veto in significant government matters.
The Constitution had become a vehicle to promote
governmental deadlock in such matters. Accordingly,
Archbishop Makarios proposed a series of thirteen
constitutional changes. These changes would have,
among other things, eliminated the restrictive
Presidential and Vice Presidential vetoes, provided
greater unity in the House of Representatives,
restricted the rights of the separate Turkish
community, and reduced significantly the Turkish
representation on the police force, in the armed
services, and in the civil service. The Turkish
Cypriot reaction was prompt and, in view of their
past expressions, not entirely unpredictable. As
might be expected, the Turkish Cypriots objected
rather strongly. Violence broke out between the

two communities on December 21, 1963, with each side accusing the other of making the first move.

What were the essential elements in this situation? First, and most obvious, the basic ingredient was communal strife. The history of suspicion and distrust between Greek and Turkish Cypriot communities is long, and the most recent developments tended to accentuate the sources of friction. Second, Cyprus was a newly independent state which had not yet had time to develop the institutions and the common traditions so essential to the consolidation of a secure base of power. It was a state recently released from colonial status and, like other newly emergent states, manifested a lingering resentment against its former rulers. This heritage of distrust provided a built-in limitation of the ability of the former colonial power to assist in resolving the tensions. Third, an essentially unworkable constitution was imposed on the new state which reinforced the existing communal frictions and did not make the task of achieving a generally acceptable government any easier. The Constitution perpetuated the divisions between the two communal groups and inhibited positive governmental action. Fourth, differences of opinion arising between the Greek and Turkish Cypriot communities were quickly supported by two outside governments, Greece and Turkey, both of which were quick to champion their respective ethnic communities. As might be expected, these outside pressures supporting the opposing viewpoints tended to make the situation even more rigid. This further reduced the possibilities for compromise and denied those governments the leeway and flexibility needed to deal with the problem. Fifth, not unexpected, was the actual outbreak of violence on December 21, 1963. Both communities acted or reacted as the case may be. The violence spread and Cyprus became an area in which some procedure or mechanism to restore the peace was urgently needed.*

---

*See Chapter 3 for a review of the actions undertaken by the guarantor powers and the United States in their attempts to resolve this dispute short of resorting to United Nations action.

COMPARISON OF SETTINGS

In Suez, in the Congo, and in Cyprus there was a potential threat to international peace and security. It is true that the dimension of the threat in each of these three cases was different. It is difficult to imagine that any two situations would be identical. It is likewise true that, in each instance, the combination of ingredients was different. This is also not at all surprising--but it still may be helpful to look at these three developing situations in which a United Nations Peace Force was later to be introduced and to see how the backgrounds compared with each other. Were there any common features? It may also be worthwhile to look at the contrasts--because a consideration of the contrasting elements may be helpful in analyzing the course of action as it unfolded. Such a review may also provide insight concerning the future possibilities of peace-keeping. In this process, it will be noted that the issues were frequently not simple. There were many forces at work, and the precise impact of conflicting currents are not always easy to distinguish or to assess.

Similarities

Turning first to a consideration of the similarities, we may note that the most obvious common denominator was the outbreak of violence. In each instance, this occurred before the peace operation was initiated. Perhaps if the peace-keeping effort had commenced before violence erupted the subsequent steps leading toward a control of the violence might have been less difficult and contained a greater promise for success. This almost automatically raises the question, can such situations be anticipated? In many cases they can; in others they cannot.* In either eventuality, there is still a

---

*Obviously, there will be situations in which no amount of advance planning or anticipation will be able to overcome the fact that U.N. action, for one reason or another, is not acceptable to the parties concerned. However, an action unacceptable at one point in time may later prove acceptable.

requirement to improve the United Nations capacity
to be able to respond promptly if such response
appears acceptable and appropriate.

In each case, the violence was considered to
pose a threat to international peace and security.
If this had not been true, the disorder would have
been a matter of purely domestic concern and, as such,
under the provisions of Article 2 (7) of the Charter,
a matter beyond the competence of the United Nations
action.* The international character of the emergency
was most clearly evident in the Suez crisis. The
relationship of the domestic and international
characteristics in the Congo and in Cyprus was
somewhat more complex.

In the Congo, the first symptoms of violence--
civil rioting and mutiny in the army--were, strictly
speaking, in the nature of internal matters. The
cause of these disorders may be traced to the
ineffectiveness of the Congolese Government which,
without adequate prior preparation, was unable to
guarantee internal security. Subsequently, the
introduction of Belgian reinforcements to restore
peace provided an excuse for the Congo to claim
external aggression. The existence of an external
threat was at least implied in the initial Security
Council resolution calling upon Belgium to withdraw
its forces.[10] Although the crisis was primarily
domestic in nature, there existed a potential threat
to international peace which, coupled with the
presence of Belgian troops, provided an international
overtone. In Cyprus, certain characteristics of the
violence were once again domestic. However, there
were definite external manifestations, e.g., the
support of the governments of Greece and Turkey to
their respective Greek and Turkish communities and
the treaty arrangements.

Another common element was the inability of the
national governments concerned to resolve or contain
the danger short of its becoming a threat to the
international peace. This was particularly true in
the Congo. It was also true in Cyprus where the
government was unable to prevent the spread of

---

*This is true unless enforcement action is
initiated under the provisions of Chapter VII of
the Charter.

violence. In Suez, the international character of
the conflict was apparent from the outset. Here the
ability or inability of the government to cope with
local disorder or to prevent such disorder from
reaching dimensions that would threaten the international peace was not an important factor. The
case was clearly one characterized by an external
attack against which the defending state was unable
to preserve its territorial integrity.

     In all three crises, it seems reasonable to assume
that the responsible leaders were interested in
finding a peaceful solution. Admittedly, there
might be certain qualifications to this preference.
For example, each of the leading figures would have
desired that any proposed solution to the situation be
written on his terms. To what degree compromise on
these terms was possible, thus bringing about a
meeting of the minds between the conflicting interests,
was in each case the key question to be answered.
But a common interest in finding a formula for
peace provided at least a hopeful element and one
which might be exploited in the search for a pacific
settlement.

     Another similarity that stands out in reviewing
these situations is the fact that each reflects
some aspect of colonialism: Egypt, the Congo, and
Cyprus all have a colonial heritage. This was
reflected in the Suez crisis when Nasser repetitiously
referred to the Anglo-French attack as an imperialist
plot designed to reinstitute colonial rule and
charged that the Israelis were serving as a willing
pawn in this process. This was the case in the
Congo, recently released from direct Belgian rule.
It was also true in Cyprus, newly independent, with
a vivid remembrance of its former colonial ties, and
still subjected to continuing imperial restrictions
on her sovereignty in the form of the British base
areas. The Suez and the Cyprus crises took place
in the Middle East; Congo in Central Africa. These
are both areas of the world in which large territories
in the past have been under colonial rule, have
been recently freed of this tutelage, and are demand-
ing further economic and political development.

     This review suggests certain cautious general-
izations. Each occurred in an area characterized by
rising nationalism, the creation of newly independent
states, and the struggle of those states to

consolidate their newly won statehood. Looking at
a broader sample, including other areas where United
Nations operations have been undertaken such as
Lebanon, Jordan, Laos, Yemen, and West Irian, it
appears that the newly emergent areas of the world
tend to provide the conditions requiring international
action. This prospect will be important to bear in
mind when considering the need to enhance the United
Nations peace-keeping ability.

What is the significance of this common colonial
backdrop? First, it invariably militates against
the former colonial power directly, and the Western
powers as a whole indirectly, in their efforts to play
a constructive role in pacifying the situation. At
the same time, it affords the Eastern bloc an
opportunity to exploit for their benefit. Because
of this limitation on taking direct action, the
West, if it is to be helpful, may have to concentrate
on supporting efforts by the United Nations or on
working through an appropriate regional organization.

Another significant question concerns the time
it takes for a particular crisis to reach a boiling
point and erupt. In Suez and in the Congo, the
violence erupted first, the matter became one for
urgent United Nations consideration, and the United
Nations responded quickly. In Cyprus, the violence
broke out, and the United Nations reviewed the
developments and then deferred to the parties most
directly concerned. When those parties were unable
to reach agreement within several months and there
was a continued deterioration, the United Nations
re-entered the picture and shortly thereafter
dispatched a peace-keeping force. In Cyprus, the
United Nations, because of the particular sequence
of events, had more time to react. However, in all
three cases, when the United Nations did decide to
respond, it was essential that the response be
prompt. This supports the case for advance preparations in order for the United Nations to be in
the optimum position to react.

This further suggests a related question,
already mentioned briefly. Could the build-up of
these crises have been predicted? The answer must
be an emphatic "yes" in all three cases. This
question is easier to answer so positively with
the benefit of hindsight--but it should also have
been possible to answer in a like manner with only

a minimum of foresight. An exceptionally acute
political sense would not have been required to see
signs of trouble in Egypt after the Suez Canal was
nationalized in July of 1956, in the Congo in the days
immediately preceding independence in July of 1960,
or in Cyprus subsequent to 1959 when an "unworkable"
constitution was imposed on a new nation divided
into two suspicious, separate communities. Accordingly,
it seems logical to argue that to the extent possible,
the United Nations should develop its capability to
react to such situations earlier in the sequence of
a developing crisis.

Differences

We have seen that there are a number of similarities in the backgrounds of violence against which
the United Nations operations have been projected.
What about the differences? Some have already been
mentioned. For example, the international character
was more readily apparent in Suez than in the Congo
and in Cyprus. In both of these latter instances,
domestic considerations were prominent. For this
reason, the Congo and Cyprus posed difficult questions
regarding the relationship of the United Nations
force to the local government. Likewise, we have
noted that Suez and the Congo erupted quickly and
required a prompt United Nations response, whereas
more time was available for reaction in Cyprus.

Another difference involves the strength of the
government directly concerned. Although this
obviously calls for a subjective judgment, certain
generalizations may be valid and prove useful for
further consideration. For example, although the
Egyptian Government was confronted with an awkward
situation in 1956, it was able to respond from a
relatively secure and stable base of power. In
Cyprus, the government was less a completely
independent agent, but it was still able to exert
its will in international affairs. In the Congo, the
government was new, untried, and unstable. Under
stress, the Congolese Government was completely
unable to maintain local order, and this influenced
its ability to act with authority and to shape
essential decisions. The strength of the government
centrally involved in the crisis situation may,
therefore, influence materially the course of the
peace-keeping operations.

SOME GENERALIZATIONS

From this review, the following tentative
conclusions may be summarized. In each situation,
there was an outbreak of violence. This outbreak
occurred before a peace-keeping effort was mounted,
not after. This does not mean that peace-keeping
operations should be initiated only after violence
has broken out; there may be situations where the
likelihood of violence can be anticipated. It merely
indicates that this was not the case in three significant peace-keeping projects and that similar situations
could occur in the future. It is also possible to
speculate that the violence might not have occurred
in the first place, or have been abated sooner, if
international action had been initiated prior to the
disruption of the peace.

In two of the cases, the domestic component was
of great significance; in the third, the international
aspects were more clearly predominant. This small
statistical sample cannot, of course, be used to
conclude that two thirds of the threats arising to
the peace in the future will have significant domestic
characteristics. But it does appear reasonable to
conclude that, in the future, the United Nations
will probably again be faced with many situations
displaying a large domestic element. In the instances
where domestic disorder was the initial ingredient
such as in the Congo and in Cyprus, there appears
to be a relationship of the internal violence to
such factors as stability of the national government,
how long that government has been independent, and
how well the government was prepared to assume the
responsibilities of independence.

In all three crises, the national governments
involved and most immediately concerned were unable,
within their own capacities, to contain the situation.
This reinforces the case for both preventive and
remedial action on a broader basis. Preventive action
might consist of such generally recognized expedients
as assisting colonial territories to prepare for
eventual self-rule or aiding weak governments to
develop a reasonably secure and effective governmental
base. In cases where the peace is threatened, it
might also include such measures as the prompt
dispatch of a United Nations presence, which could
take one of several forms running the gamut from a

small observation group to a relatively large peace-
keeping force. One step that might be taken to
increase this capacity would be to encourage advance
planning by the United Nations in the area of peace-
keeping. This is by no means intended to imply that
the United Nations has been completely negligent in
this area or that key staff officers are unaware of
this requirement.[11]

Each of these situations reveals a number of
complications that impeded a quick solution. When
considering the continuing problems in the Congo
even after the withdrawal of the United Nations
force, this statement may be a gross oversimplifi-
cation. But, here again, the very complexity of
these situations, compounded by the inability of the
governments most directly concerned to solve the
problems, argues for the development of an international capability to assist in preserving the
peace.

In each case considered, there was an element
of colonialism. This issue, combined with that
frequent handmaiden of post-colonialism, rising
nationalism, introduces difficult emotional complications. From the standpoint of the West, this
residual colonial heritage appears as a negative
factor limiting the maneuverability of both the
Western powers and, on occasion, the leaders of the
newly independent states.

All three crises developed in a different
location, and each involved outside interests
transcending the strictly local considerations. In
the future, it is difficult to imagine a dispute
arising in a strategically unimportant area. This
is true because there are few, if any, strategically
unimportant areas of the world today. The world
has become too tightly intermeshed. Thus, it is
difficult to classify the West Irian area, for
example, as strategically unimportant. West Irian
immediately becomes part of the larger picture
involving both Indonesia and the Netherlands.
Accordingly, almost any dispute arising anywhere in
the world with the potential for boiling over will
have international importance. This again, if any
further emphasis is needed, reinforces the urgency
for giving attention to international peace-keeping
machinery and procedures.

NOTES

1. See Leland M. Goodrich, "The Maintenance of International Peace and Security," International Organization, XIX (Summer, 1965), 429ff.

2. An indication of the decisive effect of this raid on Egyptian-Israeli relations is reflected in Lieutenant General E. L. M. Burns' Between Arab & Israeli (New York: Ivan Obelansky, Inc., 1962), pp. 17-21. Burns sees this as a "crucial event" in a "dismal history" and as establishing the trend that led to the Sinai hostilities in October, 1956. This view was shared by many diplomatic observers who were present in Cairo during the period 1955-56.

3. There was a general consensus within the international community for achieving a peaceful resolution. This was revealed dramatically in the statements of the representatives of a number of the member nations made during the General Assembly debate. See U.N. General Assembly, Official Records, First Emergency Session, 561st-563rd Meetings (November 1-3, 1956), pp. 1-78.

4. For a reflection of the official U.S. views, see U.S. Department of State, United States Policy in the Middle East, Publ. 6505 (Washington, D.C.: Government Printing Office, 1957), pp. 148-57.

5. T. W. Adams and Alvin J. Cottrell, "The Cyprus Conflict," Orbis, VIII (Spring, 1964), 67-68.

6. Ibid., p. 69.

7. Ibid., pp. 69-70.

8. For texts, see U.S. Department of State, American Foreign Policy, Current Documents, 1959, Publ. 7492 (Washington, D.C.: Government Printing Office, 1963), pp. 765-75.

9. Michael Wall, "Cyprus Problem = Makarios Problem," The New York Times Magazine (October 18, 1964), p. 108.

10. U.N. Doc. S/4387, July, 1960.

11.   Confirmed through conversation with United
Nations Secretariat personnel including Dr. Ralph
Bunche, Under-Secretary for Political Affairs;
Major General Indar J. Rikhye, the former Military
Adviser to the Secretary-General; and members of
the Office of General Services. The amount of
thought given to advance planning by key members
of the Secretariat Staff has been greatly under-
estimated.

CHAPTER **3** ALTERNATIVES TO
UNITED NATIONS
INTERVENTION

As the Suez, Congo, and Cyprus stories unfolded,
United Nations intervention in the form of a peace-
keeping force appeared appropriate and feasible.
What were the other alternatives for keeping or
restoring the peace? Did any of these alternatives
offer the promise for a peaceful solution? If not,
what factors suggested that United Nations action
might be useful? Why was such an approach finally
invoked? Possibly, in attempting to answer these
questions, we may get an inkling of why the course
of action ultimately adopted was taken.

THE ALTERNATIVES IN SUEZ

The immediate challenge to peace in the Suez
area was the Israeli attack in the Sinai launched
on October 29, 1956. No attempt will be made in
this context to judge the justification for, or the
merits of, that attack. Whether it was provoked or
unprovoked is incidental to the problem at hand.
It is sufficient herein to note that the Israeli
attack constituted a "breach of the peace" in the
terms of the Charter of the United Nations and posed
a direct threat to the stability of the area. We
have seen how this problem was quickly complicated
by the Anglo-French ultimatum and the intervention
by those two powers. This entire sequence occurred
within a short space of time. What were the possibilities for resolution of this problem, other than
by the United Nations, during the interval that
preceded United Nations action?

One solution that might have been possible
prior to the Anglo-French entry on the scene would
have been to permit the two countries immediately
concerned, Israel and Egypt, to settle the matter
directly between themselves in the traditional

manner--by force of arms. In such a case, barring
other complications, the decision would normally
have gone to the contestant most able and effective
in bringing the greater power to bear on the problem.
In view of the circumstances that followed immediately
and ruled out such a direct method of resolution, it
is difficult to speculate with assurance on the outcome of such a course. It is very possible, however,
that if this sequence had been allowed to run its
natural course without outside interference, the
Israeli forces would have occupied the entire Sinai
Peninsula. The Israeli capability to achieve this
objective cannot seriously be questioned.* Their
capacity to have continued their successes to the
west of the Canal is, however, subject to serious
question. Once past the Canal, the Israeli supply
pipeline to support further military operations
would have been unduly extended, and any pause to
reorganize their logistics would have afforded the
Egyptian forces a badly needed respite and a chance
to regroup. It can only be concluded that the story
of a campaign to the west of the Suez Canal would
have been a different story than that reflected by
the swiftly moving Israeli advances in the Sinai.

Under this initial assumption, i.e., two-party
hostilities without external interference, the battle
lines would likely have been stabilized along the
Suez Canal with the Israeli forces occupying the
territory on one side of the Canal and the Egyptian
forces on the other. What this would have done to
the operation of the Canal is not difficult to
speculate. Here we can imagine an international

---

*Likewise, the Egyptian ability to mount an
effective military counteraction east of the Canal,
at least during the initial operations, appeared
extremely remote. The Egyptian forces were in
complete disarray during the period immediately
following the Israeli attack and did not regain
their equilibrium until some time after the United
Nations cease-fire became effective. This assessment
is based on personal observations and on interviews
with qualified military observers in the area. This
and the related observations apply only to the
situation in 1956. The situation that subsequently
developed in the 1967 Middle East crisis, although
similar in some respects to that of 1956, also had
marked differences.

waterway not over 200 feet wide for most of its
length with the opposing military forces entrenched
on and harassing each other from the opposite banks.
To complicate the picture even further, the Canal
itself had been blocked by sunken ships and other
obstacles to navigation. Clearance of the Canal
under these circumstances without third-party
assistance would have been a very difficult, if not
impossible, task. A situation somewhat similar to
that pictured herein in fact came to pass in June,
1967.

How long could the maritime powers of the world
in 1956 have permitted this important international
waterway to remain closed before exerting pressure
on the belligerents to adjust their differences?
The concern manifested by the users of the Canal
during the period immediately following the nationalization in July of 1956 indicates that these powers
would have exerted influence to bring about a resumption of normal traffic. With such external pressure
and given the inability of either of the two contestants singly or in concert to restore freedom of
movement, some form of international effort would
probably have been required. In this hypothetical
situation of 1956, the United Nations would have
been a logical candidate to take the lead in reopening the Canal.

Another possibility in the Suez crisis would
have been to permit the contestants to fight it out
even after the Anglo-French intervention had occurred.
Here the previous picture is complicated by doubling
the number of active contestants. The following is
only one of the possible alternative results of such
an approach: the Anglo-French force in secure possession of the Canal and a strip ten miles wide on
either side; the Canal open to free passage for
international shipping (on the completion of the
necessary dredging and clearance operations); and
the Egyptian and Israeli forces separated by a
buffer zone policed by self-appointed British and
French policemen. This outcome resembles closely
the declared Anglo-French goals.[1]

How long such a solution could have been maintained strictly by force and in the face of unsym-
pathetic world opinion, the hostility of Egypt which
bitterly objected to the joint intervention, and the
resentment of the other Arab states is more speculative

It can be effectively argued that such a simple
direct answer, although satisfactory to those participants who achieved their objective, would not have
been acceptable to all and would not, therefore,
have provided the inherent stability necessary for
a lasting solution. Neither would it have been
acceptable to the other Great Powers with whose
interests it clashed. The imposition of this type
of solution might have been successful in the nineteenth century. However, such a solution was clearly
an insufficient answer to this complex twentieth-
century problem. It is doubtful that the Egyptians
would have been willing to accept complacently such
an enforced verdict. It is more probable that they
would have resorted to underground terrorist activities in the Canal Zone similar to those already
confronting the British in Cyprus. The British and
French may have then been faced with the problem of
trying to pacify an unruly, "unappreciative" populace
unwilling to accept an arbitrary enlightened rule
imposed from without. The Anglo-French position in
such circumstances might be compared to the problem
posed in trying to sit comfortably and serenely on
the back of a wild stallion. Although this is sometimes possible, the task is complicated by the fact
that the animal is unwilling to cooperate and the
seat is inherently unstable.

    The legality of such a move is not nearly so
speculative. The allied intervention was clearly
inconsistent with the provisions of the United
Nations Charter which calls upon all member states
to "settle their international disputes by peaceful
means" and to "refrain in their international relations from the threat or use of force against the
territorial integrity" of any state (Article 2).
It is extremely difficult to view the Anglo-French
action as not involving the use or the threat of
use of force. Certainly the British and the French
did have claims for compensation resulting from the
nationalization of the Canal. They also had a claim,
based on treaty and customary rights, regarding the
use of the international waterway. However, it is
doubtful that these claims were sufficient to justify the flaunting of the provisions of the Charter
of the United Nations. Furthermore, the rights
involved were susceptible to peaceful settlement.
The Egyptians did not deny either the right of
international usage of the Canal or the claim of the
Suez Canal Company for compensation. These were
publicly acknowledged.[2]

Once the Anglo-French military action was initiated, what were the alternative possibilities for resolution? Unilateral action by either the United States or the Soviet Union was not a likely prospect. Both had very real interests in the area, and because of these interests neither desired nor would willingly permit the other to dictate or actively impose a solution. The United States had, since the end of World War II, played an increasing role in attempting to prevent or contain Soviet encroachments in the Middle East. During this same period, the likelihood of the Soviets at least partially achieving their historical aim of projecting their influence into this area continued to grow. In the year immediately preceding Suez, the Soviets had made significant progress in this direction, and the sale of Soviet bloc arms to Egypt in 1955 was a significant milestone in this effort. As is true at any moment in history, the ability of either Great Power to pursue its aim in the Middle East was complicated by external factors and, at this particular time, some of the external factors were of even greater than usual importance.

The United States was caught in the embarrassing position of being at odds with her allies. In addition, a Presidential election, an event that had traditionally inhibited forceful international political action, was in the immediate offing. Fortunately, the record in this instance does not completely substantiate this old truth. Because of sympathetic and understanding public support at home, the Administration was not prevented from taking a strong and decisive stand on this difficult problem.[3] However, unilateral action would have placed the United States in direct confrontation with two of her principal allies and posed a serious strain on the Western alliance. This was something to be avoided or minimized. Accordingly, it appeared appropriate and advisable for the United States to channel her efforts through the United Nations.

Similarly, the Soviet Union had problems that reduced the threat of Soviet intervention. Hungary was in revolt, and this fact limited Soviet freedom of action. However, this limitation was not sufficient to prevent the Soviet voice from sounding off on the question of Suez. Instead, as they were once again to do in 1967, the Soviets were quite vocal in demonstrating their support for Nasser and Egypt. This support was reflected in a proposal "that Russian and American troops go to Egypt's rescue

'to crush the aggressor and restore peace,'" and in
an announcement that tens of thousands of Russian
"volunteers" were ready to go to the assistance of
Egypt.[4]

Although the Soviet Union made belligerent noises
and threatened Great Britain and France with rocket
attacks, it is very questionable whether this threat
reflected a genuine willingness to launch. The
threat appeared to be more bluster than a reflection
of serious intent. This conclusion is partially
warranted by the fact that the Soviet threat was
not made at the height of the crisis but only after
the decision of the United States to oppose the
Anglo-French action became evident and the course of
events seemed to be improving. However, despite the
tardiness of the proposal, there was a propaganda
value to be gained, and the Soviets were apparently
anxious to capitalize on it.

There were, therefore, factors inhibiting unilateral action by either the United States or the
Soviet Union. Because of these limitations on either
nation's ability to intervene directly, there was
little real possibility of either taking action alone
to resolve the crisis. Joint action by the two powers
was also not politically feasible inasmuch as the
United States could not have agreed to act in concert
with the Soviet Union in opposition to two NATO allies.
This, in effect, left some sort of international
solution as the only real possibility remaining.

Could an international solution have been achieved
on a regional basis? Such a likelihood appeared
remote because there was no appropriate regional
organization to which to appeal. The League of Arab
States, assuming it had a potential for peace-making
that is not readily apparent, would have been unacceptable to Israelis. The crisis was outside the
geographic area, and beyond the competence of NATO
and CENTO, either of which would have been an anathema
to President Nasser. An appropriate African regional
organization did not exist. The United Nations,
therefore, was the only international body that
might be competent and prove acceptable to the parties
to the conflict.

THE ALTERNATIVES IN THE CONGO

Turning to the Congo, we must ask the same

question.   There are several possible alternatives
that might be explored, but the four most likely
appear to have been the following: (1) reliance on
the Congolese authorities to resolve the problems on
their own; (2) acquiescence in the re-establishment
of Belgian political control--or encouragement of
Belgian assistance to the newly created Congolese
Government in trying to bring about the transition
to self-government in an orderly manner; (3) intervention by national powers other than Belgium; or
(4) an international approach through the United
Nations.

A lengthy review is unneccessary to demonstrate
that the Republic of the Congo was incapable of
maintaining law and order after independence. Within
two weeks of independence, there were internal riots,
mutiny in the armed forces, flight by the white
residents, a threat of secession in Katanga, and the
complete breakdown of law and order.[5] The Congolese
authorities proved unable to check this progression
of events, and a course of action continuing to
place principal reliance on the Congolese Government
to restore order contained little promise of eventual
success.   If such a course had been continued for
long, the disorders would merely have continued
unabated and the situation would have become even
more hopeless.

Against this pattern of anarchy, it was unlikely
that Belgian intervention, even if the Government of
the Congo would have been willing to accept or
acquiesce in such action, could restore stability.
Once the situation had become chaotic, the Belgians
would have faced an endless task in trying to patch
up the old order.   However, consideration of such a
possibility is purely academic because the Congolese
Government was either unwilling, or unable for
domestic reasons, to work with or accept assistance
from the Belgians.   The Belgians were stigmatized
as colonialists.   As such, they were the ready target
for invective by the many diverse and competing local
factions.   The Belgians were the declared "enemies"
even though the real enemy was something else, i.e.,
that state of anarchy which dramatically revealed
the inability of the Congolese to create an effective
government and to maintain law and order.

What about the possibility of outside intervention? Any single nation would have faced the
same difficult conditions that confronted the

Government of the Congo and would have faced the
Belgians. Congolese authorities requested assistance
in the form of U.S. troops on July 11, 1960. President
Eisenhower promptly declined, replying that forces
from the large powers should not muddy the waters.[6]
Clearly the United States was reluctant to extend
the Cold War into the heart of Africa and had no
desire to commit troops to a situation for which no
end was in sight. The Congolese Government also
indicated early in the crisis that if United Nations
assistance was not forthcoming it would have to
turn to the Bandung Treaty Powers for assistance[7]
or to the Soviet Union.[8] These expressions reflected
the desperation of the Congolese and their willingness
to turn in any direction for assistance. Nothing
resulted from these expressions, and United Nations
action rendered other appeals unnecessary or inappropriate. It is highly speculative whether the Bandung
Treaty members could have agreed to, mobilized,
transported, and conducted an effective peace-keeping
operation relying on their own resources. Regarding
the possibility of Soviet unilateral intervention,
the United States and the West could never have
allowed such a course.

Any outside nation attempting to intervene in
the Congo would have been confronted with the initial
task of creating a stable local government. Intervention without achieving this basic objective would
merely have resulted in a ceaseless diversion of the
resources of the intervening nation with no end in
sight. Even the achievement of this initial objective
would have been formidable. Political groups, other
than the local faction working with an intervening
power, would have been able to rally support from
the other internal dissidents with nationalistic
appeals. Tribal differences, threats of secession,
and the absence of the basic elements upon which
to create an effective governmental organization
combined to present a very dismal picture for the
restoration of order. A single nation attempting
to assume this burden alone would also undoubtedly
have been faced with adverse criticism from other
nations not completely agreeing with the course of
action. Such is the nature of international politics.
Accordingly, assistance to the Congo by any single
country did not appear to offer great promise for
success. Neither did such a course appear attractive
to the countries that might have fulfilled this kind
of role. However, the prospects for success, although

not promising, might be enhanced through some form
of cooperative international action. In the absence
of any other very appealing alternative, and in a
situation in which the continuation of anarchy could
extend the threat to the peace, it is not surprising
that an international solution was sought through
the United Nations.

THE ALTERNATIVES IN CYPRUS

When violence erupted in Cyprus on December 21,
1963, it was not a new phenomenon to the island.
Violence had been the order of the day during the
uneasy years that immediately preceded and led to
Cypriot independence in 1959. Independence brought
with it a temporary respite. Now disorder once again
prevailed, precisely because many of the fundamental
problems of the pre-independence period had been
unresolved with the attainment of independent statehood and with the consummation of the London-Zurich
agreements. But, despite an old familiarity with
violence, the breakdown of law and order was not a
welcome or happy turn of affairs for all parties
concerned. New efforts were obviously required to
restore the peace.

As in the two previous crises, there were, at
least in theory, several possible choices of methods
or procedures that might have been adopted to restore
order. In the Cyprus crisis, there is evidence that
the search for such alternative measures was more
extensive than in either of the former cases. The
parties involved attempted to find a solution on
their own before turning to the United Nations.
This search took the form of an extended series of
discussions, conferences, and meetings between the
interested parties. These discussions lasted from
the outbreak of rioting in December, 1963, until the
time the conferees, unable to agree on a proposed
solution, referred the problem to the United Nations
in mid-February, 1964.

The search for alternatives to United Nations
intervention was more extended in the case of Cyprus
because of the existence of a set of circumstances
markedly different from those that had existed in
either the Suez or the Congo. In Cyprus we witness
a somewhat unusual situation at this point in history
in which the status of an independent state is

guaranteed under treaty commitments by several
external powers. This arrangement might have been
more appropriate for an earlier period. The existence
of such an arrangement in Cyprus presented the opportunity for joint international action by the guarantor
powers short of United Nations intervention. But,
with the failure of the guarantor powers to reach
agreement, the promise of pacification through the
guarantee procedures proved illusory.

What were the alternatives to United Nations
action? One possibility might be to rely solely on
the Government of Cyprus to resolve the problem.
This possibility can be quickly ruled out. As the
crisis progressively unfolded and local disorder
spread, the inability of the Cypriot authorities to
maintain order, let alone resolve the basic issues
underlying the disorder, became very apparent.
Once the dispute broke into the open rekindling the
old enmities between the Greek and Turkish Cypriots,
the chances for pacification through local governmental action were greatly reduced. Only by capit-
ulating to the Turkish Cypriot demands and withdrawing
the proposals to amend the Constitution could the
Cypriot Government have satisfied the desires of the
Turkish community. This the Government of Cyprus
was unwilling to do. Alternatively, only if the
Turkish Cypriots had been willing to forego their
firm opposition to the constitutional changes could
the government forces conceivably have been able to
check the passions aroused in the December outbreaks.
In the absence of a willingness by either side to
retreat from these irreconcilable demands, the
government was helpless. Neither side by force alone
could impose its will and, even if this were possible,
an imposed solution would undoubtedly not have proved
lasting. Without resolving the basic issues in a
manner acceptable to both sides, the prospects for
a permanent solution or even a return to the pre-
December conditions were exceedingly dim.

When it became obvious that the Government of
Cyprus would be unable to resolve the crisis, what
were the chances of the guarantor powers acting
jointly to restore peace? We have noted that, in
accordance with the provisions of the Treaty of
Guarantee, Greece, the United Kingdom, and Turkey
jointly recognized the independence and guaranteed
the territorial integrity, the security, and the
provisions of the Constitution of Cyprus.[9] Three

countries, one the former colonial ruler and the
other two close neighbors with blood ties, all tied
to Cyprus by different bonds, were committed by
treaty obligations to preserve the sercurity of
Cyprus. In the event that concerted action to achieve
this objective could not be agreed upon, each power
reserved the right unilaterally to take action with
the sole aim of restoring the state of affairs
established by the treaty.[10]

In an effort to discharge these treaty obligations in good faith, the guarantor powers, under
the leadership of the United Kingdom, undertook the
search for a method to restore peace to the island.
This search met with only limited success. It did
lead to the establishment of a limited peace-making
force which helped to keep the lid on the situation
until a more comprehensive peace force could be
established. It did not lead to a settlement of the
basic problems, and it accentuated the difficulties
of reaching an agreement that would prove acceptable
to the two communities. Increasingly, the Greek
Cypriot position, which looked toward Enosis (or
independence with an unimpeded option to elect Enosis
at a later date), hardened. The Turkish Cypriot
community, on the other hand, leaned more and more
toward Taksim, or partition, as the only solution
that would protect their interests. The governments
of Greece and Turkey, supporting the demands of their
respective ethnic groups in Cyprus, became captive
to these views which were in turn reinforced by the
pressure of popular sentiment in both Greece and
Turkey. This left these two powers with little room
for maneuver during the negotiations. This proved
unfortunate because otherwise it might normally have
been expected that these neighboring states, each
with an interest in resolving this issue, would have
been able to play a positive and constructive role
in the discussions. The remaining guarantor, the
United Kingdom, was anxious but unable to formulate
an agreement acceptable to all parties. The British
had a large stake in Cyprus in the form of their
strategic bases and for this reason, as well as for
humanitarian considerations, were especially anxious
to arrive at a settlement.

The initial effort of the guarantor powers,
putting first things first, was directed toward
the immediate restoration of law and order; this led
to the establishment of a joint peace force in Cyprus

composed of Greek, Turkish, and British units on
December 26, 1963. The objective of this force was
to attempt to secure a cease-fire and restore peace.
Because of these efforts by the guarantor powers,
the Security Council which first met to consider the
Cyprus problem on December 27, 1963, in response to
a Cypriot complaint against Turkish aggression,
considered the matter briefly and then adjourned to
reconvene "when and if it was considered appropriate
by the members."[11]

Following the creation of this three-power
peace-keeping force, the United Kingdom directed its
energies toward securing a forum in which to consider
a more far-reaching solution. As a result of this
effort, a conference of the parties directly concerned
was subsequently convened in London in January, 1964.
Representatives of the two Cypriot communities were
given an opportunity to state their positions during
these deliberations. It is interesting to note that
although the London Conference was not conducted
within the immediate United Nations structure, neither
was it conducted without regard to the United Nations.
The participating governments kept the United Nations
fully advised concerning the discussions. This would
be especially important in the event that the conference was unable to reach an agreement and would
then be forced to turn the problem over to the United
Nations, as eventually proved the case. Accordingly,
Jose Rolz-Bennett, a senior official of the Secretariat,
proceeded to London as a representative of the
Secretary-General to observe the proceedings. At
the request of the four governments represented in
London, the Secretary-General also sent Lieutenant
General P. S. Gyani of India to Cyprus as his personal
representative to observe the peace-making force in
operation. The London Conference succeeded in coming
up with two proposals for an expanded peace-keeping
force utilizing contingents from several North Atlantic
Treaty countries. Both were rejected by Archbishop
Makarios.[12]

The first set of proposals, if accepted, would
have provided an enlarged peace-keeping force comprised of units from countries "friendly to Cyprus"
under a British commander who would receive his
political guidance from an intergovernmental committee
of representatives sitting in London. The force was
to have been composed of selected national contingents,
including the Greek and Turkish units then in Cyprus,

which would serve for a period of three months.
Under the second set of proposals, an international
peace-keeping force composed of national contingents
would also have been established. The duration would
likewise have been for three months, during which
time the existing treaty rights and obligations
relating to Cyprus would not have been affected.
However, during the period of concerted action, the
guarantor powers would agree not to exercise their
unilateral rights set forth in the Treaty of Guarantee.
The proposals also called for the designation of a
mediator to assist the parties in reaching a settle-
ment.13

The Government of Cyprus was unwilling to accept
either set of proposals. It did agree in principle
that an international force should be constituted
but desired that such a force be directly responsive
to the United Nations and that it not include Greek
and Turkish units. Archbishop Makarios desired that
the terms of reference should specifically refer to
the protection of Cypriot territorial integrity and
specify clearly that the force would be available
to assist the Cypriot forces in restoring normal
conditions. In effect, the indispensable prerequisite for Cypriot acceptance of a peace force
was a firm statement, most probably in the form of
a Security Council resolution, confirming the
territorial integrity of Cyprus. From the Cypriot
viewpoint, such an expression could then provide
an argument against the legality of the Treaty of
Guarantee which, as we have already noted, would
under certain conditions specifically authorize one
or all of the guarantor powers to intervene in Cyrpus.
This would support the Cypriot claim, in the event
of armed intervention by Turkey, that such action
was an act of aggression under the provisions of the
United Nations Charter. By the same token, this
argument might be extended, relying on the provisions
of Article 103 of the Charter, to declare the Treaty
of Guarantee invalid.* This line of reasoning would
deny the counterargument that the Treaty of Guarantee

---

*Article 103 States: "In the event of a conflict
between the obligations of the Members of the United
Nations under the present Charter and their obligations under any other international agreement, their
obligations under the present Charter shall prevail."

was designed to uphold both the territorial
integrity and the Constitution of Cyprus and that
action by one of the guarantor powers in accordance
with the provisions of that Treaty could not be
considered an act of agression.

During the months of January and February, the
position of the principal actors--United Kingdom,
Greece, Turkey, and Cyprus itself--may be summarized
as follows.

First, the United Kingdom actively desired and
worked toward achieving a peaceful solution acceptable
to the main participants. The British envisaged the
continuation of a unified Cypriot state with adequate
safeguards for the minorities. On the immediate
problem concerning the restoration of peaceful conditions, the British demonstrated a willingness to
continue to assist in the pacification process but,
at the same time, desired to share that responsibility
by broadening the base of the peace-keeping force.
This would be accomplished by augmenting the United
Kingdom, Greek, and Turkish units already in Cyprus
with the addition of national units from other
selected countries. These units, naturally, would
come from countries acceptable to the parties concerned, possibly from the Commonwealth countries,
NATO nations, or even from certain non-aligned
states. The British were also anxious to share not
only the responsibility for maintaining the peace
but the related financial burden as well. Fundamental to the United Kingdom position was a concern
for the continued availability of their very important strategic base complex. As the discussions
between the guarantor powers dragged on without
success, the British became more and more inclined
to look toward the United Nations for a way out.

The position of the Greek Government reflected
the views of the Greek majority on Cyprus. Greece
supported the demands of Archbishop Makarios and
presumably would have been happy to see either a
continuation of the unitary State of Cyprus, with
the proper constitutional modifications, or Enosis.
Regarding the immediate problem of restoring law
and order, Greece indicated a willingness to cooperate
in measures to achieve this end and, in contributing
toward this goal, to maintain units of the Greek
Army in the joint peace force that had been established
in Cyprus. Greece also joined the other guarantor

powers in proposing that this force be enlarged.

The position of the Turkish Government was underlined by an increasing concern over the fate of the Turkish community on Cyprus. As in the case of Greece, the Turkish position reflected the views of the less populous Turkish group in Cyprus. Concerning the immediate problem of restoring peace, the Turks were also willing to accept proposals providing an enlarged peace-keeping force. There is an indication that the Turks were hopeful for some form of U.S. leadership in leading the way out of this awkward situation. As the crisis continued with no signs of reaching an agreeable solution, the Turkish position gradually appeared to become more rigid and to look toward a physical separation of the two quarreling Cypriot communities as a sine qua non.

The Government of Cyprus appeared determined to bring about an effective unitary state unhampered by an "unworkable" constitution. This meant removing the limitations contained in the Treaty of Guarantee and revising the Constitution. Regarding the immediate question of restoring peace, Archbishop Makarios was obviously reluctant to accept any form of NATO peace-keeping force, fearing perhaps that this would lead to partition. Increasingly, the Government of Cyprus, although accepting in principle the need for an international force, leaned toward the acceptance of such a force only under United Nations auspices.

Thus, the efforts of the guarantor powers to provide an acceptable answer proved fruitless. This difficulty might have been anticipated by noting that the basic positions of the countries concerned did not provide sufficient flexibility to reconcile the divergent views. With the inability of the powers most directly involved to find an answer, what other prospects short of United Nations action were there?

One approach might have been intercession by the United States, and this course was at least partially explored. The United States was concerned over the continuation of the Cyprus crisis for humanitarian reasons, because of the possible disruptive effect of the dispute on NATO, and because of the possibility of the threat to the peace spreading. While the guarantor powers were searching for

an answer, the United States indicated a readiness
to assist although preferring to leave the solution
to those directly concerned. This willingness was
voiced by President Lyndon B. Johnson at an early
stage when he declared that he would continue to do
everything he could "to support any and all actions
proposed by the three guarantor powers which offer
reasonable hope of assisting in a peaceful solution."[14]

     The U.S. concern prompted a visit of George
Ball, the Under-Secretary of State, to London, Athens,
Ankara, and Nicosia to lend support to the proposals
of the guarantor powers. He expressed support for
the London Conference proposals for an enlarged
international force to be composed of units from
NATO countries. Although reluctant to provide
American units, the United States would have agreed
to contribute to a peace force in order to move
forward.[15] However, this question became academic
when Archbishop Makarios refused to agree to the
creation of any force with a predominately NATO
label. The Archbishop likewise turned a deaf ear
on suggestions to use NATO good offices or to accept
the services of a NATO mediator. He was adamant in
his refusal to have anything to do with NATO, apparently convinced that a NATO solution would be no
better than the Zurich agreements.[16]

     The failure of the London Conference signaled
the inability of the parties immediately involved
to resolve their differences. The failure of Ball's
mission and of President Johnson's appeals reflected
the inability of the United States to come up with
an acceptable answer. The unwillingness of Archbishop
Makarios to accept a NATO approach ruled out a regional
solution. Accordingly, no practicable recourse was
left except to appeal to the United Nations. This
was the only forum to which the parties concerned
could agree; thus, the United Nations was given
another troublesome problem.

                    CONCLUSIONS

     In each situation thus far examined, the various
alternatives to the United Nations action, for one
reason or another, proved unacceptable. The nations
involved were unable, relying on their own resources,
to resolve the problem at hand. Likewise, the possibilities of any single intervening state, group of

states, or regional organization assisting in reaching
a satisfactory solution did not appear hopeful.
Accordingly, the only real remaining possibility with
some promise of success was a form of international,
or United Nations, intervention.

The foregoing is not intended to imply that all
such situations arising in the future should be
referred to the United Nations. There may be occasions when peace-keeping action can most effectively
be accomplished under the auspices of an appropriate
regional organization. There will obviously also
be instances in which action by a particular state
may be proper and best serve the interests of the
international community at large in preserving the
peace. The arrangements and forms of organization
adopted for peace-keeping must take into account
the peculiar circumstances of the specific situation.
This has been true in the past; it will undoubtedly
continue to prove true in the future.

NOTES

1. See "Statement in the British House of
Commons by Prime Minister Eden, Oct. 30, 1956,"
reprinted in U.S. Department of State, United States
Policy in the Middle East, p. 139. There are many
who defend the Anglo-French intervention convinced
that if the British and French had been permitted
to achieve their declared objectives a logical and
lasting settlement would have been obtained. Considering such a settlement "logical" depends on one's
point of view. It would not have been logical to
the Egyptians and possibly also not to the Israelis.

2. Republic of Egypt, Ministry of Foreign
Affairs, White Paper on the Nationalization of the
Suez Maritime Canal Company (Cairo: Government Press,
August 12, 1956). Final compensation to the Suez
Canal Companies was arranged in 1958 through the
World Bank.

3. U.N. General Assembly, Official Records,
First Emergency Session, 561st and 562nd Meetings
(November 1, 1956), pp. 1-44.

4. William R. Frye, A United Nations Peace Force
(New York: Oceana Publications for Carnegie Endowment
for International Peace, 1957), pp. 10, 12.

5. Lyman M. Tondel, Jr. (ed.), The Role of the
United Nations in the Congo (New York: Oceana Publications for the Association of the Bar of the City
of New York, 1963), pp. 11-13.

6. Ibid., p. 13. For speculation concerning
the wisdom of direct U.S. assistance to the Congo,
see Ernest W. Lefever, "The U.N. as a Foreign Policy
Instrument: The Congo Crisis," in Foreign Policy in
the Sixties: The Issues and the Instruments, ed.
Roger Hilsman and Robert C. Good (Baltimore, Md.:
The Johns Hopkins Press, 1965), pp. 141-57.

7. U.N. Doc. S/4382, July 12, 1960, p. 2.

8. U.S. House of Representatives, Committee on
Foreign Affairs, Staff Memorandum on the Republic of
Congo, 86th Cong., 2nd Sess., Committee Print, 1960,
p. 11.

9. U.S. Department of State, American Foreign
Policy, Current Documents, 1959, Publ. 7492 (Washington,
D.C.: Government Printing Office, 1963, p. 770.

10. Ibid.

11. International Organization, XVIII (Spring,
1964), p. 479.

12. "U.N. Peace-keeping Force in Cyprus,"
United Nations Review, II (April, 1964), p. 6.

13. See Statement by Sir Patrick Dean, the
representative of the United Kingdom, February 18,
1964, U.N. Security Council, Official Records,
Nineteenth year, 1095th Meeting (February 18, 1964),
pp. 6-17.

14. Letter from President Johnson to General
Cemal Gursel, President of Turkey, December 26, 1963,
U.S. Department of State, Bulletin, L, No. 1282
(1964), p. 90.

15. Statement by Secretary of State Dean Rusk
during press conference on February 7, 1964, U.S.
Department of State, Bulletin, L, No. 1287, p. 283.

16. Michael Wall, "Cyprus Problems = Makarios
Problem," The New York Times Magazine, October 18,
1964, p. 108.

CHAPTER **4** THE LEGAL BASIS FOR
UNITED NATIONS
PEACE-KEEPING
OPERATIONS

The Confederacy of Delos which linked a number
of Greek city-states in an "international" organization for the purpose of preserving peace was established in 477 B.C. This appears to be the first
recorded attempt to set up an international navy and
police force.[1] In 1945, another attempt was made to
organize the international community for the purpose
of safeguarding international peace and security in
the form of the United Nations. Between 477 B.C.
and 1945 A.D., 2,422 years intervened. During this
interval, numerous proposals envisaging the use of
military forces to assist in maintaining peace were
advanced. Although many of these schemes appeared
attractive in theory and some served limited purposes,
e.g., the Governing Commission of the Saar constituted by the League of Nations, most proved difficult
to implement in practice and none provided the complete solution for peace their proponents were seeking.

Since 1945, there has been a continuing and
added interest in preserving the peace and, subsequent to creating the UNEF during the Suez crisis
of 1956, a new pattern of peace-keeping activity
has gradually evolved. The arrival of Canadian
forces along with units from other nations in Cyprus
in March of 1964 marked the eleventh time the United
Nations had embarked on a peace-keeping role.* The

---

*The previous endeavors include the following:
Indonesia (1947-48); Greece (1947-51); Palestine
(1948-); Kashmir (1948-); Korea (1950-53); Suez
(1956-67); Lebanon (1958); Congo (1960-64); West
Irian (1962-63); Yemen (1962-64); and Cyprus

review of three recent instances in this series has
led us from a consideration of the background set-
tings, through some of the possible courses of
action that might have been taken to redress the
situation, and finally to the point of United Nations
action. Each action taken was consistent with the
general objectives of the United Nations set forth
in the Charter. However, there have been differing
views regarding the legal basis for the specific
form the operation has taken and the manner in which
the actions were initiated and conducted. Constitutional questions have been raised concerning the
initial authorization and with respect to the
responsibilities of the main United Nations organs
concerned--the Security Council, the General Assembly,
and the Secretary-General. A broad interpretation
of the general as well as the more specific provisions contained within the Charter provides the
United Nations with wide latitude in taking actions
to maintain or restore the peace. A narrow interpretation, giving particular emphasis to certain
specific articles and not to the declared purposes
and assuming that what is not completely spelled out
in the detailed procedures is not legally authorized,
could severely inhibit the United Nations' capacity
to maintain or restore peace.

    The strict constructionists, represented by
the Soviet Union, France, and others, argue that
only the Security Council is empowered to authorize
the use of military forces in cases where there is
a threat to or breach of the peace and that any

(1964-   ). This list does not include such other
related activities as the Security Council consideration of Trieste (1954), the dispatch of a Security
Council subcommittee to Laos (1959), the establishment of a U.N. presence in Jordan (1958), or the
provision of good offices on the Thai-Cambodian
border (1963-64). It also does not include subsequent operations such as the expansion of the
Kashmir U.N. force in 1965-66 through the creation
of the United Nations India Pakistan Observer Mission
(UNIPOM) or the United Nations Truce Supervision
Organization (UNTSO) in the Middle East in 1967.
Again it should be noted that Korea, although
"peace-keeping" in a broad sense, is more properly
described as an enforcement action.

responsibility delegated to the Secretary-General must be strictly defined and delimited. Fortunately, from the standpoint of the international community at large, this represents the minority view within the organization. The majority view is that the Security Council has primary responsibility but that the General Assembly can act in circumstances in which the Security Council is deadlocked. Furthermore, in accordance with the views of those who subscribe to this line of reasoning, the Secretary-General can be given broad authority by either of the other two organs to act as their agent in accordance with a duly approved mandate.

Unfortunately, these differing views have not been reconciled, and they continue to constitute a serious challenge to the United Nations' capacity for maintaining peace. Despite this, however, the organization has been able to act and there has been, especially during the most recent experience, a tendency to follow the majority view with respect to the role of the principal organs involved in peace-keeping.

With the foregoing in mind, it is appropriate to take a closer look at the authorization for recent United Nations peace-keeping ventures, at the initial directives setting forth the terms for the operations, at the legal basis under which those directives were issued, and at the role and responsibility of the Security Council, the General Assembly, and the Secretary-General in this process.

LEGAL AUTHORIZATION IN SELECTED CASES

Suez

The United Nations reaction to the Anglo-French-Israeli intervention in Suez has been cited as an outstanding example of the responsiveness of that organization in meeting a threat to the international peace. This description is not unmerited. The actual story of that response has been set forth very completely in several accounts describing (1) how, on October 30, 1956, the day the Anglo-French intervention was announced, the United States requested an immediate meeting of the Security Council to consider the matter;[2] (2) how resolutions

proposed first by the United States and then by the
Soviet Union were met with Anglo-French vetoes, and
how, with the Security Council deadlocked, the
problem was turned over to the General Assembly;[3]
and (3) how the General Assembly, working under
great pressure, passed the resolutions authorizing
the creation of the United Nations Emergency Force
(UNEF). The prompt establishment of the force is
one of the better known and more reassuring episodes
in United Nations history of peace-keeping.[4]

The legal basis for that action has been well
documented:

> General authority for UNEF is to be found
> in the Charter of the United Nations,
> particularly in those provisions relating
> to the functions and powers of the General
> Assembly, the rights and duties of member
> states, and the general principles of
> international law. Particular sources of
> UNEF's legal authority are a number of
> understandings between member states and
> the Secretary-General and various agree-
> ments concluded between Hammarskjold and
> the Egyptian Government.[5]

The UNEF, in contrast to the ONUC and the
UNFICYP, was fathered by the General Assembly, not
by the Security Council. Although the Security
Council is charged in Article 24 with the primary
responsibility for the maintenance of international
peace, this responsibility is not exclusive. The
General Assembly also has a large share in the
burden for insuring the continuation of peace and
security, and the exercise of this function has
proved to be a matter of great significance in
situations in which the Security Council has been
unable to act. Suez was such a situation.

As is true for the Security Council, the
General Assembly is responsible for furthering the
purposes of the United Nations. The first listed
purpose of the organization--Article 1 (2)--is "to
maintain international peace and security, and to
that end: to take effective collective measures for
the prevention and removal of threats to the peace."
Although the subsequent provisions of the Charter
that give precision to this objective are more
specific for the Security Council, the General

Assembly has a substantial responsibility for assisting in achieving this goal. The specific Charter
provisions setting forth the powers of the General
Assembly in this area of competence are contained
in Articles 10, 11, 12, and 14 of the Charter. These
Articles authorize the General Assembly to discuss
and make recommendations on "any questions or matters
within the scope of the present Charter" (Article
10); to consider principles and discuss questions
relating to the maintenance of the peace and to make
recommendations with regard to such questions unless
the Security Council is considering the matter
(Article 11); and to recommend measures for the
peaceful adjustment of any situation likely to impair
the general welfare or friendly relations among
nations (Article 14).

It should be noted that there are certain
limitations on the competence of the General Assembly
in this sphere. Unlike the Security Council in the
case of enforcement actions, the General Assembly
can only recommend. According to Article 11 (2),
although the General Assembly is granted wide competence in discussing matters affecting the peace of
the world, any such question on which action is
necessary must be referred to the Security Council
either before or after discussion. Article 12 (1)
states, in addition, that the General Assembly is
prevented from making recommendations on disputes
or situations during the period in which the Security
Council is exercising its assigned responsibilities
unless so requested by the Security Council. This
latter provision is sometimes not interpreted
literally. For example, the General Assembly did
not feel forestalled from calling an Emergency
Session in June, 1967, to consider the Middle East
question at a time when this matter was on the
Security Council agenda.*

The General Assembly's role in the maintenance
of peace has been affirmed in the "Uniting for Peace"
Resolution, which provides that the Assembly may act
promptly and recommend actions, including collective
measures, to preserve or restore international peace
and security.6 The provisions of this resolution

----

*The General Assembly's competence to take this
step was not even seriously challenged.

were invoked during the Suez crisis of 1956 when the
Security Council was unable to act. Subsequently,
the General Assembly, in the course of its considerations, authorized the creation of the UNEF.[7] The
UNEF may properly be considered a subsidiary organ
of the General Assembly in accordance with the
provisions of Article 22, which permits the General
Assembly to establish such agencies to assist it in
performing its functions.

        As in the case of the Security Council resolu-
tions on the Congo and Cyprus, the General Assembly
resolutions concerning the UNEF contained no specific
reference to the legal basis for the action. However,
as in the Congo and Cyprus, this omission does not
becloud the juridical status of the operation. Thus,
one student of UNEF has concluded that "despite the
innovating nature of this para-military organ and
the fact that the UNEF was hastily created, . . .
the Force . . . is constructed on a solid legal
foundation.[8]

The Congo

        On June 30, 1960, the Congo became an indepen-
dent republic. Less than two weeks later, on July
12, this newly independent government appealed to
the United Nations for the "urgent dispatch" of
military assistance. Here we have, in direct form,
a request from a new state for United Nations
military assistance "to protect the national territory of the Congo against the present external
aggression which is a threat to international peace."[9]
Although this request cited "external aggression"
against "national territory," the Congo conflict
was already characterized by internal strife--a
factor which was to continue to prevail long after
the external threat no longer existed. The initial
request of the Government of the Congo was reiterated
again the next day, July 13, in a second cable which
further emphasized the extreme uneasiness of that
government.[10]

        Both messages stressed the urgent need for
outside assistance. The Security Council, in
response to an initiative by the Secretary-General,
acted swiftly and on July 14, 1960, adopted the
first Congo resolution which (1) called for the
withdrawal of Belgian troops; (2) authorized the

Secretary-General to take the necessary steps, in consultation with the Congolese Government, to provide military and technical assistance until "the national security forces may be able, in the opinion of the Government, to meet fully their tasks"; and (3) requested the Secretary-General to report to the Security Council "as appropriate."[11]

Several features of this sequence of action are worthy of note. First, the Congolese Government itself requested United Nations military assistance. Second, the request specifically identified the threat to the international peace as external aggression. Third, the appeal was referred to the Security Council on the initiative of the Secretary-General who acted under the provisions of Article 99 of the Charter.* This marked the first time this article had been invoked in the history of the organization. Thus, the Secretary-General was involved with this question from the outset. Finally, the Security Council after deliberating on the matter authorized the Secretary-General to act as its agent in taking the necessary steps to meet this threat. The Security Council response was, in this instance, prompt and positive, thereby permitting the peace-keeping operation to be initiated without delay.

By the time the Security Council resolution was adopted, the Secretary-General was already in action arranging for military forces to proceed to the Congo. General C. C. Von Horn, the Chief of Staff of the United Nations Truce Supervision Organization in the Middle East, was designated as the Force Commander. By July 18, 1960, Secretary-General Hammarskjold was able to report to the Security Council that elements of the ONUC were in place and that further arrangements on the assembly of the force were being made.[12] In this same report, the Secretary-General described the force as "necessarily under the exclusive command of the United Nations, vested in the Secretary-General under the control of the Security Council." He also indicated that the request of the Congolese Government was the

---

*Article 99 authorizes the Secretary-General to "bring to the attention of the Security Council any matter which in his opinion may threaten the maintenance of international peace and security."

sole basis for the entrance of United Nations forces
into the Congo.[13]

A second Security Council resolution, adopted
on July 22, 1960, reaffirmed the call for Belgium
to withdraw its troops and authorized the Secretary-
General "to take all necessary action to this effect."
This resolution, in an attempt to keep the Cold War
out of the Congo, further requested that all states
refrain from taking actions that might "impede the
restoration of law and order" or "undermine the
territorial integrity and the political independence
of the Republic of the Congo."[14] A provision was
included concerning technical aid in the hope that
technical efforts might assist in creating the basis
for a return to "normal" conditions.

Subsequently, when the United Nations force
was unable to enter Katanga to carry out the terms
of the July 22 resolution without using military
force, the Secretary-General considered that a new
mandate was necessary and referred the matter to
the Security Council for review.[15] This review led
to a third Security Council resolution, adopted on
August 9, 1960, which again called on the government
of Belgium to withdraw its troops. The resolution
of August 9 declared the entry of the United Nations
force into Katanga to be a necessary action; reaffirmed that the force was not to intervene in internal conflicts; and called upon the member states,
in accordance with Articles 25 and 49 of the Charter,
to accept and carry out the decisions of the Security
Council.[16]

The authority for the United Nations action was
based on the general principles and purposes of the
United Nations as set forth in the Charter; on
Article 24 of the Charter, which vests primary
responsibility for the maintenance of international
peace in the Security Council; on the provisions of
Articles 39 and 40; and on the consent of the state
involved. It is to be noted that, in the resolution
of August 9, the member states were called upon "in
accordance with the provisions of Articles 25 and 49
of the Charter, to accept and carry out the decisions
of the Security Council and to afford mutual assistance in carrying out measures decided upon by the
Security Council."[17]

Although this third resolution referred to
Articles 25 and 49 which are concerned with the
obligations of member states, none of the Security
Council resolutions identified specifically any
particular article or articles of the Charter as the
basis for the United Nations action. The Secretary-
General several times indicated his belief that the
United Nations action should be considered as
implicitly taken under the provisions of Article 40
and, in that sense, "as based on an implicit finding
under Article 39."[18] If it is necessary to cite a
more precise Charter basis for Security Council
action than that contained in the purposes, "to take
collective measures for the prevention and removal
of threats to the peace," and Article 24 which grants
the Security Council "primary responsibility for the
maintenance of international peace and security,"
then Article 40 fills the bill.[19] As will be observed
in the discussion on Cyprus, there is nothing that
specifies that Article 40 must be explicitly cited
in the Security Council resolution or that a
preliminary determination must be made under Article
39 of the existence of a threat to the peace.[20]

Aside from the question of which article does
or does not provide the specific legal justification
for United Nations action, there is another question
which defies a simple answer. Article 2, paragraph
7, of the Charter states: "Nothing contained in the
present Charter shall authorize the United Nations
to intervene in matters which are within the domestic
jurisdiction of any State or shall require the
members to submit such matters to settlement under
the present Charter; but this principle shall not
prejudice the application of enforcement measures
under chapter VII." It is clear from the wording
that enforcement measures under Chapter VII are not
to be limited by the provisions of the article.
Thus the initiation of actions under Articles 41 and
42 of the Charter which set forth the enforcement
authority is not inhibited by the domestic jurisdiction proviso. But what about Security Council
actions that are not enforcing in nature and which
are initiated as provisional measures under Article
40? This question is pertinent because both the
Congo and the Cyprus crises reflect a dominant
internal component. In large measure, both resulted
from a breakdown of internal government and continued
because of the inability of the local government to

maintain order. The external threat, in each
instance, was of lesser magnitude and secondary
importance. Furthermore, in neither case was the
action considered to be enforcement in nature.

In the Congo, the presence of Belgian troops
provided a rationalization for the Congolese Government to cite "external aggression" in their appeal
to the United Nations. It also provided the Soviet
representative to the Security Council with an excuse
to attempt to label the Belgians aggressors. However,
this objective was never achieved, and the essential
characteristic in the Congo was local anarchy. This
situation was described by the Secretary-General as
a breakdown of law and order, the consequences of
which posed a threat to peace and security and
thereby the justification for United Nations intervention. Hammarskjold further stated that, in his
opinion, whether this was a matter of conflict
between two parties, under the circumstances, was
legally not essential for justifying the action
taken.[21] The restoration of internal law and order
was to continue to be the task of the United Nations
action long after the question of evacuation of
Belgian troops had been resolved.

We may note at this point that the picture in
Cyprus is somewhat similar. The central problem
concerns the restoration of local stability. However,
simultaneously, there has existed the possibility of
external action by one of the guarantor powers.
This has provided the government of Cyprus, and those
governments sympathetic to the Cypriot position, with
some basis for claiming the existence of a threat
of external aggression. Whether action by Turkey,
under the terms of the Treaty of Guarantee, could
properly be called aggression or not is a legally
debatable point.

This still leaves the following question: Was
the United Nations action in the Congo, and later
in Cyprus, contrary to the provisions of Article 2
(7)? The answer to this question must be in the
negative. Since the inception of the United Nations,
there has been a tendency to interpret this originally
designed limitation on the authority of the various
organs narrowly. Thus, in situations presenting a
threat to international peace, the United Nations
has felt competent to act. The organs of the United

Nations "have quite clearly been concerned with the attainment of the major objectives and purposes of the United Nations and have shown an unwillingness to accept any interpretation of Article 2 (7) which would prevent action from being taken in a situation deemed to be of international concern in terms of these purposes."[22] However, in another sense, the domestic limitation would not be applicable in any event in Cyprus or in the Congo because, strictly speaking, no "intervention" took place. In each instance, the host government was free to accept or reject the United Nations assistance.

The bases for launching a United Nations peace-keeping operation in the Congo were thus contained in three initial Security Council resolutions adopted in conformity with the provisions of the Charter. Although the General Assembly was later to get into the act when certain matters were taken up by that organ, the over-all direction of the Congo operation continued to remain primarily under the cognizance of the Security Council. Subsequently in the course of this operation, other legal problems such as the use of force, the relationship with the host government, and similar matters, would arise. However, it may be concluded that, at the outset, the operation was based on a solid legal framework resting directly upon pertinent provisions of the Charter.

Cyprus

Shortly after internal disorders broke out in Cyprus on December 21, 1963, the situation became a matter for United Nations attention. On December 26, the Government of Cyprus forwarded a complaint to the Security Council citing acts of Turkish aggression,[23] and, on December 27, the Security Council formally convened to consider the charges. The Cypriot complaint reviewed the events and indicated that, in order to counter aggressive actions by Turkish military units, Greek troops had moved into Nicosia. This brought about a direct confrontation of Greek and Turkish units and consti-tuted a potential threat to the continued peace of the area. The Security Council listened to the charges and countercharges presented by the represen-tatives of Cyprus and Turkey and thereupon adjourned, agreeing to reconvene "when and if it was considered appropriate by the Members."[24]

The absence of further action or recommendations
by the Security Council at that time reflected the
hope that the matter could be resolved without
further recourse to, or specific action by, the
United Nations. In this respect, the Security
Council was obviously influenced by the fact that,
on the day preceding the Security Council review,
the Government of Cyprus had accepted an offer by
the three guarantor powers to establish a peace-
making force to assist in restoring order. Subsequently, as we have seen, it became obvious that
the efforts of the guarantors would be insufficient
to contain the disorders, much less to resolve the
underlying issues. Accordingly, the matter was
referred back to the United Nations on February 15,
1964, at which time the United Kingdom representative
requested an early meeting of the Security Council.[25]
Simultaneously, Cyprus also asked for an emergency
meeting and cited "the increasing threat of Turkish
aggression."[26] The British request was motivated
by the failure of the London Conference to arrive
at any general agreement and the continued deterioration of security on the island. The Security Council
thereupon, in accordance with its primary responsibility for ensuring peace and security, undertook a
review of the situation in a series of meetings
lasting from February 18 to March 4, 1964.[27] These
meetings culminated with the initiation of the United
Nations peace-keeping operation launched under the
provisions of a resolution unanimously adopted on
March 4, 1964.[28] That resolution called for the
creation of a United Nations peace-keeping force,
the size and composition of which would be determined
by the Secretary-General in consultation with the
governments of Cyprus, Greece, Turkey, and the United
Kingdom. This resolution became the underlying
directive for the United Nations Forces in Cyprus
(UNFICYP).

The fact that this resolution was unanimously
adopted is significant. First, it indicated Great
Power agreement or at least their acquiescence,
otherwise the veto would have prevented approval.
However, although Great Power agreement or acquiescence was obtained in the voting, there was an
undercurrent in the Security Council consideration
that indicated that the Soviets and some of the
other delegations had reservations concerning some
of the procedural aspects. Second, despite this,
there is reason to believe that the vote of the

Security Council reflected the views of the great majority of the members of the United Nations concerning the need for collective action.

The resolution adopted noted that the situation in Cyprus was "likely to threaten international peace and security" and specifically referred to Article 2, paragraph 4 of the Charter which calls upon all member states to refrain "from the threat of use of force against the territorial integrity or political independence of any State, or in any other manner inconsistent with the purposes of the United Nations."[29] This basic responsibility of the member states is set forth clearly in the Charter and, although the principal parties directly concerned in this dispute were the two Cypriot communities, each of the states playing a supporting role in the drama was a member of the United Nations. It was, therefore, appropriate to remind them of their Charter obligations. However, neither the basic resolution creating the UNFICYP nor a second resolution of March 13, 1964,[30] referred to any other specific Charter provision. What then is the legal authority for such a force? In seeking to answer this question, it becomes apparent that several Charter provisions pertain.

As in the case of UNEF and ONUC, the authority for the United Nations to engage in peace-keeping may be found both in the general principles and in certain specific Articles of the Charter as well as in the consent of the parties involved. One of the major hopes of the United Nations, as set forth in the initial passages of the preamble to the Charter, is "to save succeeding generations from the scourge of war." Thus, the achievement of international peace is the first and earliest identifiable goal of the United Nations. Consistent with this aim, Article I (1) of the Charter describes the initial purpose of the United Nations as the maintenance of "international peace and security, and to that end; to take effective collective measures for the prevention and removal of threats to the peace" (emphasis added).[31]

More specific authority for the Security Council to act is contained in Article 24 of the Charter, which grants to the Security Council primary responsibility for the maintenance of international peace and security "in accordance

with the Purposes and Principles of the United
Nations." This grant of authority is followed by
the statement that the specific powers granted to
the Security Council for the discharge of these
duties are contained in several subsequent chapters,
including Chapter VI which concerns the pacific
settlement of disputes and Chapter VII which outlines,
among other things, the enforcement measures that
can be adopted. The following question arises: Is
the reference to the specific powers granted to the
Security Council limiting in nature? It is generally
accepted that no such limitation exists, and this
view has been borne out in a number of United Nations
actions to date.[32]

A related question is whether, prior to the
initiation of peace-keeping measures of the non-
coercive variety by the Security Council, i.e., of
the type envisaged in Article 40 of the Charter
which provides for provisional measures to maintain
peace, any explicit determination under the provision
of Article 39 of the Charter or a specific reference
to Article 40 is required. Article 39 states: "The
Security Council shall determine the existence of
any threat to the peace, breach of the peace, or
act of aggression and shall make recommendations,
or decide what measures shall be taken in accordance
with Articles 41 and 42, to maintain or restore the
international peace and security." The fact that
Article 40, concerning provisional measures, follows
Article 39 raises the question whether a specific
determination in accordance with Article 39 must
precede action initiated under the provisions of
Article 40. It is generally agreed that no explicit
preliminary determination is necessary, nor is any
explicit reference to Article 40 required.[33] This
view has been reinforced by the United Nations
practice in the Congo and in Cyprus.

Accordingly, there appears to be no reason to
deny that a sound legal basis exists for the creation
of the United Nations Force in Cyprus. That legal
foundation is contained in the pertinent Charter
provisions and in the Security Council resolutions
adopted in accordance with these provisions.[3] The
legality of the operation has been further bolstered
by the consent of the parties concerned, Cyprus, the
guarantor powers, and the nations providing units
to the force.

THE QUESTION OF DELEGATION OF
SECURITY COUNCIL AUTHORITY

In the discussions prior to the adoption of the
Cyprus peace-keeping resolution, another question
arose concerning the manner in which the Security
Council proposed to discharge its peace-keeping
responsibility. This same question, in varying
forms, had arisen on previous occasions in which the
United Nations peace-keeping competence was discussed.
During the debate that preceded the adoption of the
resolution, the **representative** of the Soviet Union
questioned the main operative paragraph (paragraph
4) of the March 4 resolution. That paragraph
authorized the Secretary-General to establish the
force and to appoint a commander who would report
directly to him.[35] The Soviet delegate contended
that the provisions of this paragraph would establish
procedures circumventing the Security Council and
that such action was not consistent with the basic
provisions of the Charter. The French representative,
reflecting a similar concern, lent support to this
viewpoint.[36] Accordingly, a separate vote was taken
on this paragraph and it was accepted by a vote of
8 to 0 with the Soviet Union, France, and Czechoslovakia abstaining. The entire resolution was
thereupon unanimously adopted.

Several things are of interest concerning the
voting and the discussions preceding them. First,
the Soviet delegate, while questioning the provisions
of paragraph 4, agreed in general with the collective
effort and endorsed the resolution as a whole. In
pursuing this course, the Soviet representative
stated that he was influenced by the views of the
Cypriot Government and the assurances of the
Secretary-General that (1) the UNFICYP would be
approved for a limited time--3 months; and (2) no
financial obligations were to be placed on those
members of the United Nations not contributing
forces.[37]

It is interesting to note at this point that
the Soviet position on the matter of peace-keeping
in Cyprus reflects some ambivalence. The Soviets
maintained, first, that the Cypriot problem was one
of domestic concern and that the Cypriots were fully
capable of settling their own affairs.[38] Certainly,

the latter portion of this allegation is open to
question. In addition to this debatable assumption,
the Soviets indicated, second, that the proposed
action was inappropriate because the Security Council
could not divest itself of its basic authority and
delegate the responsibility for peace-keeping to the
Secretary-General. Thus, in voting for the final
resolution, the Soviets found themselves in the
position of saying one thing and doing the opposite.
This was not the first time that they appeared to be
going in two different directions at the same time,
nor would it be the last.[39]

A similar ambiguity had been evident earlier
in the Soviet attitude toward the "Uniting for Peace"
Resolution. The Soviets opposed the adoption of
that resolution on parallel grounds, maintaining
that only the Security Council, under the provisions
of Chapter VII of the Charter, was competent to set
up an international armed force.[40] This objection
was again registered by V. V. Kuznetsov during the
General Assembly discussions surrounding the Suez
crisis.[41] Despite this objection, however, the
Soviets merely abstained on that occasion and did
not vote against the creation of the UNEF.[42] Once
again, in the Congo crisis, the Soviet representative
voted for the establishment of the ONUC despite the
fact that, as later with UNFICYP, the Secretary-
General was deputized to act for the Security Council
in establishing a United Nations force.[43]

Regarding the Soviet charge that the Security
Council had illegally delegated its own authority
to the Secretary-General, the International Court of
Justice, in reviewing the Congo episode in connection
with rendering an advisory opinion on financing,
stated the following:

> In the light of such a record of reiter-
> ated consideration, confirmation, approval
> and ratification by the Security Council,
> and by the General Assembly, of the
> actions of the Secretary-General in imple-
> menting the resolution of 14 July, 1960,
> it is impossible to reach the conclusion
> that the operations in question usurped
> or impinged upon the prerogatives con-
> ferred by the Charter on the Security
> Council.[44]

This opinion should be equally valid for Cyprus as for the Congo. Likewise, in reviewing the UNEF operation, the International Court indicated that that operation constituted a proper action by the General Assembly.[45]

The Soviet view that only the Security Council is competent to establish and direct a peace-keeping effort was restated by Zorin, the Soviet delegate, to the Eighteen Nation Disarmament Commission in Geneva. Referring to the United Nations operations in Korea, in the Middle East, and in the Congo, he stated, "In all these cases the armed forces set up were not established in accordance with the United Nations Charter but in violation of it."[46] Fortunately, from the standpoint of keeping the peace, the Soviet Union has demonstrated a sufficient flexibility to permit the Soviet delegates in the United Nations to acquiesce, by abstention in the voting, in the creation of a United Nations force in one instance (UNEF) and to vote in support of resolutions that authorized the Secretary-General to create such forces on two subsequent occasions (in the Congo and in Cyprus).*

In fairness to the Soviet position, it must be remembered that one of the underlying concepts generally accepted during the meetings in San Francisco at which the Charter was drafted was that the Great Powers would bear the main burden for maintaining the peace and that this authority would be exercised primarily through the Security Council. However, this should not be construed to preclude the Security Council from exercising its peace-keeping powers through the agency of the Secretary-General as was the practice in the Congo and in Cyprus. It should likewise not be interpreted to preclude the General Assembly from exercising a similar responsibility, under the provisions of the "Uniting for Peace" Resolution, when the Security Council is unable to act, as was the case for UNEF.

---

*The Soviets also agreed that the Secretary-General establish a new peace-keeping observer group (UNIPOM) in the Kashmir in 1965 and expand the operation of UNTSO in the Middle East in 1967.

Returning to the specific case in Cyprus, we note that UNFICYP was created in response to directives from the Security Council. Under the general Charter provisions, particularly Article 1, and the specific authority conferred by Article 24 of the Charter, the Security Council was legally competent to act in the manner in which it did. Furthermore, the Security Council was acting within its authority when it requested the Secretary-General to establish the UNFICYP. Article 98 of the Charter authorizes the Secretary-General to "perform such functions as are entrusted to him" by either the Security Council or the General Assembly. In addition, the Security Council is fully authorized to "establish such subsidiary organs as it deems necessary for the performance of its functions" (Article 29). Whereas the Soviet delegate professed a reservation concerning the procedure adopted and the derogation of strict Security Council responsibility, the subsequent unanimous passage of the resolution, the acquiescence of the Soviets in this procedure, and the actual implementation of the peace-keeping resolution all support the legality of this action.

SOME CONCLUSIONS

From this brief review, it may be noted that in each instance the United Nations force was created through action of an appropriate United Nations organ, either the Security Council or, in the event the Security Council did not act, the General Assembly. Both organs acted within the scope of their authority as set forth within the Charter.[47] The action undertaken was compatible with the principles and purposes of the Charter and consistent with the specific charter provisions concerning the maintenance of international peace. The validity of the United Nations peace operations is further substantiated by the general consensus with which these actions were greeted.

As already noted, the first article of the Charter clearly acknowledges the United Nations responsibility for maintaining international peace and security and for taking effective collective measures as set forth in Chapters VI and VII to achieve that end. The primary responsibility of the Security Council in this endeavor is set forth in Article 24, and this provided the basis for the

Security Council to act in the Congo and Cyprus.
However, as demonstrated in the Suez crisis, and,
in part in the Congo, the General Assembly has
competence to act whenever the Security Council is
unable to respond. The General Assembly authority
is contained in Articles 10, 11, 12, and 14 of the
Charter which, taken together, provide that agency
with broad authority to consider and make recommendations concerning matters affecting international
peace.

One significant distinction between the Security
Council and the General Assembly authorities under
the Charter provides that the Security Council may,
under certain conditions, make decisions that are
binding on the member states whereas the General
Assembly is limited to recommendations. This is
true with reference to enforcement actions initiated
by the Security Council under the provisions of
Chapter VII. However, enforcement was not in question
in the type of operations represented in the three
cases in question, even for those the Security
Council initiated. The UNEF, the ONUC, and UNFICYP
were not created to take enforcement measures against
a recalcitrant state; they were created to assist
in containing a threat to the peace. The measures
adopted were more comparable to the provisional
actions envisaged in Article 40 of the Charter than
to the enforcement measures foreseen in Articles 41
and 42. Both the Security Council and the General
Assembly have adequate powers to initiate such
measures in dealing with disputes or situations.
The Security Council authority is explicitly contained
in Article 40; the authority of the General Assembly
is not contained in any such detailed provision but
is more broadly based within the general Charter
provisions granting powers to that organ.

The creation of a United Nations force in these
three cases then could have been initiated by either
of these two United Nations organs. Properly, the
matter should first be referred to the Security
Council by the parties directly involved, the
Secretary-General, or any of the member states for
consideration. If the Security Council is unable
to act or make recommendations, the matter could
then be referred to the General Assembly under the
"Uniting for Peace" Resolution provisions, as was
done in the Suez crisis. The "Uniting for Peace"
Resolution merely sets forth a procedure under the

authority already contained in the Charter by which the General Assembly may be asked to consider and make recommendations concerning a specific problem that threatens the peace.

The role of the Secretary-General will be covered in more detail in subsequent chapters. However, it should be acknowledged in the present context that both the Security Council and the General Assembly may, under the provisions of Article 98 of the Charter, properly request or, in practice, direct the Secretary-General to establish a peace-keeping force and act as the executive agent, responsible to the Security Council or the General Assembly. Such an administrative procedure would obviously be essential in providing day-to-day direction to the UNEF, the ONUC, or the UNFICYP. Likewise, as we shall subsequently see, there does not appear to be any doubt that the appropriate United Nations organ, the General Assembly or the Security Council, maintains control of the force. This is achieved by providing the Secretary-General with certain guidelines for action and requiring him to report on his activities. In this process, the over-all direction and control is exercised by the responsible United Nations organ. At the same time, the Secretary-General is able to supervise the daily operations and thereby provide a greater degree of continuity and efficiency than would be otherwise possible. It will be important to bear these general observations in mind when we turn later to consider command and control arrangements for the future.

It is significant that on three recent occasions United Nations action appeared appropriate and, in each instance, a measure of agreement was possible, in either the Security Council or the General Assembly, enabling the United Nations to respond. The fact that international action was needed is hardly surprising; the fact that agreement within the United Nations was possible is significant. The challenge was there and the United Nations was able to respond. That response in the three instances considered was based on solid legal authorities which, in turn, have been reinforced by the precedents set in these cases themselves.

However, despite the validity of the legal arguments, it is obvious that not all members of the United Nations agree. This is amply verified

by a review of the Soviet position and the records
of recent discussions within the Committee of 33,
the Special Committee on Peace-Keeping Operations.
The Soviets, their bloc allies, and France challenge
the competence of the General Assembly and the
Secretary-General. The United States and a great
majority of the other members defend the authority
of these two organs. Most of the "non-aligned"
states appear to agree with the United States view
but are unwilling to challenge the Soviets or to
vote for a reaffirmation of peace-keeping principles
in the face of adamant Soviet opposition.

This lack of general agreement has great significance. It is a central and fundamental factor
which cannot be ignored. It becomes a limiting
factor that must be taken into account fully when
we discuss the possibilities for enhancing United
Nations peace-keeping capabilities. Clearly it is
futile to propose measures that obviously cannot
gain general acceptance.

NOTES

1. Lord David Davies, The Problem of the
Twentieth Century (London: Ernest Benn Ltd., 1930),
pp. 62-64.

2. U.N. Doc S/3706, October 30, 1956.

3. U.N. Security Council, Official Records,
Eleventh Year, 751st Meeting (October 31, 1956),
p. 22.

4. For two very good summaries of this sequence
of action, see William R. Frye, A United Nations
Peace Force (New York: Oceana Publications for
Carnegie Endowment for International Peace, 1957);
and Gabriella Rosner, The United Nations Emergency
Force (New York: Columbia University Press, 1963).

5. Rosner, op. cit., p. 37.

6. Initial operative section of Resolution A,
General Assembly Resolution 377 (V), November 3,
1950.

7. General Assembly Resolution 1000 (ES-1),
November 5, 1956. For text of this resolution, see
Appendix A.

8.   Rosner, op. cit., p. 37.

9.   U.N. Doc. S/4382, July 12, 1960.

10.   King Gordon, The U.N. in the Congo (New York: Harper, 1962), p. 16.

11.   U.N. Doc. S/4387, July 14, 1960. For text, see Appendix A.

12.   U.N. Doc. S/4389, July 18, 1960.

13.   Ibid.

14.   U.N. Doc. S/4405, July 22, 1960. For text, see Appendix A.

15.   U.N. Doc. S/4417 and Add I/Rev. 1.

16.   U.N. Doc. S/4426, August 9, 1960. For text, see Appendix A.

17.   Ibid. For a discussion supporting the obligatory character of Articles 25 and 49 on the member states, see E. M. Miller, "Legal Aspects of the United Nations Action in the Congo," American Journal of International Law, LV (January, 1961), 6-7.

18.   Security Council, Official Records, Fifteenth Year, 920th Meeting (December 13-14, 1960), p. 19. This interpretation is supported by D. W. Bowett, in United Nations Forces: A Legal Study (New York: Frederick A. Praeger, 1964), p. 180.

19.   Miller, op. cit., pp. 4-5. For another view on the application of Article 39 to the Security Council action in the Congo, see Arthur Lee Burns and Nina Heathcote, Peacekeeping by U.N. Forces (New York: Frederick A. Praeger, 1963), p. 26.

20.   Based on a study of practices during the first ten years of United Nations operation, one authority was able to conclude that the Security Council has displayed flexibility in exercising its functions under the provisions of Articles 39 and 40. See Leland M. Goodrich and Anne P. Simons, The United Nations and the Maintenance of International Peace and Security (Washington, D.C.: The Brookings Institution, 1955), p. 369. The subsequent

experience of the Security Council in the second ten
years of United Nations operations, particularly in
the Congo and Cyprus, confirms this conclusion.

21.   U.N. Doc. S/4389, July 18, 1960.

22.   Leland M. Goodrich and Edvard Hambro,
Charter of the United Nations Commentary and Documents (rev. ed.; Boston, Mass.: World Peace Foundation,
1949), p. 121.

23.   U.N. Doc. S/5488, December 26, 1963.

24.   International Organization, XVIII (Spring,
1964, 479.

25.   U.N. Doc. S/5543, February 15, 1964.

26.   U.N. Doc. S/5545, February 15, 1964.

27.   U.N. Security Council, Official Records,
Nineteenth Year, 1095th-1102nd Meetings (February
18-March 4, 1964).

28.   U.N. Doc. S/5575, March 4, 1964.   For text,
see Appendix A.

29.   Ibid.

30.   U.N. Doc. S/5603, March 13, 1964.   For
text, see Appendix A.

31.   For an effective presentation of the case
for broad use of this authority to justify collective
United Nations action, see John W. Halderman, "Legal
Bases for United Nations Armed Forces," American
Journal of International Law, Vol. 56, No. 4 (October,
1962), pp. 971-96.

32.   For a comprehensive analysis that supports
this view, see Goodrich and Hambro, op. cit., pp.
204-7.   Although the analysis of Goodrich and Hambro
was based on a review of the Charter and of the
events up to 1949, subsequent developments since
1949 more than confirm the conclusions reached by
these two authorities.

33.   Goodrich and Simons, op. cit., pp. 367-72.

34.   One authority finds that the wording of
the March 4 resolution "suggests that the constitutional basis is to be found in Chapter VI of the
Charter, probably Article 36 (1), and not in Chapter
VII." Bowett, op. cit., p. 553.

35.   U.N. Security Council, Official Records,
Nineteenth Year, 1095th-1102nd Meetings (February
18-March 4, 1964).

36.   Ibid.

37.   Ibid.

38.   Ibid.

39.   See, for example, the records of the
Security Council meeting on the Middle East situation,
October 25, 1967, during which the Secretary-General
proposed to augment the U.N. observer strength along
the Suez Canal. U.N. Doc. S/PV. 1371, October 25,
1967.

40.   For an analysis of the Soviet view on the
use of international military forces, see Lincoln
P. Bloomfield, International Military Forces (Boston:
Little, Brown, 1964), pp. 47-56.

41.   U.N. General Assembly, Official Records,
First Emergency Special Session, 567th Meeting
(November 7, 1956), pp. 127-28.

42.   U.N. Doc. A/3276, November 4, 1956.

43.   U.N. Doc. S/4387, July 13, 1960.

44.   International Court of Justice, Reports
of Judgments, Advisory Opinions and Orders, 1962,
"Certain Expenses of the United Nations, (Article
17, par. 2 of the Charter) Advisory Opinion as of
July 20, 1962," p. 177.

45.   Ibid., pp. 170-75.

46.   ENDC/PV55 (June 13, 1962), p. 55. For
another statement of the Soviet position, see U.N.
Doc. S/5811, July 10, 1964. Although this statement
was made in 1964, it still reflects the basic Soviet
views on this subject and has been frequently
reaffirmed since that date especially in the

considerations of the Special Committee on Peace-Keeping Operations and during the Special Political Committee meetings on this item. See, for example, U.N. Doc. A/SPC/PV 574, December 1, 1967.

47.   It is interesting to note that, in actual practice, each organ must determine its own juris-diction. Thus, the International Court of Justice has stated that "as anticipated in 1945 . . . each organ must, in the first place at least, determine its own jurisdiction." International Court of Justice, Reports of Judgments, Advisory Opinions and Orders, p. 168.

PART **II**

THE NATURE OF THE PEACE-KEEPING FORCE

CHAPTER	**5**	PATTERN OF
		PEACE-KEEPING
		OPERATIONS

Before taking a look at some of the specific
problems arising in connection with peace-keeping,
it will be helpful to review the pattern of activity
that has evolved during recent operations. In so
doing, we must note that since 1945 the United Nations
has responded to a number of different situations in
which the peace has been threatened (listed in note
at beginning of Chapter 4). These responses have
varied widely in character, from the dispatch of
small cease-fire observer groups (Indonesia and
Kashmir) to the creation of a sizable field force
which at its peak consisted of about 20,000 troops
(Congo). The most sweeping response, however, was
that in Korea, where the United Nations command at
one time was composed of elements totaling more than
500,000 men.* The purpose and mandate of these
separate actions varied widely. Even a partial
listing of the activities undertaken would cover a
range running from the modest objective of observing
and reporting on a cease-fire to supervising a border
and reporting incursions, overseeing a truce line,
providing a buffer presence between opposing forces,
supervising the disengagement of foreign troops from
a local situation, assisting in the restoration of
local law and order, bolstering indigenous security
forces, and, on the one occasion that transcended
peace-keeping, engaging in active military hostilities
to counter aggression.

---

*Korea is not considered to be a "peace-keeping"
operation within the definition set forth in Chapter 1.
The character and nature of the U.N. Force in Korea
differed markedly from that in Suez, in the Congo, and
in Cyprus. Korea is listed merely for completeness in
enumerating the responses to situations where a threat
to the peace developed.

In reviewing this list of activities, it is at once apparent that most of the operations appear to fall within a pattern of a limited enterprise, the Korean action being a notable exception. We have already noted that the action in Korea resulted from the existence of a peculiar set of circumstances prevailing at that time. It is questionable whether identical circumstances will ever recur. It is even more questionable whether action of a similar nature could be sanctioned within the present international environment. If we accept this as a working hypothesis and rule out for the present actions on the order of Korea, which in any event can scarcely be considered to be within the commonly accepted definition of peace-keeping, what are the likely directions for United Nations peace-keeping efforts in the future? Before attempting to answer this question and advancing suggestions for improvement, we must first examine the patterns of action developed in the past. Although the experiences of the UNEF, the ONUC, and the UNFICYP will continue to occupy the center of our attention, it will be useful at this point to expand our view to include some of the other recent United Nations experiences as appropriate.

PEACE-KEEPING SINCE 1956

Six new and distinct United Nations peace-keeping efforts have been launched since 1956.* The problem in each has been different and the degree of success achieved has varied. However, the force mandates, although addressed to different undertakings, have had common elements. The operations have been based on consent and the objectives have been limited. Generally, the mandates have been restricted to recognizable and attainable goals; that this is true

----

*Two others are not so new and distinct. In 1965, the Security Council authorized the expansion of the observer group in Kashmir (UNMOGIP) to meet the additional responsibilities created by the outbreak of hostilities in that area and at the same time a new but related group (UNIPOM), since disbanded, was established. In June, 1967, the capacities of the existing observer group in the Middle East were augmented to fulfill an expanded role in that area growing out of the recent hostilities.

implicitly acknowledges that there might be more
comprehensive goals the United Nations could not
reasonably expect to achieve. This is an unfortunate
fact of international life. We will look at each of
these operations in turn.

Suez

    We have seen that the objective in Suez (1956)
was to "secure and supervise the cessation of hostilities" and thereafter provide a border patrol and
buffer force along the truce lines. The achievement
of these goals involved the consent of the parties
concerned and was not to be obtained by direct military action. The United Nations action was designed
to remove or reduce a potential source of friction.
This action was effective in maintaining a qualified
peace for a period of over ten years. During that
interval, hostilities were limited to occasional
minor incidents. The fact that the basic underlying
differences were not reconciled or that violence
broke out anew after the UNEF was withdrawn does not
diminish the contribution of UNEF to the stability
of the area during the period of its existence. It
merely demonstrates that, providing the parties agree,
a United Nations presence may be helpful. It also
reminds us of the limitations of the United Nations
role. Obviously, the United Nations did not have
the capacity to dictate or enforce the final terms
of settlement, which might have precluded hostilities
in June, 1967. However, lacking this power, the
UNEF provided a stabilizing influence and possibly
inhibited the renewal of hostilities at an earlier
date.

Lebanon

    The objectives of the 600-member United Nations
Observer Group in Lebanon (UNOGIL) in 1958 were even
more modest. The observer group was charged with
spotlighting and deterring the infiltration of personnel and supplies across the Lebanese border.[1] Despite
the Lebanese desire for a stronger force mandate, the
UNOGIL was restricted to observation and reporting
and could not, without exceeding its authority,
invoke stronger action. The operation continued
under this mandate until December, 1958, when the
government of Lebanon determined that a serious

external threat no longer existed whereupon UNOGIL
was terminated.

For one seeking to extract useful lessons from
past experiences, UNOGIL presents a confusing picture.
The basic political issues involved were complex and
are difficult to untangle. The charges and countercharges by Lebanon, the United Arab Republic, and
other interested states were difficult to substantiate
initially, and the situation, from the United Nations
standpoint, became further confused with the U.S.
landings in Lebanon after which the United Nations
action became even more ambiguous. However, Lebanon
again presents the picture of a limited operation,
the sending of qualified military personnel to observe
and report on a complicated and threatening situation
that promised to get out of hand. Fortunately, a
nucleus of experienced military observers was immediately available in the United Nations Truce Supervision Organization (UNTSO) to undertake this mission.
The ready availability of these observers enabled
UNOGIL to become operational without delay. This
fact has significance in considering measures for
enhancing future peace-keeping.

The Congo

We have observed that the initial mandate given
to the ONUC was not unlimited. At a time when local
law and order ceased to exist and when the Belgian
forces, the only force on hand with even a remote
capability for restoring order, were being asked to
leave, the Secretary-General was authorized to provide
military assistance until Congolese security forces
could assume the responsibility for internal security.
Although the difficulty of the task given to the
Secretary-General was apparent and no completion date
was set, many who supported the United Nations action
appeared to be thinking in terms of a relatively short
emergency operation. Such an assumption was not
warranted initially nor subsequently as the United
Nations mission was broadened and extended. Four
years later, when the ONUC was eventually terminated,
it was still a moot question how well the Congolese
security forces could "meet fully their task," one
of the objectives set forth in the initial Security
Council resolution.[2] Even at that date, the Congolese
had difficulty in maintaining stability throughout
the entire country.

The task of the ONUC as it evolved became at once more inclusive and more difficult. During its existence, it assisted in safeguarding Congolese unity, territorial integrity, and political independence; preventing civil war; eleminating foreign military personnel, and maintaining internal security. How well these tasks were fulfilled is still only partially answered. However, the groundwork laid by the ONUC did permit a return to somewhat normal conditions by 1964 when the force was withdrawn. Before this occurred and the ONUC was terminated, the United Nations became engaged in two other peace-keeping ventures, the first in West New Guinea and the second in Yemen.

West New Guinea (West Irian)

The dispute between the Netherlands and Indonesia over West New Guinea (subsequently redesignated West Irian) was settled peacefully in 1962 after an agreement was negotiated between the two parties. The agreement in this instance was reached in part as a result of an initiative by the Secretary-General and was facilitated by the creation of a United Nations force and a United Nations Temporary Executive Authority (UNTEA). The UNTEA, which was supported by a 1,500-man Pakistani military contingent, provided the key for reaching a solution. In establishing a neutral interim administration for West New Guinea, a face-saving device was created that facilitated the transfer of the disputed territory from the Dutch to the Indonesians. At the same time, appropriate assurances were given for the eventual exercise of the right of self-determination by the local Papuans who were involved in the real estate transfer. The mission of the military component on this occasion was to supervise a cease-fire between the contestants and to provide security for the UNTEA during the interim period when control of the territory was being transferred from one party to the other. Although this operation was limited in size and scope and the wisdom of the terms of the political settlement may be argued, it is nevertheless true that the United Nations action contributed toward a peaceful solution.

Yemen

As these arrangements were being effected in

West New Guinea, the United Nations was asked to
provide a peace-keeping presence in Yemen. In September of 1962, a coup led by Yemeni army officers
succeeded in overthrowing the Iman and establishing
a republic. This marked the start of a continuing
struggle between the republican forces supported by
the United Arab Republic (UAR) and the opposing
tribesmen, backed by Saudi Arabia, who maintained
allegiance to the Iman. This dispute promised to
fester indefinitely with the constant possibility of
erupting into greater violence at any moment. It
was not until April, 1963, that an agreement was
reached under which both the UAR and Saudi Arabia
undertook to cease their activities in support of
the opposing factions. A United Nations Yemen
Observation Mission (UNYOM) was thereupon established,
its primary task that of observing compliance with
the disengagement agreement. The UNYOM, relatively
small by the Suez and Congo peace-keeping standards
and further hampered by delay in compliance by the
parties involved, did, in providing a United Nations
presence, serve to restrict the scope of the
belligerent activity.

Although the mandate and authority of the UNYOM
was limited, the Secretary-General was able to an-
nounce after its termination in September, 1964,
that "the mission did contribute to a reduction of
international tension in the region of its operation
and to some improvements in the internal security
situation in Yemen."[3] With the withdrawal of the
UNYOM and following direct negotiations between the
United Arab Republic and Saudi Arabia, the prospects
for a settlement of the basic issues appeared, for
the moment, encouraging. In any event, the presence
of the UNYOM on the scene facilitated bilateral
negotiations which eased tensions in this trouble
spot at least temporarily.

Cyprus

The most recent "major" United Nations effort
in peace-keeping has been the creation of the UNFICYP
in Cyprus. Once again, in a different setting and
under somewhat different circumstances, the United
Nations was embarked on an effort to restore the
peace. The mandate of the UNFICYP, as we have seen,
was directed initially toward facilitating an end
to the fighting and then toward restoring normal

peaceful conditions. The actions engaged in by the
UNFICYP to achieve these objectives have taken a
variety of forms ranging from observation and patrol
to the restoration of essential public and governmental services. The fighting has been at least
temporarily contained and an uneasy peace, but not
a complete return to normalcy, prevails.

Since the initiation of the action in Cyprus
and even as that action has continued, the United
Nations was called upon to expand its military
observer group in the Kashmir (1965), to establish
an additional group of observers in that same area
(1965), and to enlarge the United Nations Truce
Supervision Organization to meet a fresh challenge
in the Middle East (1967). In each case, the new
force mandates have paralleled and extended the
existing directives--to observe and report. At the
same time, there has been a widespread and well-
documented belief that by their mere presence the
United Nations blue-helmeted military observers
inhibit further violence.

THE ACTIVITIES OF PEACE-KEEPING FORCES

The activities of the UNFICYP have been typical
of peace-keeping operations. The initial and immediate task has been to contain violence. This is
essentially a military or paramilitary operation
involving the use of military forces. This phase of
the effort is essentially a holding operation. It
is directed toward alleviating the symptoms of the
trouble but not necessarily toward providing a complete cure for the underlying causes. It is a
necessary prerequisite to further steps to restore
normal conditions. However, additional nonmilitary
measures may be required in the continuing attempt
to reach a more lasting solution.

The first steps, involving the use of armed
forces, set the stage for complementary economic,
social, and political actions designed to promote a
return to "normal" conditions. Thus, the United
Nations undertook a sizable technical program to
reopen the Suez Canal and restore normal maritime
passage even as the UNEF was taking up its positions
along the armistice lines. In this manner, one of
the principal sources of friction was removed and a
contribution made to the stability of the area.

Similarly, the restoration of public services in the
Congo and the attempts to re-establish normal economic
activities in Cyprus supplemented the paramilitary,
police-type activities conducted by the ONUC and the
UNFICYP. Taken in concert, the military or police
operations and the related technical, economic, and
social measures helped to create a better environment
in which to seek a resolution of the basic issues.

In this sense, the efforts of the military forces
engaged in peace-keeping operations such as the Congo
and Suez have been the first in a sequence of steps
that may be necessary before the more basic problems
can be resolved. Complementary civic operations
involving technical, economic, and social assistance
may very well be required as well. In part, the
military forces themselves play a role in these supplementary undertakings indirectly. For example,
by their very presence in Cyprus the United Nations
troops helped to stabilize the situation thereby
permitting the agricultural workers to harvest crops
that would otherwise have gone unharvested. However,
the military forces have also participated more
directly in these supplementary activities by distrib-
uting relief supplies, aiding refugees, and assisting
in the resumption of public services. Hopefully
these military, paramilitary, and nonmilitary activities will help to create a favorable environment in
which other efforts, designed to resolve the basic
political issues, can be effective. Hopefully, at
the appropriate time the United Nations may, through
the extension of good offices, conciliation, or
mediation, provide the mechanism needed to restore
peace. The experiences in the Congo and in Cyprus
in part reflect this progression.

Civilian Operations in the Congo

The first ONUC military forces arrived in the
Congo shortly after the Security Council decided to
act. These forces promptly directed their energies
toward the immediate task of restoring order. However, the problem that faced the ONUC was broader
than could be resolved by military or policing
measures alone. It could not be resolved without
addressing such fundamental tasks as the restoration
of essential government services and the re-establishment of a functioning economy. The task confronting
the new Congolese governmental authorities was

difficult enough at the moment of independence in
July, 1960, before internal security had disintegrated.
Even then, the Congo was faced with a critical shortage of trained Congolese nationals and a shortage of
trained administrators and technicians of any
nationality to administer the public services and
maintain a functioning economy. Until the situation
deteriorated completely, this deficiency was partially
alleviated by the presence of Belgian technicians.
However, with the complete breakdown in order resulting in the flight of the Belgians, the need for
administrators, technicians, and technical assistance
became even more acute.

     To meet this severe emergency, a prompt and
conprehensive program of technical assistance was
mandatory. Obviously, the first step was to determine
the essential requirements of the situation and then
to establish priorities and mobilize whatever assistance could be brought to bear. This was achieved
by organizing a civilian operation, the counterpart
to the military operation. Sture Linner, who had
been designated Resident Representative for the
Technical Assistance Board and had already arrived
on the scene early in July to investigate a technical
aid program to the Congo, was named to head this
effort under the title of Chief of Civilian Operations.
To assist him, a consultative group composed largely
of senior officials from the United Nations specialized agencies was established. The experts who
comprised this group were responsible to the Chief
of Civilian Operations and not to their respective
specialized agencies. This group was charged with
recommending, assisting in the initiation of, and
overseeing the essential programs required. The
creation of the consultative group was a unique and
effective response to the demands of the situation.

     This organizational scheme provided for the
integration of operations in theory and worked well
in practice. It insured that the many different
programs undertaken would be fitted into a common
over-all scheme and reduced the possibilities of
overlap, duplication, and wasted effort. It did
much to restore a semblance of normalcy to the chaotic
situation. Disrupted public services were restored,
emergency food shipments were initiated, telecommuni-
cation services were resumed, and health questions
were resolved. Problems in agriculture, trade,
transportation, and nearly every other field of

economic activity were likewise resolved to the
extent possible.[4] These efforts produced some major
achievements, and the over-all effect was to create
an improved environment in which attempts could be
made to solve the basic political questions. The
accomplishments produced by the civilian operations
in the Congo emergency action, when considered in
the light of the circumstances prevailing, must be
judged as remarkable.

Three-Pronged Approach in Cyprus

      In Cyprus, the UNFICYP experience once again
demonstrates that the introduction of police forces
alone may not provide a simple, immediate, or complete remedy. It again illustrates the fact that
the military or police action, although an essential
and necessary first step, may well have to be supplemented by additional measures. This requirement was
at least implicitly recognized by the Security Council
and reflected in the original mandate for UNFICYP
which set the sequential goals of containing the
fighting, assisting in the restoration of law and
order, and contributing to the return of normal
conditions. The military forces of UNFICYP have the
primary role in achieving the first of these objectives; a vital but not necessarily exclusive role
in promoting the second objective; and an important,
but even less exclusive, responsibility for the third
goal. It is in the latter two areas that the police
activities of the United Nations force have had to
be supplemented. In recognition of this need, U Thant
at an early stage in the Cyprus operation noted:

      The mere presence of the United Nations
      Peace-keeping Force in the island and its
      day-to-day efforts at the military level
      . . .are not alone enough to effect the
      kind of improvement in the over-all sit-
      uation which can really bring about a
      basic relaxation of tension and a better-
      ment of deplorable conditions of fear,
      insecurity and distress.[5]

He also confirmed that such an improvement was
vital to achieve a peaceful solution, outlined a
program to promote these objectives,[6] and subsequently
appointed Galo Plaza of Ecuador as his Special Representative in Cyprus to lead these efforts.

Among the steps initiated to supplement the
military activities of the UNFICYP have been efforts
to restore public services, provide for the normal
continuation of agricultural activities, assist in
reopening factories that had been shut down, and
facilitate the resumption of trade and commerce.
The UNFICYP has provided the good offices for restoring
electric services, assisting in the harvesting of
crops, opening the channels for relief and refugee
assistance, assisting the resumption of law courts,
and restoring of postal services. An essential seed-
cleaning plant was reopened through the efforts of
United Nations personnel; citrus groves abandoned by
their Cypriot owners were saved; and the barley and
wheat crops were harvested. This list could be extended at length, limited only by the number of
activities normally undertaken in the functioning
of a semi-modern economy.[7]

However, despite the foregoing and despite the
fact that the UNFICYP has been operating since March,
1964, all is not completely well. Although much has
been accomplished by the United Nations presence in
Cyprus as evidenced by the improved security position
and the easing of economic restrictions, many of the
basic problems remain essentially unresolved. Furthermore, the mediation effort has been unable to
date to bring about a political settlement. Until
this is achieved, Cyprus will remain a troubled
island.

The United Nations action in Cyprus demonstrates
the three-pronged approach to peace-keeping. First,
there has been the introduction of an international
military force to contain the fighting, to prevent
further armed clashes, and to create the conditions
for a return of law and order. Second, there has
been implementation of those additional measures
designed to restore normal economic and social conditions, a process intended to further reduce the tensions. Finally, with a diminution of disorder and
an approach to normal conditions, there has been the
attempt through the use of good offices, conciliation
techniques, and mediation efforts to resolve the
underlying problems and provide a lasting solution.

DURATION AND TERMINATION

The mandate for most United Nations peace-keeping

operations has been open-ended in the sense that no
set time period has been specified in the terms of
the authorization. This appears logical when one
considers that it is exceedingly difficult to anticipate precisely when the desired objective will be
achieved. Cyprus proved to be an exception to this
general practice. In this instance, UNFICYP was
authorized originally only for a limited period--three
months. From the record of the debate at that time,
this appears to be the maximum period for which agreement was possible. The practice of extending the
basic authorization for limited periods has prevailed
since the original authorization was approved, and
this has necessitated regular and frequent reconsideration of the mandate by the Security Council.
Initially, the force extensions were in three-month
increments but subsequently the period for each
renewal was extended to six months.* The Security
Council returned to the practice of a three-month
extension in December, 1967,[8] but has more recently
reverted to the six-month period.

While a relatively short-term period of authorization ensures frequent reconsideration of the operation and may serve to put additional pressure on the
parties to resolve their differences more quickly,
it is not conducive to long-range planning. It is
also not realistic to assume that a complex situation,
and one in which violence has broken out, can be
resolved within a short, specified time period.
Accordingly, it would appear desirable in most cases
to leave the mandate open-ended or, at a minimum, to
provide for a more extended term than three, or even
six, months.**

Although peace-keeping operations are designed
to pave the way for pacific settlement, this may
take a considerable period of time. The United
Nations Military Observer Group in India and Pakistan
(UNMOGIP) has been in operation since 1948 and the

---

*This change occurred with the fifth renewal in
June, 1965.

**There will, however, be certain situations in
which it may be desirable to maintain a short deadline in the hope that this may prove to be an added
incentive to the parties to negotiate.

problem of Kashmir has not been resolved. The United
Nations Truce Supervision Organization (UNTSO) has
been in existence for a similar period. The UNFICYP
is now over six years old. The existence of peace-
keeping operations over such prolonged periods has
raised the disturbing question of whether, by containing the immediate disturbances to the peace,
these operations have relieved the pressure on the
parties concerned to reach a more lasting settlement.

Hopefully, a given peace operation will be terminated when the conditions threatening the peace no
longer exist, or are abated to the extent that an
international presence is no longer required. This
sequence was followed, under differing circumstances,
with respect to the United Nations operations in
Indonesia, Greece, Lebanon, the Congo, Yemen, and
West Irian. However, this is not the only way a
United Nations peace-keeping presence may be
terminated.

The UNEF is a case in point. The UNEF operations
were abruptly terminated, and in a manner not clearly
envisaged beforehand by many of those most immediately
concerned, when one of the parties directly involved
withdrew its consent.[9] UNEF in the words of Major
General Indar Rikhye, the last Commander, "ceased to
exist" on the morning of May 18, 1967, when UAR troops
moved up to the Israeli frontier and by their presence
prevented the UNEF from continuing to discharge its
functions.[10]

The termination of the UNEF was unique in the
history of United Nations peace-keeping and has
raised some basic and still unanswered questions.
If one of the parties to a consent-type operation
can, with a minimum of advance notice, withdraw its
consent at any time during the course of the operation, what does this promise for the stability of
this type of effort for achieving peace? Are troop
contributors likely to provide forces for an operation
that may be called off on short notice?[11] At a minimum, this suggests that in the future there should
be a common understanding both on the duration and
the manner in which an operation is to be terminated.

SUMMARY OF ESSENTIAL CHARACTERISTICS

From this brief review, it is apparent that the

dimension and scope of recent United Nations peace missions have varied widely. The functions performed have covered a wide spectrum of activity running the complete gamut from a more or less passive to a more active, direct role; from observation and reporting on a potential source of international friction to the prevention of further hostilities, the restoration of internal order, and the promotion of conditions for peaceful settlement. Although it is difficult to assess the effectiveness of each of these operations precisely and objectively, they have all in varying degree contributed to the cause of world peace. This being so, and anticipating that a similar wide range of activities will be reflected in future operations, we may profitably look at the characteristics of these recent actions. What are the essential features?

First, it is apparent in this expanded review of recent operations that each was initiated in response to a specific threat to, or actual breach of, the international peace. Each situation had international overtones. Each emergency, from Suez to Cyprus, constituted a very real potential threat extending beyond the immediate scene of action. In none of these instances could the United Nations be accused of intervening lightly. Although several of the operations, such as the ONUC, originated in a setting in which a large measure of domestic disorder prevailed, none was initiated in the absence of a potential threat to the international peace.

Second, in Lebanon, West Irian, and Yemen, just as we have already noted for Suez, the Congo, and Cyprus, the parties directly concerned were confronted with problems beyond their immediate competence to resolve. If this had not been true, the action by the United Nations might appropriately have been limited to reminding the parties to settle the matter by peaceful means of their own choice. Thus, each crisis presented a challenge that required a more comprehensive peace effort than the parties themselves could provide.

The United Nations actions involved the use of comparatively modest-sized forces. If an observer group was sufficient, a Congo-size force was not created. A careful review of each of these past efforts suggests that a conscious attempt was made to tailor both the size of the force and its activi-

ties to the requirements of the particular situation.*
In Lebanon and Yemen, the size of the United Nations
response was limited to comparatively modest observation groups; in the Congo, a police force of 20,000
was created. In Yemen and Lebanon, the mission was
restricted primarily to observation; in the Congo,
the United Nations forces were given the more encom-
passing role of assisting in restoring law and order.

In none of these situations was the force designed to take enforcement action. Only in the single
instance of Korea did the mission of an international
force approach that of collective security. Since
Korea, even the efforts of the largest United Nations
force assembled, the ONUC, has been restricted to a
more limited role. The principle of not initiating
the use of force and restricting its use to precisely
defined situations of self-defense appears now to be
the general rule. Consistent with this de-emphasis
on the use of military force has been the emphasis
on the promotion of peaceful and stable conditions
and on the effort to create an atmosphere conducive
to a real and lasting settlement.

Despite the "limited" mandates and missions that
have characterized the period since 1956, sizable
international forces have been used on occasion:
20,000 troops in the Congo; 6,000 troops in Cyprus;
and 5,000 to 6,000 in the Middle East. This obviously
has had implications for the future. The United
Nations and the staff headquarters have gained in
experience in mobilizing and directing fairly large
military forces. Many countries have contributed
forces to the United Nations, and the personnel assigned to these units have acquired valuable information and experience in the actual conduct of peace-
keeping operations. Precedents have been established
for use of forces in the future. Unfortunately, each
of the operations, including the UNEF, ONUC, and
UNFICYP, was improvised on short notice and launched
hurriedly to meet an emergency. In spite of this
inherent disadvantage, the response of the organization has been creditable. Additional advance planning
may in the future at least partially alleviate the
handicap imposed by the short notice involved.

_____

*This conscious effort was reinforced by
financial as well as political considerations.

In each of these operations, the role of the Secretary-General has been significant, and that role has been gradually expanded to encompass additional new responsibilities. The Secretary-General has several times been charged with creating a peace-keeping force and providing executive direction. This has made the Secretary-General and his staff key actors in peace-keeping. They have gained more and more experience as these responsibilities have been exercised. To some extent, the expanded role of the Secretary-General has been abetted and made possible by the two individuals who occupied the office of Secretary-General in this time period. Dag Hammarskjold, in the crucial Suez-Congo stages, and subsequently U Thant have, largely through their impartiality, their neutrality, and above all their concern for the maintenance of peace, lent their support to the development of a more effective peace-keeping capacity by the United Nations. In addition to exercising initiatives, they responded to the many demands placed on their office in a highly profes-sional and competent manner. In no other field has the capacity of the Secretary-General and his staff been tested under more difficult circumstances and the response reflected more dramatically than in the creation of the UNEF and the ONUC.

Paralleling the increased responsibility of the Secretary-General has been the developing role of the middle and smaller powers as the instruments for peace-keeping. These countries have provided the national contingents that comprised the bulk of the peace-keeping forces in every operation since Korea. Starting with UNEF, the precedent has been established that the Great Powers would not be asked to provide force contingents. This ground rule was followed in Lebanon and in the Congo. The sole exception to it has been in the use of British forces in Cyprus, which occurred as a natural development from the unique position of the United Kingdom with respect to Cyprus and the fact that British troops were already fulfilling the major role in the peace-keeping effort at the time the United Nations action commenced. The rationale behind this practice has obviously been to keep the Cold War out of peace-keeping by reducing the possibilities of Great Power friction. For their part, the Great Powers have evidenced a willingness to accept this role just as they have been willing to see each of these peace-keeping operations under-taken. The operations so far have thus been initiated

with either the positive or passive consent of the
permanent members of the Security Council. From
this, it may safely be concluded that these actions
either served the purposes of the permanent members
or, at the very minimum, did not run counter to their
objectives. If this had not been true, it is doubtful
whether these operations would have gotten off the
ground.

In each peace-keeping effort of this last decade,
the parties most directly concerned have agreed on
the need to act and consented to the form of action
taken. This was first evidenced in the Suez crisis
and has been true for every peace-keeping operation
since that time. The principle has had several
overtones for United Nations forces. First, it means
the United Nations force should not have to fight its
way onto the scene of operations. The cooperation
of the host state should make this unnecessary and
permit the United Nations force to deploy more quickly
than if it had to be transported in a fighting configuration or fight its way into the operational area.
However, the consent of the host state does not confer
on the United Nations force unlimited privileges nor
does it confer on the United Nations the right to
interfere with the otherwise sovereign operations of
the consenting state. Likewise, the consenting state
does not have the right to veto United Nations actions
taken in accordance with the agreed force mandate.[12]

Finally, the United Nations peace missions have
been designed to provide a neutral presence and an
impartial authority, and thereby create the environment for a reconciliation of basic differences.
Although it has not always been easy to maintain
complete and absolute impartiality in some situations,
the United Nations forces have generally adhered to
this principle with circumspection. The actual record
leaves little room for criticism.

Although the size and form as well as the scope
and methods adopted have varied greatly on occasion,
each operation served useful purposes. The continuation of hostilities or the outbreak of renewed
fighting was avoided for a period of years (Suez);
observer forces have focused the spotlight on potential trouble or recent conflict areas and, to varying
degrees, have served to inhibit further unilateral
action (Lebanon and Yemen; Kashmir and the Middle
East); a potential cause for conflict has been

eliminated under conditions serving the best interests of both parties concerned (West Irian); and internal disorders that promised to spread beyond national boundaries have been contained (Congo and Cyprus). In each instance, the United Nations attempted to provide an alternative to the continuation of an unsatisfactory situation. Each instance has demonstrated its capacity, at least in certain circumstances, to take concerted action and to play a positive role in the preservation of peace.

NOTES

1. U.N. Doc. S/4022, June 11, 1958.

2. U.N. Doc. S/4387, July 14, 1960.

3. U.N. General Assembly, Official Records, Nineteenth Session, 1964, Suppl. No. 1 A (A/5801/Add 1), p. 8.

4. For a more detailed summary of these operations, see King Gordon, The U.N. in the Congo: A Quest for Peace (New York: Harper, 1962), particularly pp. 63-64, to which I am indebted for much of the foregoing, and the successive Progress Reports on the United Nations Civilian Operations in the Congo.

5. U.N. Doc. S/5671, April 29, 1964, p. 5.

6. Ibid.

7. For a review of these activities, see United Nations Doc. S/5671, April 29, 1964, and the periodic reports by the Secretary-General, U.N. Doc. S/5764, June 15, 1964; S/5950, September 10, 1964; S/6102, December 12, 1964; S/6228, March 11, 1965; S/6426, June 10, 1965; S/7001, December 10, 1965; S/7350, June 10, 1966; S/7611, December 8, 1966; and S/7969, June 13,1967.

8. U.N. Doc. S/RES/244 (1967), December 22, 1967.

9. For a summary of this sequence of actions, see U.N. Docs. A/6669, May 18, 1967, and A/6669/Add 2, June 19, 1967.

10. Interview with General Rikhye, November 27, 1967. It should be noted that the UAR intent was communicated to General Rikhye by Brigadier Ezz-El-Din Mokhtar of the UAR Army the preceding evening. When asked what action he planned to take on receipt of this communication, General Rikhye replied that he would promptly forward it to the Secretary-General from whom he took his orders.

11. The concern of one troop-contributing nation, which is perhaps typical, was reflected in the statement of the Canadian representative to the United Nations on the subsequent occasion for the extension of the UNFICYP. Ambassador Ignatieff took that occasion to note that, in voting for the resolution to extend the mandate, his delegation did so "on the clear understanding" that the authorization would be for a specific period and that any changes in this "would involve prior consideration by the members of the Security Council." He also noted that "not only the participants in UNFICYP, but all Member States and particularly the members of the Security Council have an interest in a clear understanding on the matter." This statement was not challenged. U.N. Security Council, Provisional Verbatim Records, S/PV/1362, June 19, 1967, p. 31.

12. Another limitation on the extension of the principle of consent concerns the host state's right to determine the national units to be incorporated within the United Nations force. Although it is incumbent on the United Nations to attempt to secure national contingents acceptable to the host state in order to eliminate further possible points of friction, the host state, at least in theory if not always in practice, does not have veto power concerning the national contingents. For a comprehensive statement of this principle of host government consent, including the application of the composition of the force, see the "Summary Study of Secretary General on the Experience Derived From the Establishment and Operation of UNEF," particularly the Concluding Observations and Principles from the Report of the Secretary General, U.N. Doc. A/3943, October 9, 1958.

CHAPTER	**6**	PROBLEMS OF FORCE CREATION

Once violence breaks out, more than words are required to restore peace. There are and will continue to be circumstances in which words can be translated into accomplishments only when backed by action. One such positive form of response is the provision of military forces for peace-keeping.

THE PROVISION OF MILITARY FORCES FOR CYPRUS

Cyprus furnishes a case in point. When the troubles continued in Cyprus in the spring of 1964 and the United Nations decided to act, the Secretary-General was faced with the unenviable task of seeking contributions, both financial and manpower, to create a peace-keeping force. The task of securing volunteers is generally involved and thankless, and this instance proved no exception. However, the prospect facing U Thant at that time was not entirely dark. There were some positive aspects.

Positive Factors

First, the basic problem was not new. The Secretary-General and his staff had been confronted with the necessity of rounding up national contributions on short notice on two prior occasions i.e., UNEF and ONUC. The earlier experience was to prove of value in furnishing guidance applicable to the current crisis. The United Nations staff was thus enabled to work with greater speed, knowledge, and assurance than otherwise would have been possible. Likewise, it may be expected that the experience gained in Cyprus will be of future use in the event that similar action is again required.

Second, there was another plus factor working
for the United Nations in creating a force in
Cyprus. When the United Nations assumed this
responsibility, a peace force already existed in
Cyprus. The bulk of that force consisted of British
troops but it included units from the other two
guarantor powers, Greece and Turkey, which gave it
an "international" character. Possibly by building
on this existing structure the United Nations could
further internationalize the operation and create a
more representative force. This in effect is what
happened.

Finally, a number of nations had contributed
forces to previous peace-keeping operations. Ten
states had provided contingents to the UNEF; thirty-
four nations had contributed manpower to the ONUC.
The nations that had supported past peace operations
constituted a potential pool of states experienced in
peace-keeping. The problems involved were familiar.
The fact that they had, on one or more occasions,
evidenced a willingness to assist in international
efforts to meet an emergency might reflect a
predisposition to respond favorably on subsequent
occasions. Furthermore, several countries had
already advised the Secretary-General that they were
currently maintaining, or were planning to maintain,
units earmarked for possible emergency use in the
future. Among these states were Canada, the
Netherlands, and the four Scandinavian countries.
During the course of 1963, Canada provided the
United Nations Secretariat with detailed information
on Canadian stand-by forces which would be available
under certain conditions to support United Nations
operations. Similarly, in an address to the General
Assembly on September 24, 1963, the Minister of
Foreign Affairs for the Netherlands made an offer of
Dutch marine units. In like manner, the Scandina-
vian countries were in the process of creating United
Nations stand-by forces, earmarked for ready use,
which might be used jointly as a Scandinavian brigade
or individually as separate contingents in future
United Nations operations.

The Problem of Availability of
Stand-By Units

However, the act of creating and earmarking
national stand-by units alone does not give the

United Nations a carte blanche to use these forces
automatically when a need arises. Obviously, any
country earmarking a national contingent will desire
to reserve the right to decide whether that unit can
be made available for a particular United Nations
operation depending on the circumstances existing at
the time of the operation. A political judgment on
the part of the contributing state must be made at
the time the operation is launched. There will also
of necessity be other conditions attached by the
earmarking country concerning the size and the nature
of the forces and the time of their being made
available. For example, the offer by the Netherlands
specified that a first contingent of 300 marines
could be ready within twenty-four hours; that additional units could be made available within the next
few days; and that Dutch officers could be provided
for United Nations staff duty if the marines were
included in the United Nations force.

There are other complications involved in providing national units to an international force.
These complications vary from country to country.
They depend on the nature of the constitutional
provisions governing the use of the national defense
forces and the composition of those forces, i.e.,
whether composed of volunteers or regular personnel.
Generally, parliamentary consent is required to send
a national contigent abroad. This is true in the
case of Canada where the government, on contemplating
the provision of forces to a United Nations operation,
must advise the Parliament and secure approval for
the operation and then issue an Order-in-Council to
initiate the required action. The forces are then
provided from pre-designated regular Canadian
Defense Forces units.

Similarly, Ireland, a country whose citizens
have long been recognized for their reluctance to
turn their backs on a good internal battle, has
legal restrictions on the use of Irish soldiers outside the Emerald Isle. As a result of Irish
participation in recent United Nations actions,
these restrictions were reviewed and partially
modified by amending the basic law governing the
use of Irish forces. The revised law now permits
contingents of the Permanent Defense Force to be
sent outside the home state as part of an international force providing that a resolution is passed

by the Dail Eirean and provided further that the
international force has been duly created "by the
Security Council or the General Assembly of the United
Nations for the performance of duties of a police
character" (emphasis added).[1]

The procedure for the Scandinavian countries is
somewhat more involved. Here, parliamentary consent
has been necessary even to create the stand-by units.
These units are composed of volunteers, not regular
forces, and under the present authority can be committed to serve overseas in a peace-keeping role for
a maximum period of six months. At the end of this
six-month period, the volunteers must be returned
home, discharged, and replaced by a new contingent.
Obviously, such a requirement introduces certain
problems for the continuity of the peace-keeping
mission if the operation is of extended duration.
The six-month limitation is premised on the hopeful
assumption that effective and lasting results of the
peace-keeping effort can be obtained within that
minimum period.

In view of the uncertainty of securing forces
for operations after a breach of the peace has
occurred, there has been much thought given to
proposals to give greater assurance that forces
would be promptly available under United Nations control when needed. The difficulty lies in giving
effect to these suggestions. The possibility of
making military forces readily available to the
organization was initially considered in San Francisco
in 1945. The general acceptance of this principle
was reflected in the adoption of specific provisions
in the Charter to achieve this goal. These provisions,
contained in Chapter VII (Article 43), specified that
the forces would be provided in accordance with the
terms of agreements to be consummated between the
providing countries and the Security Council. In the
interim and pending the conclusion of such agreements,
the permanent members of the Security Council were
given a special responsibility for maintaining the
international peace and security (Article 106).
Because of the political circumstances existing since
1945, it has proved to be impossible to conclude
these arrangements. Neither have the major powers
been successful in exercising the interim grant of
authority to maintain the peace.

Because of the inability to assure adequate forces
to the organization as originally envisaged, a number
of alternative suggestions have been advanced.
Generally, these suggestions envision the provision
of limited forces for restricted purposes. Among
such proposals was one by the then Secretary-General,
Trygve Lie, in June of 1948, calling for a "United
Nations Guard Force" of relatively modest size--1,000
to 5,000 men.[2] The Secretary-General intended that
this force would be available for limited peace-keeping
functions, guard duty, observation, the administration
of truce terms, and duties of a similar type. However,
even this modest proposal was unacceptable in the
form originally outlined. Although the complete
plan was not accepted, it did stimulate thought in
this area. Under the General Assembly resolution
finally adopted, a United Nations Field Service of
300 guards and communications personnel was
subsequently created within the Secretariat to
assist the operation of United Nations Field Missions.[3]
In retrospect, Trygve Lie's proposals and the response
evoked did not provide much encouragement for the
proponents of a greater United Nations peace-keeping
capacity.

Another step in this direction, one based at
least partially on the experience provided by the
Korean action, was the "Uniting for Peace"
Resolution of 1950. In accordance with the terms of
this resolution, each member was encouraged to maintain trained, equipped, and organized units within
its national forces for service with the United
Nations upon recommendation of the Security Council
or the General Assembly. The Collective Measures
Committee, created by the "Uniting for Peace"
Resolution, further endorsed this goal in subsequent
periodic reports before it lapsed into inactivity.[4]
Although this resolution encouraged the earmarking
of national military contingents for United Nations
service, and the Collective Measures Committee invited
the member states to provide information on the steps
actually taken in this regard, the responses were
generally not encouraging. Sixty member states were
polled. Seventeen states failed to respond; two
merely acknowledged the inquiry; and twenty-one
replies were negative to noncommittal. Of the
remaining twenty replies, some were hedged, and only
four (Denmark, Norway, Greece, and Thailand)
"actually set aside any forces then in existence

without a great many strings attached."[5]   Thus,
until the creation of the UNEF, the history of
earmarking forces for United Nations operations
had not been very promising. However, Suez, the
Congo, and then Cyprus have given a new impetus
to suggestions along this line.

The Composition of UNFICYP

The Security Council resolution recommending
that the Secretary-General establish a peace force
in Cyprus was no surprise to U Thant. The Secretary-
General and his staff had been aware of the
possibility of United Nations involvement in Cyprus
since the initial troubles in December, 1963.
Following his discussion with the Permanent Representative of Cyprus and in response to a request from
that individual, joined by the representatives of
Greece, Turkey, and the United Kingdom, the Secretary-
General had earlier appointed Lieutenant General
P. S. Gyani of India as his personal representative
to observe the situation in Cyprus. The presence of
General Gyani was most helpful in keeping the
Secretary-General informed on the developing situation
and perhaps may have contributed toward alleviating
some of the tensions as well. The Secretary-General
also sent a member of his headquarters staff, Jose
Rolz-Bennett, a very capable and experienced civil
servant, to London in January, 1964, to observe the
efforts of the guarantor powers to resolve the issue.

Although the Secretary-General was able to
anticipate the possible need for a United Nations
force, the March 4 resolution provided the actual
go-ahead signal. Two days later, U Thant informed
the Security Council that General Gyani had been
appointed to command the force and that discussions
had already been initiated with several governments
for force contingents.[6] The discussions rapidly
centered on Austria, Brazil, Canada, Finland,
Ireland, Sweden, and the United Kingdom as likely
troop contributors. At the same time, the Secretary-
General established a goal of 7,000 for the initial
strength. By March 9, the United Kingdom advised
that it was prepared to match manpower contributions
from other countries up to a total of 3,500, thereby providing a basis for the 7,000 force desired
by the Secretary-General. Canada, Sweden, Finland,

and Ireland promptly indicated a willingness to
supply contingents pending the clarification of
certain questions pertaining to the organization,
status, directives, duties, and duration of the
force.   Sweden also expressed an understandable
unwillingness to be the only neutral nation
represented.   Brazil, a nation with a notable record
in supporting past efforts, did not respond in this
instance, and Austria, another prospective contrib-
utor, required additional time for review of the
matter.[7]

Some of the countries willing to provide
national units to the Cyprus force evinced a concern
over the financing inasmuch as the Security Council
had stipulated that the costs would be underwritten
by the tenuous means of voluntary contributions.
If such contributions were not forthcoming, conceivably the troop-contributing countries could be left
holding the bag and thus liable for costs normally
reimbursed by the United Nations.   To meet this
concern, the Secretary-General attempted to secure
advance commitments of financial support.   Fortunately, he was able to get prompt responses from
the larger financial contributors, the United States
and the United Kingdom, and was thus able to reassure
the prospective force contributors.

The discussions of the Secretary-General and his
staff representatives with the countries that
ultimately provided contingents resulted in a
continuous dialogue until the various conditions and
qualifications surrounding the operation were
resolved.   This was a typical and necessary exercise
in the creation process.   Despite the difficulty
of conducting extensive and detailed negotiations
under the pressure to create a force quickly, the
UNFICYP was established and became operational on
March 27, 1964, with Canadian and British troops.
Advance contingents of the Swedish and Finnish units
joined the force on the following day, and the complete contingents of Sweden, Ireland, and Finland moved
into positions during the period from the 10th to
the 30th of April.   By the end of April, UNFICYP
represented a substantial force which was composed
as follows:

Military

Austria	10
Canada	1,087
Finland	1,000
Ireland	636
Sweden	889
United Kingdom	2,719

Police

Austria	28
Total	6,369

Subsequently, during the month of May, a Danish contingent of 1,000 officers and enlisted personnel, an Austrian field hospital, and additional Swedish troops joined the United Nations force. The British contingent was reduced accordingly, providing an over-all force total of 6,411 men as of June 8,1964.[8] Thus, another enterprise in peace-keeping was under way.

COMPARISON OF FORCE CREATION IN CYPRUS, THE MIDDLE EAST, AND THE CONGO

Certain similarities may be detected in the manner in which the UNEF, the ONUC, and the UNFICYP were assembled.

Force Creation Under Pressure

Each effort led to an ad hoc arrangement. Negotiations to secure force commitments were hurried, conducted under the pressure of mounting an operation swiftly to preclude the possibility of further deterioration of a dangerous situation, and complicated by the number of parties involved.

The circumstances surrounding the establishment of UNEF in early November, 1956, and the activities that both immediately preceded and followed the General Assembly Resolution of November 4, 1956, are illuminating. The Secretary-General was requested to submit a plan for the organization of UNEF within 48 hours.[9] For the first time, the Secretary-General

and his staff were, on short deadline and under
trying circumstances, asked to create a force, secure
the consent of the parties involved, move the force
to the area of operations, and issue the necessary
guidelines and operational instructions. It is truly
a tribute to the persons involved in this undertaking
that the UNEF was created, was transported to the
scene of action, became operational, and successfully
undertook its mission. The force at one time or
another included units from ten states: Brazil,
Canada, Colombia, Denmark, Finland, India, Indonesia,
Norway, Sweden, and Yugoslavia.

Despite the abruptness with which the crisis
erupted and the rapid sequence of events that followed,
the number of members offering forces was reassuring.
Canada, Colombia, Norway, and New Zealand responded
on the same day the resolution was adopted. Sweden,
Denmark, and Pakistan submitted offers on the
following day; Finland, Ceylon, India, Czechoslovakia,
and Rumania on the next day. Subsequently, promises
were received from Burma, Yugoslavia, Brazil, Iran,
Ethiopia, Peru, Afghanistan, and Laos. Still other
commitments were available if they had been required
or requested.[10] Such a response was heartening and
demonstrated both the substantial approval of the
United Nations action and the measure of international
support that can be mustered in a crisis situation.

The creation of ONUC was likewise a hurried and
frantic operation. Chaos already reigned in the Congo
and if this situation were to be contained remedial
action was required promptly. The longer the
situation was allowed to continue unabated, the more
difficult and extensive would be the efforts required
to restore peace. During the initial days of force
creation and assembly, the Secretariat members faced
with the responsibility of getting this undertaking
going learned to do without their full eight-hour
sleep nightly. For several days after the passage
of the initial resolution, it is questionable whether
the key staff members slept at all.

Here again, the preliminary efforts looking
toward the eventual creation of a composite force
actually preceded and anticipated the action of
the Security Council. Under the circumstances, it
is fortunate that such an initiative was displayed.
As the situation in the Congo progressively worsened,
the Secretariat staff monitored closely the unfolding

events. During this period, Ralph Bunche, then serving as the Secretary-General's personal representative in the Congo, maintained close liaison with the Congolese authorities. It was to him on July 11, 1960, that Patrice Lumumba turned for technical military assistance. This was followed by the formal cabled appeals to the United Nations on July 12 and 13.

In an effort to prepare for the action that might, and did, follow, the Secretary-General met with the representatives of nine African states * on the day preceding the request for military assistance to discuss measures that could be taken to assist the Congo. These discussions continued after the Congolese request was received and basic agreement was obtained on a general plan for the operations that were to follow. By the time the Security Council met on July 13, four of these states--Ghana, Guinea, Morocco, and Tunisia--had promised contingents to any operation authorized by the Security Council.[11]

With the adoption of the resolution of July 14, 1960, the momentum of the operation increased. On the same day, Dag Hammarskjold asked the United States, the Soviet Union, the United Kingdom, Italy, and India for food and transport and named Major General C. C. von Horn of Sweden, who had been serving as the Chief of Staff of the United Nations Truce Supervision Organization in the Middle East, as commander of the operation. Within 24 hours, 600 troops were en route to the Congo from Ghana and Tunisia. Four days later, the United Nations force consisted of contingents from Ethiopia, Ghana, Morocco, and Tunisia and numbered 3,500 troops. The force build-up continued rapidly. By July 31, it consisted of 11,155 troops from Ethiopia, Ghana, Guinea, Ireland, Liberia, Morocco, Sweden, and Tunisia.[12] Eventually, at peak strength the force approximated 20,000 men and, during its four-year existence, personnel and specialized technicians were provided from 35 countries.[13]

---

*Ethiopia, Ghana, Guinea, Liberia, Libya, Morocco, Sudan, Tunisia, and the United Arab Republic.

Pattern of Force Contribution

It is significant to note that the names of certain countries appear and reappear when reviewing the
lists of peace-keeping forces. Prominent among
these are Austria, Brazil, Canada, Denmark, Finland,
India, Ireland, Norway, and Sweden--all of which
have contributed units to two or more peace-keeping
operations. This list can be expanded to include
the following states, which have provided units to
support at least one United Nations peace undertaking:
Colombia, Ethiopia, Ghana, Guinea, Indonesia, Iran,
Liberia, Mali, Malaysia, Morocco, Netherlands, Nigeria
Pakistan, Senegal, Sierra Leone, Tunisia, the United
Arab Republic, and Yugoslavia. In total, the list
is long and, although mistaken conclusions regarding
the support for peace ventures· may be made on the
basis of the number of contributing states, the number
is nevertheless impressive. The number could be extended even further if we were to add to it those
countries that have made military observers available
on occasion.

It is likewise noteworthy that the names of the
permanent members of the Security Council do not
appear among the list of force contributors. An
exception to this is the United Kingdom which
because of its historical role in Cyprus, its treaty
relationship with that country, and the presence of
British peace maintenance forces on the scene,
provides a significant force contribution and
substantial logistic support to the UNFICYP. Although
the permanent members, notably the United States and
the United Kingdom, have on occasion and because of
their military capacity furnished logistic support
to the peace-keeping efforts, they have not normally
provided units for "front-line" operations. This
has been by deliberate design in an effort to keep
such situations isolated from the East-West conflict
and thus to avoid the dangers of Great Power com-
petition and direct confrontation.

UNEF set the pattern for not using force components from the Great Powers. ONUC maintained the precedent and, although it proved difficult to keep the
Cold War out of the political vacuum that followed the
Belgian withdrawal from the Congo, "a consent emerged
among the vast preponderance of member states that
the operation, like the Emergency Force in the Middle
East, should be an exclusive endeavor of states not

directly involved in the Cold War."[14] This was one
of the reasons why the Secretary-General in his
efforts to secure force commitments turned initially
to the African countries to provide the bulk of the
forces required.* This principle was adhered to
throughout the Congo crisis and has been continued
with the Cyprus exception already noted.

The action by the Secretary-General in looking
toward the African states to furnish forces for the
ONUC provides another precedent that could prove
useful on occasion in the future. When feasible,
troop contributions from countries within the
region in which the situation or dispute occurs offer
certain advantages. First, personnel from the region,
other considerations apart, may normally be expected
to arrive more quickly at the scene of trouble. This
could prove to be significant in initiating a police
action promptly. It also offers a potential advantage
for the continuing operation in terms of force
rotation, the logistic supply for those items from
national sources, the emergency evacuation of
personnel, and the expeditious handling of other
matters of strictly national responsibility. Second,
providing they are politically acceptable to the
parties concerned, neighboring or nearby countries
may bring with them a special regional knowledge or
understanding that could contribute to the success
of the mission. Third, particularly in the case of
the Congo, reliance on the neighboring states offered
an opportunity to foster a regional feeling which
could, in turn, have wider implications for the
future of the entire area. Possibly, the fostering
fo such a regional consciousness might lend impetus
to or accelerate the development of constructive regional institutions. Finally, there is the possibility that intraregional associates might be more
acceptable to the state or states directly involved
in the crisis than other more distant states. If
this is so, keeping the matter "within the family"
may avoid the problems created when a stranger steps
into a domestic dispute. On the other hand, there

_____

*Among the other reasons were to attempt to
handle this matter on a regional basis, to get forces
that might be near to the scene of the action, and
perhaps to play down any black-white complication.

are circumstances in which it may be highly desirable
to have a wider geographical representation of contingents in order to maintain the international character of the operation or to ensure impartiality.
There may also be situations, such as in the case of
the UNEF, where contingents form some of the neighboring states would not be acceptable to one of the
parties.

OBSERVATIONS REGARDING
FORCE CONTRIBUTIONS

The experience of the United Nations to date in
attempting to secure commitments of national force
contingents on short notice clearly demonstrates the
difficulties arising when operating under emergency
conditions. Some of the confusion that prevails at
the time an operation is mounted could be avoided by
advance planning. This planning should be of a considerably longer-range nature than that carried out
by the Secretariat staff, laudable though these
efforts were, in trying to anticipate and prepare to
implement a Security Council or General Assembly
directive that was already imminent. Longer-range
preparations should take into account (1) the possible, or probable, future situations that might
require a peace-keeping presence; (2) which countries
might be likely to respond in a particular situation
to a call for forces; and (3) which countries could
provide the required type of units. Although much
can be done in this direction, it must be recognized
that the possibilities are not unlimited because not
all future circumstances can be predicted with
certainty.

The most recent operations provide certain
precedents with respect to political factors involved
in creating a United Nations force. These precedents
substantiate the important role of the middle and
smaller powers in providing national contingents.
At the same time, they demonstrate the limited role
of the Great Powers. These observations concerning
the UNEF, ONUC, and UNFICYP are generally applicable
to the "lesser" United Nations peace efforts, e.g.,
Yemen and West Irian. Although the precedents
developed are not inviolate, they do offer useful
guidelines for advance planning. Based on the actual
experience and practice in peace-keeping to date, on
the continuing active concern of such states as

Canada, the Netherlands, and the Scandinavian
countries in developing capacities to anticipate
future force calls, and on the problems involved
with the active participation of one or more of the
Great Powers, it would be well to anticipate a major
role for the middle and smaller powers in providing
forces. It is these countries which in all likelihood
will be called upon in the future for peace-keeping
forces. Fortunately, the list of nations that have
displayed an interest in earmarking forces or that
have provided contingents is impressive.

Whether any single nation will authorize the
use of its national forces for any particular occasion
will depend on constitutional considerations and a
political decision made at the time. That decision
must take into account the force objectives as
reflected by the pertinent United Nations resolutions
and the debates surrounding the adoption of those
resolutions. Likewise, if the United Nations mandate
changes either through evolution as the operation
progresses or by the adoption of a new directive in
response to changing conditions or to reflect a new
consensus, the contributing states may consider it
necessary to review their original consent.* If the
contributing countries at any time during the
operation disagree with the reviewed force mandate,
they may elect to withdraw their national contingents.
Such judgments were made by certain of the African
states during the Congo operation, and some
contingents were withdrawn from the ONUC. However,
states should exercise great restraint in the
withdrawal of units already committed to an operation
because such action could both jeopardize the current
action and set an unfortunate precedent for future
peace-keeping operations.

There are other considerations that might require
a state to withdraw forces committed to an international operation. For example, an entirely new

---

*This raises the question of the scope of the
original consent. There may be circumstances
arising where a modification of the original mandate
could be considered to be encompassed within the
terms of initial consent. On the other hand, there
may well be changes in the mandate that clearly
go beyond the original consent.

situation might arise that imperils the security of the contributing nation and necessitates the return of its national contingent. This occurred when India was forced to withdraw its forces from the ONUC to meet a Communist Chinese threat on its northwest frontier.

It is interesting to note that the motives for particular states to provide forces for an operation may vary considerably. By far the majority of the states that have contributed units for peace-keeping operations have undoubtedly done so for worthy and commendable reasons. It is not inconceivable that there may be instances, however, in which other motives prevail, e.g., personal aggrandizement of the national leader, state prestige, a desire to extend national influence within a given region, or an effort to export a particular political philosophy. In such circumstances, it might be expected that the task of the Secretary-General in insuring an impartial United Nations attitude would be more difficult.

In the last analysis, the composition of a peace force must take into account a number of political and legal factors--both national and international. On the national side, there may be constitutional and political considerations that inhibit the provision of national contingents for a particular operation. Certain preliminary steps may be taken to ease the adverse political implications, to simplify or remove the constitutional restrictions, or to anticipate the actual procedures to be followed in contributing national forces.

On the international side, political and constitutional questions are also of concern in force creation. The constitutional question was addressed in Chapter 4. The over-riding political questions from the international standpoint, apart from the basic constitutional question on the legality of peace-keeping which has a political taproot, concern the composition and acceptability of the force. What will be the mix of national units? What nationalities are acceptable? What will be the proper balance of national contingents? The answers to these and similar questions are important because the correct answers may do much to insure the success of the operation. The final decision as to the precise composition of the United Nations force must take into account the implications of the national

origin of the individual contingents. Whether the
"right" country will be able to provide the "right"
type of unit is another factor of importance. A
compromise may be necessary in the end taking into
account those countries which are willing to provide
forces, the type of units offered, and the type of
units actually required. These latter questions will
be addressed in the next chapter.

NOTES

1. Hidejiro Kotani, "Peace-keeping: Problems
for Smaller Countries," International Journal, XIX
(Summer, 1964), 311-12.

2. U.N. General Assembly, Official Records,
Third Session, 1948-49, Suppl. No. 1 (A/565), pp.
XVII-XVIII.

3. "Report of the Special Committee on a United
Nations Guard," U.N. General Assembly, Official
Records, Fourth Session, 1949, Suppl. 13 (A/959).

4. U.N. General Assembly, Official Records,
Sixth Session, 1951, Suppl 13 (A/1891); Seventh
Session, 1952, Suppl. 17 (A/2215); Ninth Session,
1954, Annex 19 (A/2713).

5. William R. Frye, A United Nations Peace Force
(New York: Oceana Publications for Carnegie Endowment for International Peace, 1957, p. 59.

6. U.N. Doc. S/5579, March 6, 1964.

7. U.N. Doc. S/5593, March 12, 1964.

8. U.N. Doc. S/5764, June 15, 1964.

9. For a detailed description of this sequence,
see Frye, op. cit., pp. 1-20.

10. Ibid., pp. 21-22.

11. For much of the infomation concerning
these first days of the Congo operation, I am indebted
to observations by Dean Andrew Cordier of the School
of International Affairs, Columbia University, and
the book by King Gordon, U.N. in the Congo: A Quest
for Peace (New York: Harper, 1962). Both individuals

were intimately acquainted with the Congo operation.
Dean Cordier, as a principal deputy to Dag Hammarskjold, played an importnat role in the negotiations
that led to the creation of a United Nations force
and later served for a period as the Secretary-General's personal representative on the scene in the
Congo. Subsequently, he returned to United Nations
headquarters in New York, where he continued to
maintain a close association with the Congo operation.

12. U.N. Docs. S/4389/Add 4, July 20, 1960,
and S/4389/Add 6, July 31, 1960.

13. Ernest W. Lefever, Crisis in the Congo
(Washington, D.C.: The Brooking Institute, 1965),
p. 15.

14. Lyman M. Tondel, Jr. (ed.), The Role of the
United Nations in the Congo (New York: Oceana
Publications for the Association of the Bar of the
City of New York, 1963), p. 16.

CHAPTER **7** FORCE COMPOSITION
AND ORGANIZATION

The preceding chapter was concerned primarily
with the political and legal questions of force
creation. This chapter will consider some additional
aspects of force creation that are likewise of great
importance and which directly affect the operational
efficiency and, ultimately, the success of the force
created. It will consider, first, the type and kind
of contingents required; and, second, how these individual contingents can be conbined and organized
into a single command. Once the various countries
decide to contribute units, an integrated United
Nations operation does not automatically follow.
There still remain the complex organizational
problems of constructing a balanced military force
and creating an adequate organizational structure.

FORCE COMPOSITION

It is obvious on reflection that the efficiency
of any military or paramilitary force cannot be
measured merely by adding the sums of the capabilities
of the component units. By a careful selection of
the subordinate units to be incorporated into the
collective command, that command can be assured a
capacity greater than the total of the individual
unit capacities. Conversely, by an ill-chosen
grouping of components, the over-all organization
may not achieve the maximum efficiency possible.*

---

*This and the related observations are based
partly on the writer's military experience, his
study of and association with peace-keeping at the
United Nations headquarters level since 1965, and
interviews with persons who have had direct
experience with or in peace-keeping operations.

Very conceivably it could end up with a capacity even less than the simple aggregate of the unit capabilities. Accordingly, the proper selection of component elements is an especially important consideration in constituting an international force. This consideration has both quantitative and qualitative implications. For this reason, the process of force construction entails more than the automatic acceptance of offers of force contingents from those states that are "politically acceptable" and willing to contribute to the common effort.

The quantitative implications relate both to economy and to effectiveness of operation. Obviously, the size of the force should be no larger than that required for the specific mission. Otherwise, the financial burden would be increased unnecessarily. The recent history of the financing of peace-keeping operations underscores the desirability for keeping the financial costs at the lowest level possible. It is also desirable, from the standpoint of operational as well as financial efficiency, that the over-all force be no larger than required to achieve the force objectives. A force larger than necessary places an unnecessary additional responsibility on the commander, his staff, and the supporting logistics structure. Thus, excess numbers can be counter-productive in terms of over-all efficiency. Furthermore, by their very nature, it is sometimes desirable that United Nations peace-keeping forces should be as unobtrusive as possible. To the extent that supplemental personnel over and above those actually needed are introduced into the operational area, the United Nations presence would become more noticeable. However, there will be other occasions, e.g., in Cyprus, where the visible presence of the blue beret force is useful.

A peace-keeping command should also be qualitatively balanced. The operational force should be assembled with care to insure that the type of units best suited to undertake the particular undertaking are included. This requires that a proper ratio between the support and operational units be achieved. There should also be an appropriate balance within the supporting elements themselves. If this equilibrium is not achieved, again the operational capacity may suffer. This "correct" balance can only be determined in relation to the specific mission the force will be called upon to perform. Therefore,

the first step in developing a proper force structure
is to examine and clarify the mission that is to be
fulfilled. This may or may not prove to be a simple
matter.

Clarification of Force Mission

The UNEF mission was relatively straightforward.
The United Nations resolutions and the related
General Assembly discussions provided adequate
guidance to ascertain the mission with some precision.
Simply stated, the purpose of that force was "to secure
and supervise the cessation of hostilities." During
the history of the UNEF, the initial mandate remained
unchanged. The UNEF was designed primarily as a
buffer force and given police, patrol, and observation
responsibilities to discharge the function. It was
not intended to be a combat force, nor was it supposed
to become involved in internal affairs. These objectives were unambiguous, clearly understood, and provided broad but well-defined guidelines for designing
the force.

However, the identification of the mission
and the determination of the force composition
necessary to fulfill that mission may not always be
as simple, especially in the confusion surrounding
the initiation of an operation. Furthermore, the
mission may change as an operation unfolds. This
was true in the Congo where the tasks of the ONUC
were progressively expanded. Initially, the mandate
of the ONUC was merely to permit the withdrawal of
the Belgian troops and to provide a local security
force until the Congolese national security force
could assume this responsibility. This modest and
uncomplicated sounding mandate proved difficult to
fulfill because of the collapse of the government
of the Congo and its continued inability to relieve
the international force of internal security responsibilities. When additional complications arose
with the secession of Katanga, the original mandate
had to be reviewed and revised. From this point on,
it became virtually impossible for the ONUC to remain
completely detached from Congolese internal affairs
because almost any act, or inaction, would accrue to
the benefit of one or the other internal faction.
The evolving, and increasingly more comprehensive,
nature of the mission was reflected in the additional
functions with which the ONUC was charged with the
passage of time. Obviously, the initial composition

of ONUC was geared to the originally announced
objectives. As these objectives changed during the
course of the operation, it was necessary to re-tailor
the force. Additional capabilities in the form of
armored scout cars, personnel carriers, and tactical
air units were introduced to provide the ONUC with
a capability consistent with its enlarged objectives.

The mission of the UNFICYP as outlined in the
original Security Council resolutions appears to be
less complicated than that which finally evolved for
the ONUC but more complex than that of UNEF. UNFICYP
was charged with using "its best efforts to prevent
a recurrence of fighting" and with contributing
"to the maintenance and restoration of law and order
and a return to normal conditions."[1] This mandate
implied interposition, patrolling, and observation.
The force was constructed to perform these activities.
Because of the communal nature of the underlying
difficulties in Cyprus, the UNFICYP has had to display
some ingenuity in accomplishing these tasks and, at
the same time, in complying with the Secretary-General'
charge to "avoid any action designed to influence
the political situation in Cyprus except through
contributing to a restoration of quiet and through
creating an improved climate."[2]

The key to determining the mission of any
specific operation must be, in the first instance,
the United Nations resolution creating the force.
If this directive is not clear, possibly the discussions surrounding its adoption may shed additional
light and reveal the will of the organization. If
neither the basic resolution nor the surrounding
discussions provide sufficient enlightenment concerning the intent, the Secretary-General must then
either make his own interpretation or refer the
matter back to the appropriate organ for clarification. The Secretary-General has on occasion,
when he believed he generally understood the intent
of the organization, taken the first course of action
and provided his own interpretation of the force
mandate. However, if a question arises concerning
the interpretation of the Secretary-General, it is
incumbent on the appropriate organ to clarify promptly
its intention. The second procedure has also been
utilized on occasion. It was followed during the
initial days of the Congo action when Dag Hammarskjold
felt the need on several occasions to request that
the Security Council clarify or redefine the original

mandate. In any event, a full and complete understanding of the precise mission to be achieved is a
first essential in creating a properly balanced force.

Establishing Balance

     What, precisely, do we mean by a balanced force?
First, we mean that the line elements must include
the proper mixture of operational units to insure
that the basic capabilities to do the job are present.*
Second, "balance" also applies to the ratio between
the line, or operational units, and the supporting
echelons. This ratio will not be the same in every
situation. In fact, it is difficult to visualize
two different situations in which identical force
structures would be appropriate. If there is too
great a proportion of operational units in relation
to the supporting units, the operational units cannot be effectively supported and employed. Conversely,
it is undesirable to have an excess capacity in the
number of supporting elements for they then will
become an uneconomic resource. However, if there is
to be an error in arriving at the appropriate proportion of operational to support units, the margin
of error should be on the side of the operational
forces in order to provide a reserve operational
capacity against emergency situations. During
emergencies, the supporting services can be extended
temporarily. This period cannot be prolonged indefinitely without in turn affecting and degrading the
operational effectiveness of the combat elements.
This principle is elementary. Any western movie fan
can verify that the wagon train can hold out against
the circling Indians temporarily. It cannot hold
out indefinitely as its ammunition supply becomes
exhausted. Finally, there must be a proper balance
within the logistic structure in order to meet the
twin requirements of economy of operation and operational efficiency.

---

     *In this chapter, the words "line," "combat,"
and "operational" have been used interchangeably when
referring to force units despite the fact that,
strictly speaking, "combat" is not a particularly
desirable or descriptive word for use in reference
to operational units on a peace-keeping mission.

The Battalion as the Basic Operational Unit

Let us examine first the operational side of
the force structure. What are the required or
desirable components? There is a wide measure of
agreement among those who have taken part in United
Nations peace-keeping operations that the basic operational unit should be a "normal" infantry battalion.[*]
There are several arguments to support this view.
First, this is the most appropriately armed and
equipped unit to meet the wide variety of situations
with which peace-keeping forces might be confronted.
Second, the use of infantry battalions as opposed
to composite units will preserve the fundamental
advantage of organizational integrity. However,
despite the general view of persons who have served
in operations such as the UNEF and ONUC concerning
the suitability of the infantry battalion as the
basic stepping stone in creating a United Nations
force, it should be noted that the word "normal"
when applied to an infantry battalion covers a lot
of ground. Strictly speaking, there is no single,
standard model. Battalions vary considerably among
different armed services with respect to the numbers
of personnel, equipment, organization, and training.
The personnel strength may vary from 500 to 1,000;
the equipment may include a wide diversity of weapons,
different in size, caliber, and capability; and the
organization may consist of four, five, or six companies depending on the number of rifle companies
and whether separate headquarters, support, or heavy
weapons companies are included. In spite of these

---

[*]This view was reflected at the conference
convened in Ottawa in November, 1964, to consider
certain military and technical matters related to
peace-keeping operations. The conference was attended
by representatives of 23 nations that had participated
in previous United Nations peace-keeping operations
and in many respects was a landmark in (1) highlighting
many of the problems involved in present peace-keeping
activities, (2) providing a forum for the exchange
of useful information concerning measures that might
be initiated or pursued in developing national
capacities to respond to future operations, and
(3) evidencing the widespread interest in and support
of peace-keeping operations.

differences, however, there are sufficient similarities to consider this unit as the logical basic
building block.[3]

The infantry battalion is an extremely versatile
and useful basic tactical unit. It is also the
smallest tactical unit that, when augmented by the
addition of certain administrative and staff personnel,
can be given more or less self-contained capacity.
By making use of this capacity to the extent possible,
the normal administrative burden at the international
force level may be reduced. The next smaller unit,
an infantry company, will not afford this same
advantage nor can it readily be augmented to do so.
Constructing a force composed entirely of company-size
units would multiply the administrative load by
increasing the number of units involved without any
offsetting advantages.

The use of company-sized elements could also
create pressures toward multiplying the number of
units represented in the international force. Many
of the smaller nations that are unable to furnish
a larger unit might be able, and anxious, to provide
company-size units. Although broadening the international base might be politically desirable, it
would greatly complicate the problem of force integration and adversely affect the over-all administrative effectiveness. More important, however,
would be the adverse implication for operational
efficiency. In terms of operational effectiveness,
the use of multiple units of different nationalities
would materially increase the problems of command
and control, and greater efforts would be required
to coordinate the actions undertaken to assure the
success of the mission.

If we accept the battalion as the basic organizational unit, what are the implications arising
from the fact that the "normal" organization may
vary considerably from one country to another?
Does this mean that the adoption of such a yardstick
in force assembly is valueless? The answer is
definitely no. Despite the disparities between the
1st Battalion of the Queen's Own Rifles of the Royal
Canadian Army and a Danish, an Irish, or a Malaysian
infantry battalion, there are sufficient likenesses
to provide a high degree of uniformity and to justify
using this as the basic unit for building a force.

What are the essential characteristics of
the "normal" battalion? A look at the 1st Battalion
of the Queen's Own Rifles will provide us with the
vital statistics of one such typical unit.[4] The
over-all strength of this battalion is 650 personnel.
It is armed and equipped with an imposing array of
the "usual" small arms and light armament associated
with ground forces. The Table of Organization lists
four rifle companies, a headquarters and a headquarters
company, and a support company. The support company
is charged with providing operational and administrative
support for the entire battalion and consists of a
mortar platoon, an assault pioneer platoon, a maintenance platoon, an administrative platoon, and a
garrison platoon. The battalion as a whole possesses
a substantial tactical and operational capacity and
is organized to insure a certain degree of self-
sufficiency. It is readily adaptable to many different
types of operations and it can function effectively
under a wide variety of conditions. This same statement could be generally applied to a Danish, an
Irish, or a Malaysian battalion. However, if the
comparison were to be extended greatly, further
qualifications would have to be made to reflect
national differences relating to size, organization,
equipment, and training.

For maximum effectiveness in responding to
peace-keeping emergencies, the basic units should
be air transportable. This means that the personnel
should be trained in air movements and that the
organic equipment including at least some vehicles
should be capable of being transported by air so
that the unit can be moved in a tactical configuration.
For this reason, small, versatile vehicles such as
1/4-ton vehicles should be used to the extent possible.
The battalion headquarters should contain the normal
staff elements: S1 (Personnel); S2 (Intelligence, or
Information); S3 (Operations); and S4 (Supply); and
be augmented by special staff sections as necessary.
For example, a special communications section could
be set up if this function is not included within
the S4 (Supply) echelon. In addition, the existing
staff sections might have to be augmented, particularly in the supply and administrative areas, to
enhance the capacity of the unit to operate indepen-
dently from its national military system. In this
connection, the addition of a battalion surgeon and
a medical section may be highly desirable and,
depending on the national religion or religions, a

chaplain and a chaplain's section might be added.

This "normal" infantry battalion should contain
a full complement of communications equipment, extra
technicians, and adequate spare parts to permit a
minimum of 90 days initial operation in the field
before resupply becomes effective. It should plan
to take its entire complement of organically assigned
equipment to the field. Obviously, the communications
equipment assigned will vary in amount and type
between different national forces. However, all
contingents should have the capacity to provide line
(telephone) communications down to platoon level in
static situations and radio communications to other
subordinate elements. At a minimum, each squad should
be provided a walkie-talkie tie to its platoon headquarters.

The infantry battalion is then a logical basic
stepping stone in creating a peace-keeping force.
National contributions of smaller size, e.g., companies or platoons, although they may serve to
broaden the structure, to get more countries into
the act, and to create a broader base of support
for the United Nations operation, are relatively
inefficient. Reliance on such units would multiply
the problems in administration and supply with a
corresponding loss of operation effectiveness. On
the other hand, an international force constructed
on the battalion building block concept may be
tailored to fit the requirements of almost any
situation taking into consideration the factors of
locale, geography, terrain, climate, and distances
to the scene and within the scene of operations.
The infantry battalion, either with its organic
equipment only or augmented as necessary, can provide
a readily mobile and adaptable unit for peace-keeping.
However, in the final analysis, the key to the success
of any unit lies in its personnel, not its equipment.
The most important single element is the well-trained
and disciplined soldier. With such troops, dependable
platoons, companies, and battalions can be constructed.

The Role of Support Units

Let us turn to consider the supporting structure.
The efficiency of the line elements will depend in
large measure upon how well they are supplied and
provided with the means to act. The effectiveness
of a rifle squad as an observation post can be greatly

enhanced if it has a communications link with its
platoon command post. On the other hand, ·that same
rifle squad may serve no useful purpose in observation if it lacks the means to relay its findings to
the next higher echelon. In like manner, if the
operational needs of that infantry squad are not
properly and promptly met, the unit will be unable
to operate effectively. For this reason, it is
essential that the appropriate balance, both in
type and number, of support to combat troops be
achieved. Communications technicians, logistics
personnel, medics, vehicle repairmen, and other
supporting troops must be available within the
over-all organization in sufficient numbers to back
up and satisfy the requirements of the operational
units.[5]

     International peace operations present difficult
and unusual problems in this respect. During national
military operations, an infantry battalion will
normally operate as part of a regiment, within a
division, within a corps, within an army. Each
higher echelon has within its structure elements
that support the basic battalion. Generally these
services become progressively more specialized and
sophisticated as one proceeds up the chain of command.
Thus, under normal conditions, an infantry unit might
have to send its weapons to the division ordnance
company for certain repairs and its engineering
equipment to the division engineers for maintenance.
However, separate battalions, serving as part of an
international force, will not be able to call on
their national regiment, division, or corps supply
trains for assistance. This deficiency must therefore be rectified within the United Nations force
structure which must fill the gap left by the absence
of regimental and divisional trains. This becomes
an even more critical factor when additional complications resulting from differences in unit
equipment and the lack of standardization are introduced. For this reason, the logistics organization
within an international force composed of different
national contingents must insure a larger and more
comprehensive supply and maintenance capacity than
would normally be expected from the size of the
force alone. To facilitate maintenance and resupply
under such conditions, the maximum amount of equipment standardization between contingents is desirable.

In addition to the logistic support elements,
such as maintenance and supply units, certain combat
(operational) support elements may also be required
by the international force. For example, motorized
reconnaissance units, tanks, or aircraft may be
required. The selection of the type and number of
such units for a particular occasion cannot be
accurately predetermined. This will depend on the
mission and the peculiar requirements of the situation.
However, in order to be in a better position to secure
and to move such units promptly to an operation where
needed, they should, just as in the case of the
initial contingents, be earmarked in advance.

FORCE ORGANIZATION

Assuming that the proper mix of units has been
made available to the United Nations for a particular
operation, how should these units be organized?
What type of organization is best fitted for the
specific circumstances? This question is related
to the problem of command and control. However,
command and control as well as the role of the
Secretary-General and his staff will be discussed
in the next chapter. This section will be concerned
only with the mechanics of organization for field
service.

Organizational Pattern in Three Selected Cases

Fortunately, in considering these questions we
can draw on the experiences encountered in the three
recent United Nations peace-keeping operations.
The pattern of organization that developed in these
three operations, to some extent by trial and error
and not similar in each instance, appears to be
fundamentally sound and offers a model for the future.
This model may have to be altered slightly to con-
form to the particular requirements of a given situation, but such re-adjustments can be affected without undue loss of momentum.

The United Nations Emergency Force in the Middle East

Looking first at the UNEF (see Figure 1) and
the organization that evolved during that operation,

FIGURE 1

Organization of UNEF

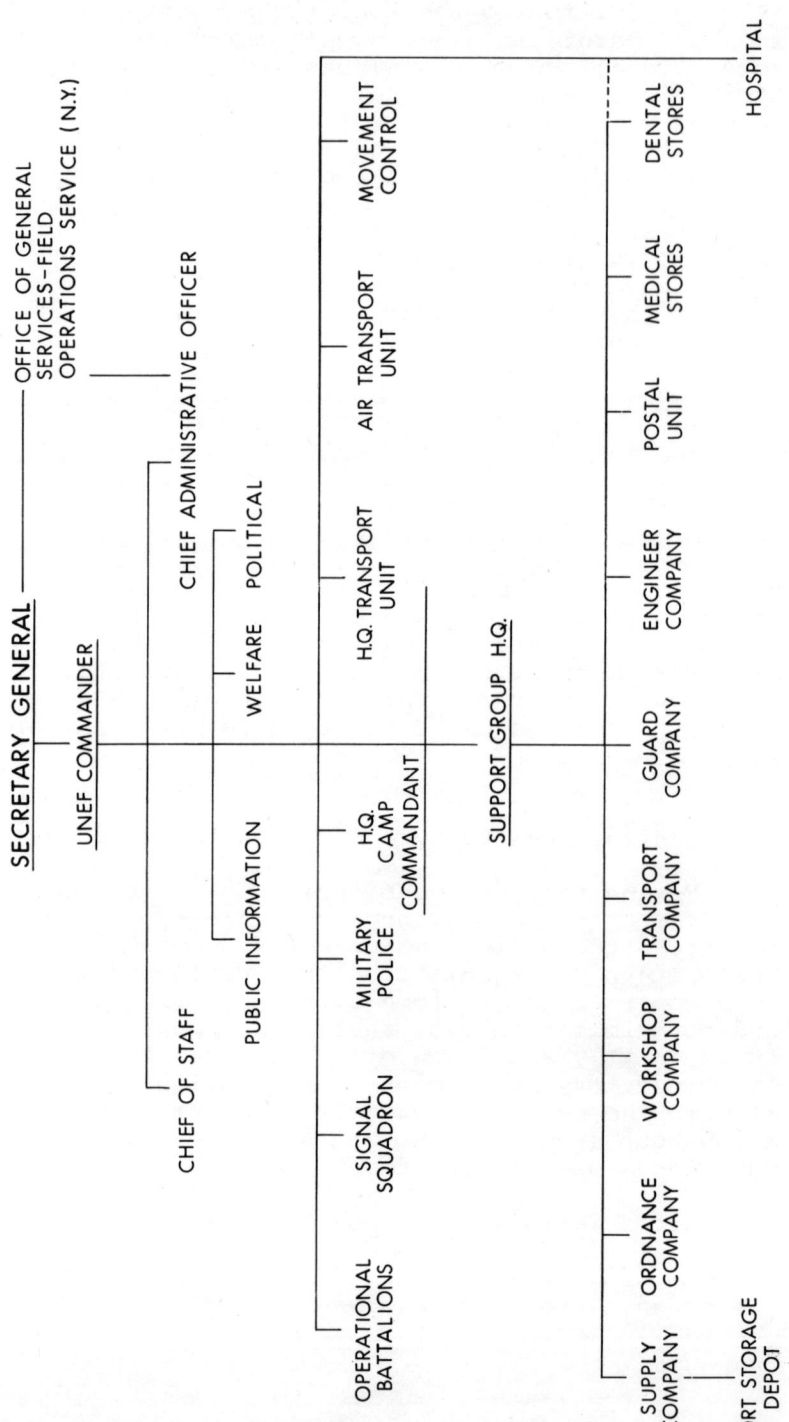

we see that the UNEF commander was directly responsible to the Secretary-General who in turn was
responsible to the General Assembly. The Commander
of UNEF exercised his authority over all elements
of UNEF--both operational and support. He was
assisted in this task by a military Chief of Staff
and a Chief Administrative Officer, the latter
being concerned with the logistics side of UNEF
operations and responsible also to the Field
Operations Service of the United Nations Headquarters.
The Commander of UNEF exercised direct control over
the operational forces, the operational battalions,
and the direct operational support units such as the
signal squadron. He exercised control over the
remainder of the supporting maintenance and logistics
units through a maintenance area commander who, with
his headquarters and the bulk of the maintenance
activities, was located at Rafah in Sinai. This
general organizational approach was well adapted to
the needs of UNEF and, with various slight modifications and adaptations to meet new or changing
requirements, served the United Nations purposes
well. From a military standpoint, the organizational
structure provided the basis for clear and distinct
command lines.

     The organization of UNEF was modified in the
light of actual field conditions during the course
of its twelve-year existence. These modifications
served to improve and perfect the structure, and the
conclusion that the organization of UNEF served the
functional needs of the command seems justified.
UNEF provided the experience and a model framework
for future United Nations forces. However, no
organizational scheme is ever perfect. There is
always room for further improvements. General
Rikhye, based on his extensive experience in peace-
keeping and on his experience as the last Commander
of UNEF, feels that future United Nations Force
Commanders should be given even greater responsibility
in supervising the logistics system and that this
should be reflected in organizational changes to
insure that the Chief Administrative Officer is
responsible more directly to the Force Commander.6

The United Nations Force in the Congo

     A somewhat similar organizational pattern was
adopted for the ONUC (see Figure 2). The Force
Commander exercised direct command over the opera-

FIGURE 2

Organization of the ONUC

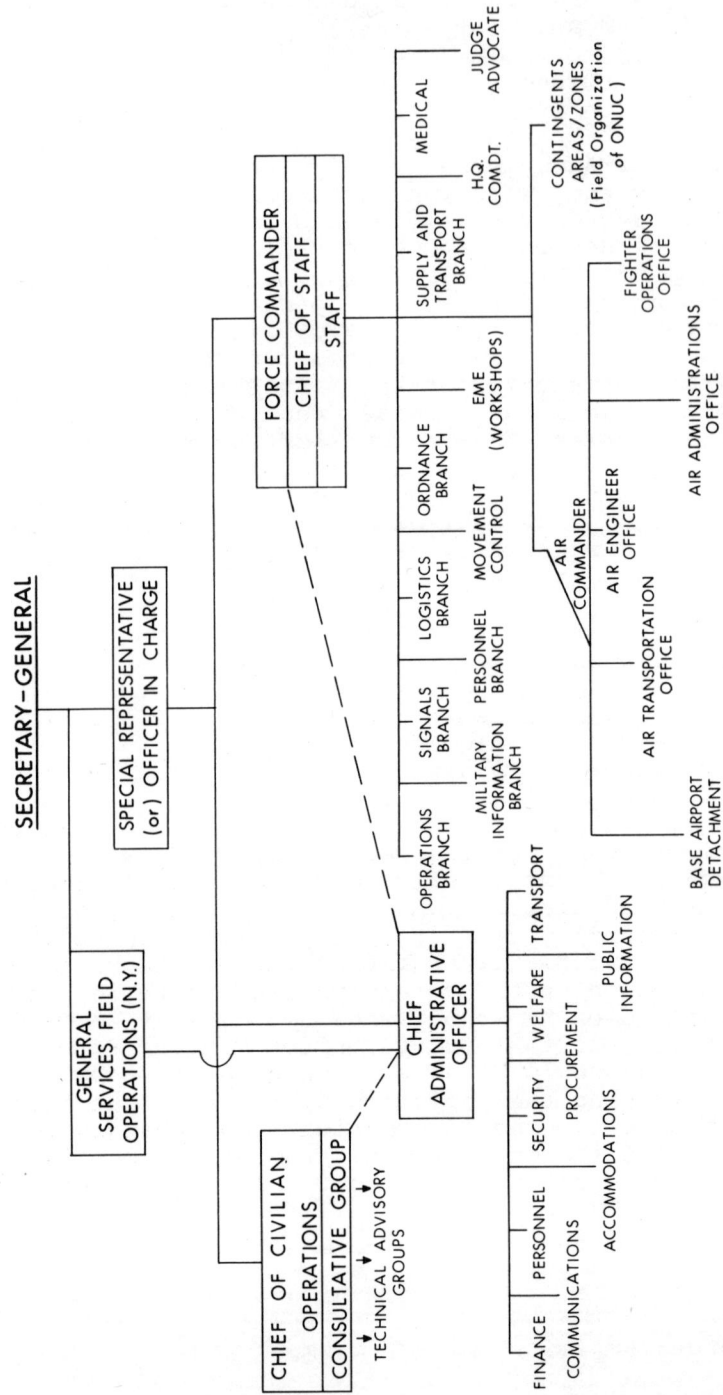

NOTE: Although there is no direct line between the Secretary-General and the Force Commander, on occasion the Force Commander reported directly to the Secretary-General on operational matters.

tional and operation support units. Subordinate,
but reporting directly to the Force Commander, was
the Air Commander under whom the air service and
activities were grouped. It should be noted that,
in contrast with the UNEF, the civilian activities
of the ONUC were more extensive and the Chief
Administrative Officer charged with supporting both
the civilian and military operations was also responsible to the Field Operations Service in New York.
In effect, this created two lines of authority and
responsibility for the Chief Administrative Officer,
one to the representatives of the Secretary-General
in the field, the Special Representative and the
United Nations Force Commander, and the other to
the Field Operations Service in New York. Such dual
lines of responsibility create a situation likely
to result in confusion and conflict. Although there
were difficulties because of this in the Congo, the
fact that such difficulties were held to a minimum
is a tribute to the personnel involved and the fact
that close coordination and liaison were established.
The Chief Administrative Officer was made responsible
for the financial matters in connection with the
United Nations operations in the Congo as well as
for all procurement to support both the military
and the civilian activities. It should also be noted
that, because the Congo supply and operational requirements were different from those of Suez, the organizational pattern established had to be adjusted to
reflect these differences. This may be expected in
any operation. Another distinctive feature in the
Congo was the creation of the post of the Special
Representative, later designated the Officer-in-
Charge, who represented and reported to the Secretary-
General on political matters. This proved to be an
essential and important post.

The United Nations Force in Cyprus

        The UNFICYP organizational structure (Figure 3)
resembles to a high degree that used in the Congo
and reflects the experience gained in the latter.
A comparison of the organizational chart of the
UNFICYP with that of the ONUC reveals few basic
changes. An office similar to that of the Officer-
in-Charge (Congo) reporting directly to and representing the Secretary-General on political matters
was established for Cyprus. However, in Cyprus, in
contrast to the Congo, the military Force Commander
reports directly to the Secretary-General and not

FIGURE 3

Organization of UNFICYP

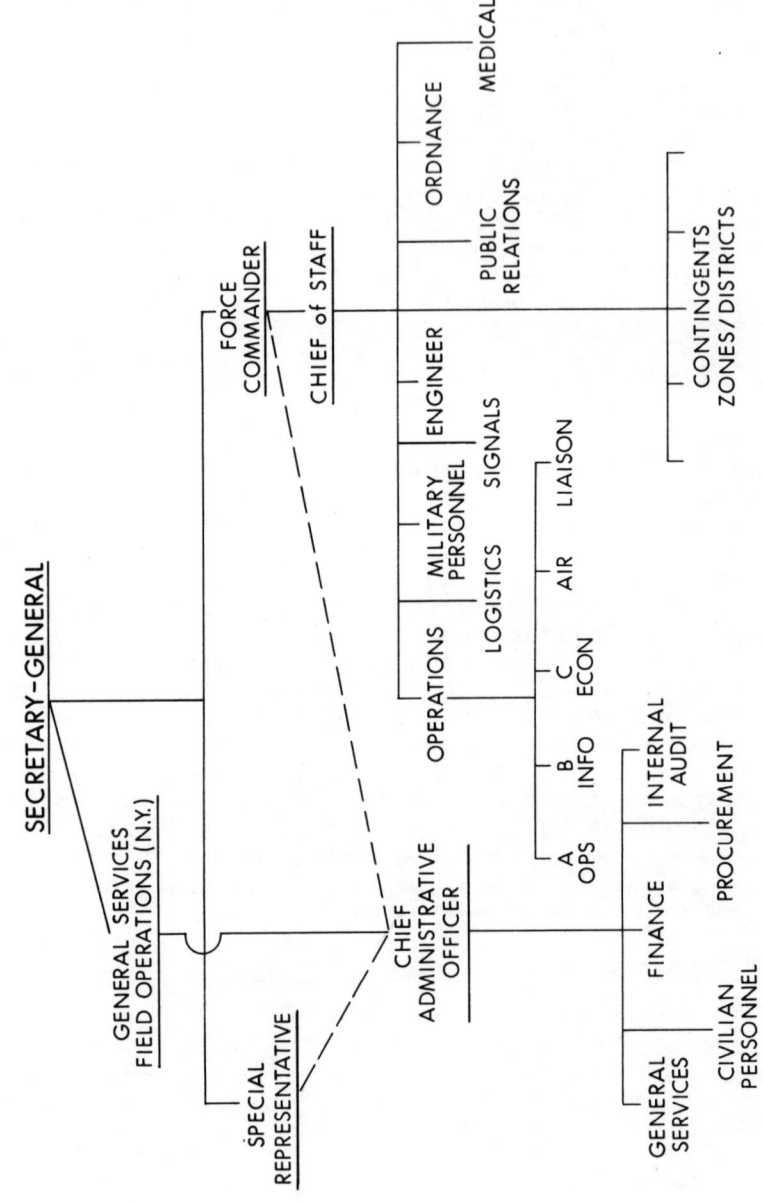

through the Special Representative. The Chief
Administrative Officer and his staff remain little
changed from the Congo, their responsibility to
support the military forces, however, being not as
formidable as in the Congo. This has resulted at
least partially from the fact that the United Nations
forces in Cyprus have been able to draw upon the
existing United Kingdom logistics system. This has
proved to be most advantageous. The organization
of the UNFICYP itself appears to parallel that of
the ONUC except that the air activities, which are
not as extensive in Cyprus, are a responsibility of
the headquarters operations staff and are not placed
under a separate air commander. In Cyprus also,
the present zonal structure of the organization is
reflected in the organization chart.*

Concluding Observations

     From an organizational standpoint, the internal
alignments of the UNEF, the ONUC, the UNFICYP all
proved satisfactory and survived the test of actual
operations. Each bore a resemblance to the other
two, and taken together they offer a rough pattern
for any future peace-keeping operation. The possible
model for such an operation is shown in Figure 4,
but it should be noted that this model is a guide
only and can be changed as required. The important
considerations to be borne in mind in establishing
an organizational framework are the following:

     1. The Force Commander should be given
     direct command authority over all of the
     operational and the combat (operational)
     support elements. The lines of authority,
     both upward and downward from the Force
     Commander, must be clear and unambiguous.

----

     *In August, 1965, following a reduction in
force which occurred when a portion of the Irish
contingent was repatriated and not replaced, the
Nicosia Zone was eliminated and the UNFICYP reorgan-
ized. Under this reorganization, all districts and
contingents reported directly to force headquarters.
The elimination of the zonal headquarters permitted
an economy in manpower.

FIGURE 4

Organizational Model for Future United Nations Forces

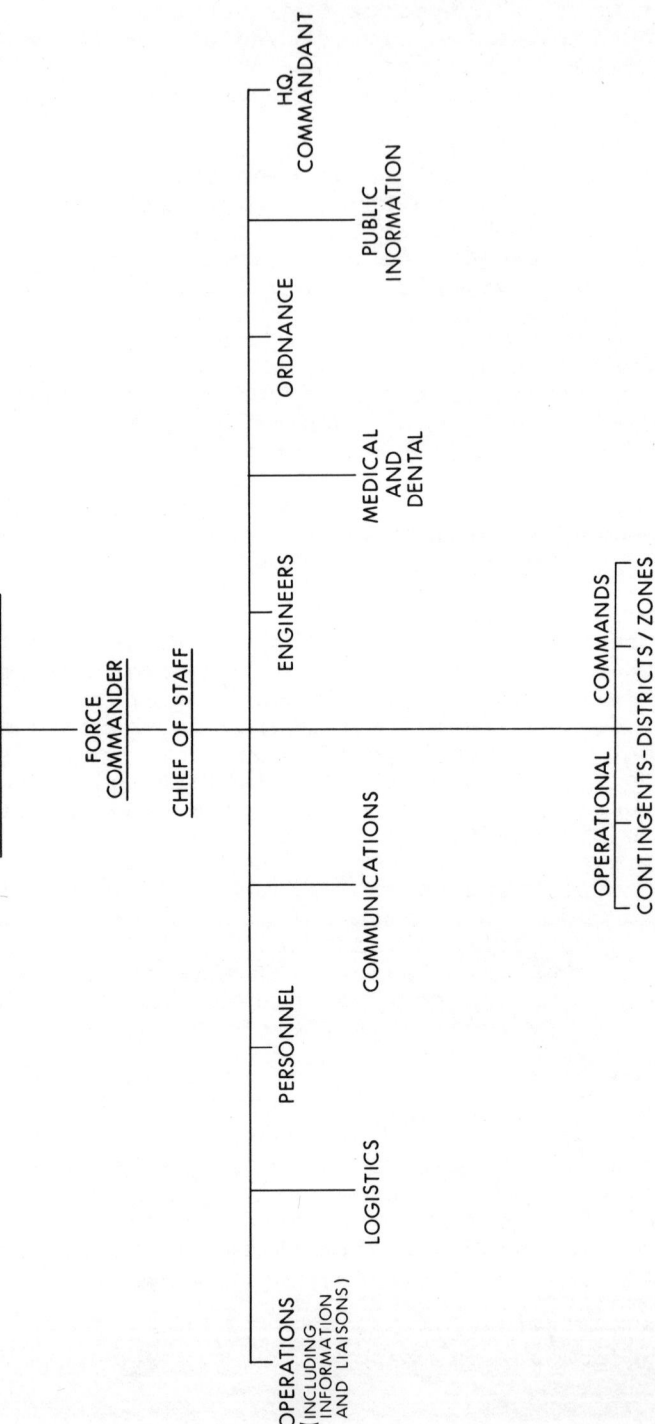

2. The Commander's immediate responsibility for logistics matters may, as in the
case of UNEF, be exercised directly
through a support area commander in the
event that such proves feasible and desirable. Alternatively, this responsibility
may be discharged directly by relying on the
the logistics and supply sections of the
force headquarters to provide staff guidance and to determine requirements which
in turn will be fulfilled by a separate
supply and procurement service (such as was
done by the Field Services in the Congo).
In the final instance, the decision as to
which approach to adopt will depend on both
scope of the support activities and geographic considerations.*

3. The size of United Nations force headquarters should be the minimum required to
administer and direct the operations. A
normal tendency in any headquarters establishment, military or civilian, is to
expand the staff beyond the optimum size
required. This is in accordance with
Parkinson's Law, which provides a scien-
tific explanation for the tendency of a

---

*General Rikhye, the most recent Commander of
UNEF, who is well qualified to comment on the role
and authority of a United Nations field commander,
believes that the commander's control and responsibility over logistics matters must be enhanced.
Although the arrangements worked satisfactorily for
UNEF, General Rikhye feels that this may be attributed
to the fact that good working relationships were
actively sought by both the Force Commander and the
Chief Administrative Officer. According to General
Rikhye, much of the success of this system was due
to the personalities and attitudes of the individuals
concerned and did not derive primarily from the
organizational arrangements. He believes that this
places too great a reliance on fortuitous assignments
and on personalities. He suggests that, for future
operations, the Force Commander be given complete
control over logistics as well as operational matters
instead of relying on a system of coordinated
responsibility.

bureaucratic enterprise to expand and
become self-perpetuating. However, expansion beyond the point of need creates a
loss of efficiency, and this obviously
should be avoided.

4.   The command and force structure must be
flexible enough to permit adjustment to the
requirements of different operations. Even
within a given operation, the requirements
may change as the operation continues.
Accordingly, the number and type of both the
operational and the operational support
elements may have to be re-tailored during
the course of operations. This in turn may
require some adjustments in the district
and zonal arrangements. Likewise, the supply
structure established to support a field
force must take into account the fixed geographic factors and the physical facilities
and resources locally available as well as
the operational force requirements. Thus,
the UNEF set up a port detachment in Port
Said to handle surface shipments arriving
at that location and to expedite the movement of such supplies to the main logistics
base at Rafah. In similar manner, an air-
head was established at El Arish. The size
of the UNEF logistics structure was also
readjusted as the requirements and the size
of force were reduced. It is undoubtedly
true that any preconceived organization for
future operations, if it is to be satisfactory, will have to be adaptable to the
peculiar requirements of the operation.

5.   The Force Commander may report directly
to the Secretary-General as in the UNEF and
the UNFICYP or through the Special Representative as in ONUC, where an extensive
and coordinated civilian-military effort
was required. With either pattern, the
essential element is that the line of command be well understood and adhered to by
all personnel concerned.

NOTES

1. U.N. Doc. S/5575, March 4, 1964.

2. U.N. Doc. S/5653, April 10, 1964.

3. This conclusion and the supporting observations are consistent with the findings contained in a series of papers prepared by the International Information Center on Peace-keeping Operations (IPKO), World Veterans Federation, Paris. See, for example, the Annex contained in Monograph No. 4 in which the battalion is described as "the most useful unit from an operational point of view" (p. 15). Colonel Nils Stenqvist, The Swedish U.N. Stand-by Force and Experience (Monograph No. 4; Paris: IPKO, August, 1967). The IPKO series also describes in some detail the actual experiences of various contingents in United Nations field operations.

4. See Canadian Operations in Support of the United Nations (Document No. 12; Paris: IPKO, March, 1967). This paper summarizes "the organization and training of Canadian military forces earmarked for service on United Nations Peace-keeping Operations." Additional specific details on the Queen's Own Rifles battalion were contained in an informal working paper prepared for the Ottawa Conference, 1964.

5. See Major General I. J. Rikhye, Preparation and Training of United Nations Peace-Keeping Forces ("Adelphi Papers," No. 9.) London: Institute for Strategic Studies, April, 1964, p. 6.

6. Interview with Major General Indar Rikhye, November 27, 1967.

CHAPTER **8** COMMAND AND CONTROL

Since World War II, with the advent of military
capabilities carrying the promise of instant and
devastating destruction, much attention has been
given by military men and militarily oriented
statesmen and scholars to the subject of command
and control. This has been dictated by the international strategic environment and the need to insure
prompt and effective control of, and response by,
national strategic forces. The concern over the
regulation of these strategic forces having such
great destructive capacities has been reflected in
the desire to create completely effective command
and control systems to insure that such forces are
not launched prematurely or accidentally. There
has also been a parallel concern with developing
effective systems to guarantee the ability to launch
such forces if the decision is made to unleash them.

However, the problem of providing reliable
command and control is not peculiar to strategic
forces and national military establishments. It is
an essential requirement for any military or
paramilitary operation. It is no less a necessity
for a United Nations peace-keeping effort than it
is for the direction of strategic forces of the
major powers, even though the consequences of a
breakdown in the regulatory system may not be quite
as disastrous in the first instance. Ultimately,
the success of any operation will depend on the
abilities of the military forces involved to fulfill
their mission, and the command and control system is
an important factor affecting this ability. Although
a successful operation cannot be guaranteed by
providing a reliable command system alone, it is
doubtful that any operation can succeed without
such a system.

Command and control is exercised through the
command line. It is therefore intimately connected

with the type of command structure. The organization
adopted must be simple and uncomplicated enough to
permit directions and instructions to flow swiftly
from the top to the bottom, and for responses at
the operating levels to be reflected upward to the
higher command levels. The organizational structure
and the command line must be well understood by all
personnel concerned. The organizational system
suggested in the preceding chapter provides one
arrangement that can be adopted to meet the command
requirements for possible future crises.

THE THEORY OF COMMAND AND
CONTROL OF UNITED NATIONS FORCES

General Theory

Command and control proceeds from top to bottom.
Orders and directions issued from the highest levels
are followed by response and implementation at the
lower levels. However, this is not an entirely
one-directional operation. Directions from on high
are not conceived in a vacuum; they are developed,
taking into consideration, among other things, the
impact on the operating echelons, the capabilities
of those units, and the experiences encountered in
the field of operations. Thus the avenue by which
orders are transmitted downward is a two-way street
and allows responses to directions to be reflected
upward as well.*

This two-way street must therefore be able to
accommodate two essential functions: the issuance
of orders and the supervision of their execution.
The first without the second leads to a breakdown
in the system and eventually to failure of the
operation. The correct proportion between promul-
gation of commands and supervision of their fulfillment has been estimated to be in the order of 10 to
90 per cent ratio, the 90 per cent weight being
given to supervision and follow-up control and,
surprisingly, not to the initial and more dramatic

---

*These and the other general comments on command
and control are consistent with established military
doctrine.

aspect of issuing commands.* Regardless of the
precise weight of effort given to command as opposed
to control, both are essential. Neither command
without control nor control without command leads to
efficiency, and, although they may not be equally
weighted halves of one system, the natural linkage
of the two words reflects their ultimate insepara-
bility.

Application to United Nations
Peace-Keeping Forces

Looking at command and control for United
Nations peace-keeping, we note that the apex of the
command line lies within the organ which, on behalf
of the United Nations, initiates the particular
operation. This organ, either the Security Council
or the General Assembly as the case may be, representing and reflecting the will of the governments
of the member states, sets forth the force mandate,
usually in rather broad terms, in an appropriate
resolution. However, it is neither desirable nor
possible for the Security Council or the General
Assembly to exercise control over all of the varied
and detailed aspects of a particular operation.
Although the Security Council has its Military Staff
Committee, there is nothing in the record of
performance of the Military Staff Committee so far
to justify the conclusion that it is the proper
agency to give executive direction to a field
exercise. Neither the Security Council nor the
General Assembly has the administrative and service
staff to provide day-to-day supervision and support
of a peace-keeping operation.

Such facilities are, however, available in the
office of the Secretary-General. With his staff and
advisers, technicians, and administrators, he has
the capacity for providing continuous supervision
and logistics support to field operations. Thus,

---

*The 9:1 ratio is obviously merely a rough
approximation. However, it is a commonly accepted
approximation within the armed services and is
included in the suggestions on "how to succeed in
the armed forces" passed on to newly commissioned
officers.

the Secretary-General has been asked by the General Assembly in the case of Suez, and by the Security Council in the instances of the Congo and Cyprus, to exercise executive direction for and in the name of the responsible United Nations organ. This, we have seen, is in accordance with the provisions of Article 98 of the Charter, which states that the Secretary-General "shall perform such other functions as are entrusted to him by these organs."

The role of the Secretary-General in providing executive direction to the United Nations operations has been characteristic of recent United Nations actions. In one sense, the Secretary-General has been the key to the entire operation and he bears the ultimate responsibility for giving political direction to the force. He may be assisted in this process by an advisory committee composed of representatives selected from those member states which have an interest in or are contributing in some form to a particular operation. This device was adopted in the Suez operation with encouraging results. The committee, advisory in fact as well as in name, was limited to such a role and could not bind the Secretary-General to a course of action. Despite this, the use of this committee provided a useful link in keeping the Secretary-General attuned to the will of the responsible organ and in securing recognition and a broad base of support for the Secretary-General's action by the countries most directly concerned with the operation. The merits of an advisory committee were subsequently demonstrated when a similar institution was created for the Congo operation.

The Secretary-General is assisted in exercising day-to-day supervision of the force by the Secretariat, a sizable permanent and, on occasion, augmented staff complete with field extensions.* Since Suez, he has also been assisted by a military adviser

---

*The elements of the Secretariat which have been most concerned with and involved in giving support to the Secretary-General are (1) the Office of the Under-Secretaries for Special Political Affairs, (2) the Office of the Military Adviser to the Secretary-General, and (3) the Office of General Services, particularly the Field Operations Service within that office.

located in and attached to his executive office.
The military adviser has invariably been an officer
intimately familiar with international operations
by multi-national forces who is immediately available
to provide professional military advice and assistance
to the Secretary-General. Until 1966, this office
was occupied by Major General Indar Rikhye of the
Indian Army, who was assisted by one or more military
assistants. With the departure of General Rikhye to
assume command of UNEF, the office of the military
adviser was left with only a single assigned officer,
Lieutenant Colonel Lauri Koho of the Finnish Army.
Colonel Koho was later reassigned to other duties,
leaving the military adviser's office unmanned.

The staff of the military adviser's office has
at various times performed services in some respects
similar to that originally anticipated for the
Military Staff Committee in relationship to the
Security Council. Within the limitations imposed
by its size, this staff has provided a very useful
service in assisting the Secretary-General to mount
and direct field operations. It is difficult to
envision how an emergency military operation could
have been launched and directed without such assistance being available to the Secretary-General. The
possibility of strengthening this office offers
great promise in the future.

The Secretary-General may appoint the military
field commander as in the Congo and Cyprus or suggest
the commander for endorsement by the directing organ
as was done in the case of Major General E.L.M.
Burns' appointment as UNEF Commander. In either
event, it is incumbent on the Secretary-General to
provide the field force commander with terms of
reference promptly. In this process, the original
resolution of the United Nations, of necessity broad
and general, must be translated, expanded, and given
additional precision. This is accomplished in the
form of orders and directions to the Force Commander
that amplify and refine the general statement of
objectives. At the same time, extreme care must be
taken to insure that the orders issued are as clear
and concise as possible to eliminate the possibility
of misunderstanding.

The command line from the Secretary-General to
the Commander of the United Nations field command may
be direct without any intervening link in the chain.

On the other hand, there have been circumstances in
which it was considered desirable to designate a
civilian political representative of the Secretary-
General in the field, immediately subordinate to him.
In such instances, this representative serves as the
arm of the Secretary-General in the area of operations
and coordinates and provides over-all direction to
all the field activities--military and civilian.
The designation of a special representative is
particularly useful when the United Nations activities
in a specific area are either extensive or varied.
In such instances, the United Nations Military
Commander will receive his directions from the
Secretary-General through the Special Representative.

   The Force Commander is the individual who
exercises immediate command of the United Nations
military operations in accordance with the political
guidance relayed from the Secretary-General. In
general, these instructions take two forms: basic
or general guidance and more specific, detailed
directions. The basic guidance or terms of reference
may be spelled out in a set of force regulations
governing such matters as the authority of Force
Commander to issue orders; the international character,
privileges, and immunities of the force; the general
administrative, executive, and financial arrangements;
and the rights and duties of the members of the
force.[1]

   Generally, the directives to the Force Commander
are designed for internal use; of necessity, these
directives are not always available for public
dissemination. On the other hand, it is sometimes
useful to publicize some of the force guidelines.
This was the case when the Secretary-General published
an aide memoire setting forth certain guiding
principles regarding the function and operation of
the UNFICYP; it clarified a number of aspects of
command and control such as the responsiveness of
the UNFICYP Commander to the Secretary-General and
the contingents to the Commander of the Force; the
precise parameters governing the use of force; and
the relationship of the force to other United Nations
activities.[2] The issuance of such directives and
the enunciation of principles governing the operations
are essential for effective direction of the operation.

   Up to this point, the preoccupation with command
and control has been with the links between the

United Nations authorizing organ, the Secretary-
General, and the Force Commander. However, the line
does not stop at this point. The mission of the
United Nations force will not be fulfilled unless
this process is extended downward. Just as the
Secretary-General must provide the Force Commander
with appropriate guidance, the Force Commander, who
is operationally responsible for all of the functions
of the force, must establish a system to adapt this
guidance for use by the subordinate elements and
insure that appropriate, clear, and unambiguous
instructions are given to the commanders of the
operating echelons. He does this through the issuance
of force regulations, directives, and direct orders.
Force direction must be provided to the lowest
operating level, to the United Nations soldier on
his post. The ultimate aim is to insure that every
unit and each individual within those units "gets
the word."

From the Commander of the Force downward, the
directions must be even more precise and the
supervision of the execution more detailed. This is
a command responsibility. How well this responsibility
is fulfilled will depend in large part on the capacity
of the Commander. For this reason, the selection of
the Force Commander is one of the most important
considerations in organizing an international force.
The capability of the Commander will, more than any
other single factor, determine first the effectiveness of the command and control system, and second
the ultimate success of the operation.

THE PRACTICE OF COMMAND
AND CONTROL OF UNITED NATIONS FORCES

So far we have been concerned primarily with
the theory of a United Nations command and control
system. How does the theoretical model compare
with the actual practice?

Command and Control in Three
Selected Peace-Keeping Missions

Just as in other facets of peace-keeping
activity, the actual experience of United Nations
forces in the field has done much to shape the
arrangements that have evolved.

The Middle East

The experience of the UNEF has played a major
role in command and control evolution. The plan for
the UNEF, drafted by Dag Hammarskjold and accepted
by the General Assembly, placed the responsibility
for the operation in the hands of the Secretary-
General. The General Assembly resolutions governing
the operations were broad, and the Secretary-General
was given wide latitude in executing these directions.
At his request, an Advisory Committee, composed of
representatives from Brazil, Canada, Ceylon,
Colombia, India, Norway, and Pakistan, was established
to assist and advise him in discharging this function.
The committee proved to be a very useful institution
in providing a link to the General Assembly. It
was chaired by the Secretary-General, held meetings
usually at his call, and provided him a measure of
assistance and support. Hammarskjold took cognizance
of the views reflected in the committee meetings,
but he was not bound by them. In his summary study
of the operation of the UNEF, he endorsed the use of
such a committee for future operations and suggested
that it would be useful for all countries contributing
forces, if they were not too numerous, to be
represented.[3] It was also during the Suez experience
that a Finnish general was drafted to serve as the
first Military Adviser to the Secretary-General, an
institution that gradually took on permanence.

The line of authority from the Secretary-General
proceeded directly to the Commander of the Force,
initially Major General E. L. M. Burns, in whose
hands rested the direct command of the UNEF. The
Force Commander under the Secretary-General was
endowed with full command authority for field
operations.[4] General Burns' responsibilities and
authority covered the multitude of tasks involved
in creating, fielding, directing, and supporting
the UNEF effort. In fulfilling his tasks, he was
aided by his immediate staff which was composed of
officers from the various nations participating in
the UNEF. The command arrangements, considering
the ad hoc manner in which they were effected,
proved satisfactory for the operation. With minor
modifications, they have continued relatively
unchanged to the present and set a pattern for
subsequent operations.[5]

The Congo

     The command and control arrangements adopted
for the ONUC profited from the experience gained in
the UNEF. However, the command problem in the
Congo was in many respects more complicated for a
number of reasons. The size of the force was
larger; there were more national contingents; the
distances involved were greater; the United Nations
civilian operations were greatly expanded and the
relationship of these operations to the military
forces was more complicated; the relationship with
the local inhabitants was more complex; and the
mandate was more difficult to fulfill. A further
complication was introduced by the fact that the
countries that voted to establish ONUC did not all
share the same view regarding the terms of the
mandate.[6]

     Because of these complications, the UNEF
pattern of command and control had to be modified
to the new circumstances. A Special Representative,
later designated as the Officer-in-Charge, was
appointed to head the effort in the Congo. The
Special Representative exercised control over both
the military and civilian operations in the name of
the Secretary-General. He became an additional
link in the military chain of command and was
responsible for insuring that proper directions were
transmitted to the Force Commander. In reviewing
the Congo operation, it is difficult to see how any
other arrangement could have been effected because
of the necessity to coordinate two separate and
supporting efforts, one civilian and one military,
both working side by side in one geographic area.
The appointment of a Special Representative meant
that one individual could decide any differences
arising between two arms of the endeavor within the
immediate area and without referring the matter to
United Nations Headquarters in New York. For example,
the Special Representative could reconcile such
important matters as the appropriate distribution
of jeeps when the estimated needs of the military
and the civilian sides of the operation exceeded
the total available. However, even more significant,
he could coordinate the United Nations efforts to
fulfill the basic objective of restoring peaceful
conditions. The institution of the office of
Special Representative also provided an arrangement

that insured civilian political control inasmuch as the military commander was subordinate and responsive to those charged with the political execution of the endeavor.

The United Nations operation in the Congo provides several interesting examples of what can happen when directives lack clarity. One instance, which occurred early during the initial confusion of getting the operation under way, arose in connection with the interpretation of the mandate of the ONUC. To what extent did the initial Security Council resolutions authorize or permit the use of force by the ONUC to effect a United Nations presence in Katanga after the secession of that province in August, 1960? Interpretations of the intent behind the resolutions varied. Accordingly, the Secretary-General felt it necessary to return to the Security Council for clarification of his mandate and, until this was accomplished, the ONUC was delayed in the discharge of its responsibilities in Katanga.[7]

The Congo experience demonstrated the difficulties that can arise when directives are inadequate or unclear. In September, 1961, the ONUC resumed operations in Elizabethville to expel the mercenaries. Bitter fighting resulted and neither side was able to claim victory. However, the important question in this context was whether that operation was authorized. There is considerable doubt on this point, and a final answer may never be forthcoming. The essential elements in this case concerned the instructions conveyed to Conor Cruise O'Brien, the United Nations Representative in Elizabethville, by a political officer of the United Nations, Mahmoud Khiari, which directed O'Brien to resume action in Katanga. There is much mystery as to the origin of these instructions and, after Dag Hammarskjold's death, his immediate staff assistants at United Nations headquarters in New York denied any knowledge concerning the issuance of such instructions. In any event, a United Nations operation was initiated, not very successfully, and under questionable authority. Such a situation should obviously be avoided in the future and emphasizes the need for effective command and control.[8]

There should be no doubt at the moment any operation is launched concerning the specific mission

to be undertaken or the validity of the orders
directing the operation. Obviously, one method to
assist in achieving this goal is to insure that
orders are received and authenticated only within
the command line and not transmitted by personal
representatives, staff assistants, or high-ranking
couriers, unless there are clearly over-riding
circumstances. Normally, if there is an officer-in-
charge in the chain, orders from the Secretary-
General should be directed through, and not around,
him. Furthermore, no level of the command line
should be by-passed except in the case of an extreme
emergency. Such emergencies will happen only in
very rare instances. No matter how worthwhile or
well thought out the directive, if an intermediate
commander is by-passed, the entire operation may
be imperiled or undermined. The reasons for this
are fairly obvious. The intermediate commander may
either be aware of other considerations that would
put a different light on the enterprise, or he may
have planned, or already have initiated, other
actions that would be at cross-purposes or neutralize
the proposed undertaking.

Cyprus

     The pattern and practice of command and control
in the UNFICYP bears the print of the ONUC system.
It had the advantage of benefiting from the experiences of both the UNEF and the ONUC. The guiding
principles for the command arrangements were
expressed very succinctly by U Thant:

     The Force is under the exclusive control
     and command of the United Nations at all
     times. The Commander of the Force is
     appointed by and responsible exclusively
     to the Secretary-General. The contingents
     comprising the integral parts of it take
     their orders exclusively from the Commander
     of the Force.[9]

     Although the UNFICYP command system has the
stamp of the ONUC structure, there were alterations
made to adjust to a new situation which contained
new elements. A Special Representative of the
Secretary-General was not appointed at the outset
in Cyprus. However, subsequent to the inauguration
of activities by the UNFICYP, U Thant deemed it
desirable to have a top-level political officer on

the scene. This officer would be in a better
position to conduct negotiations on the implementation of a comprehensive program to restore normal
conditions.[10] On May 11, 1964, Galo Plaza of
Ecuador was appointed to fill this post. Unlike
the Officer-in-Charge in the Congo, he was on a
level with the military commander of the United
Nations Force, Lieutenant General P.S. Gyani. Both
individuals reported directly to the Secretary-
General for operations within their competence.
This relationship continued when both Galo Plaza
and General Gyani were succeeded by Carlos A.
Bernardes and Lieutenant General A. E. Martola,
respectively.

The logistics support operations in Cyprus are,
like those in the Congo, under the Chief Administrative Officer, who takes his orders from New
York but is responsible for coordinating logistical
support services with the military commander on
the spot. It should be noted that the support
services in Cyprus are of a much lesser magnitude
than those that existed in the Congo, and this
difference is reflected in the organizational
modifications. Furthermore, whereas in the Congo
the Chief Administrative Officer was responsible
for providing major logistics support to the military
forces and for establishing lengthy supply lines,
the UNFICYP has been able to draw extensively on
existing United Kingdom logistics lines. This has
eased the problem of resupply and simplified the
task of logistics coordination. In this new setting,
the Chief Administrative Officer has been made
primarily responsible for supplying only those items
peculiar to the United Nations force, such as the
familiar blue berets. He has not been required to
arrange for the supply of the bulk of military
equipment and rations. In general, partially as
a result of the experience gained in previous
operations and in part due to the different physical
environment, the command arrangements in Cyprus
have proved to be well adapted to the needs of the
force.

General Complicating Factors

One special problem arising in connection with
exercising command of force composed of several
different nationalities should be mentioned. Just

as in the other aspects of force operations, the
multi-national character introduces difficulties
that otherwise might not be encountered. Command
is normally a national matter, and some countries,
in recognition of this basic fact, have specific
prohibitions precluding their military forces from
taking orders from nationals of another country.
For example, Canada has regulations that do not
permit Canadians to be subject to the command of
non-Canadians. What happens then when Canadian
units are called upon to serve in a force under the
command of an Indian general? Fortunately, as the
record of Canadian participation in international
peace-keeping efforts amply testifies, a modus
vivendi has been found during actual operations to
permit living with this restriction and still
allowing effective command and control to be
exercised. This has been accomplished by using
Canadian officers on the Force Commander's staff to
transmit force directives. Such practices have
permitted international operations to be accomplished
with relative efficiency. However, in the future,
it would be desirable for those countries with
these or similar limitations to redesign their
regulations in order to remove any doubt about the
responsibilities of their units in the international
command.

     A related complication arises from the fact
that command and control are intimately linked with
discipline, another element that is usually a matter
of exclusive national concern. Discipline is
essential to insure that control is effective at
all levels. Yet, by the law of most countries, the
discipline of their national forces can be exercised
solely by the national commanders. On the one hand,
discipline is essential to proper control and can
only be enforced by national authority and, on the
other, the requirement is for control by the international Force Commander; how can these apparent
irreconcilables be reconciled? Fortunately, again,
a working solution has been found. In actual
practice, the national commanders have assumed
responsibility for enforcing discipline within their
units as the occasion has required. This is
probably not the ideal solution, but it has permitted
the United Nations forces to maintain discipline
and to conduct extended operations with reasonable
dispatch. The best solution, from the standpoint
of the Force Commander, would be to entrust to him

the enforcement of discipline to the degree necessary in support of his command authority. Under the present circumstances, this is too much to hope for.

Still another complication to effective command is the language problem. Obviously, when some interpretation of directives between elements of the same force is required during transmission, a possibility for error exists. It was not unusual during the ONUC operation for three different languages, normally French, English, and one other, to be used in transmitting an order from the force headquarters to a subordinate operational unit. On occasion, this led to misunderstanding. Whether misunderstanding occurred or not, there was an additional burden on all personnel concerned to insure that instructions were relayed and interpreted correctly.

COMMUNICATIONS

An important adjunct to command and control is communications. No review of this subject can be complete without addressing this related aspect, and no command and control system can be made to work effectively without proper and adequate communications. Furthermore, no commander will ever willingly admit that he has sufficient communications with which to direct his operation. In the simplest instance, a voice command given directly and personally by the commander to a subordinate is perhaps the best method of communication possible. However, the distances and complexities involved in United Nations operations rule out such a simple procedure except in occasional instances. Thus, effective radio, telephone, and other communication resources must be made available if the proper command and control is to be exercised. In United Nations actions, this is essential from the predeployment, through the deployment, the operational, and the post-operational or terminal phases of the operation.

In the predeployment period, fast and reliable communication facilities are needed between the United Nations headquarters and the countries providing contingents and to the advance echelons arriving at the future scene of action. This is a critical phase during which rapid and careful coordination is required. Decisions concerning the

provision of units, the character and composition
of the units to be provided, the dispatch of advance
parties, the securing of diplomatic clearances, the
coordination of transportation, and the movement of
national units must be made and relayed to those
concerned. Subsequently, as the actual deployment
commences, the communication resources will have to
be augmented to provide links between the various
national defense establishment headquarters and the
initial assembly bases, the deployment bases, the
en route bases, and the advance reception bases.
Fortunately, national systems may be utilized to
meet a portion of these requirements, at least up
to the time of departure of national units from
their home bases. From this point forward, international circuits may have to be used to augment the
national capabilities. The international facilities
may, in turn, have to be supplemented by the
resources of the agency (e.g., the USAF, the Royal
Canadian Air Force, a commercial air carrier)
conducting the air deployment. Usually, those
national military air forces with the capability to
effect the deployment, such as those of the United
States and Canada, also have the capacity to fly in
mobile units to provide such temporary links as the
system may require.

Subsequent to the arrival of the first United
Nations elements in the area of operation, communications must again be available between the
advance reception area, the United Nations forces
headquarters, and the operational sites. This
requirement may be met by using local facilities,
by establishing a United Nations system, or by some
combination of the two. In either event, one of the
first units in the field should be the communications
squadron to establish the required facilities as a
first order of business. From a practical standpoint, this squadron or element should be provided
by one nation rather than attempting to establish a
composite multi-national unit. This is desirable
in order to have an effective and reliable communications outfit in action at the earliest possible
moment and to avoid the problems that would arise
from using incompatible equipment. For this reason,
the country to furnish this resource should be
designated as soon as possible in order that a
communications plan may be developed and implemented
early in the operation. The plan itself must take
into account the size of the force, the number of

units involved, the local facilities available, the distances involved, and the terrain at the scene of action.

To assist in achieving an early operational capacity, communications personnel will have to accompany the advance party to the area; the remaining personnel which follow should bring with them an initial supply of spare parts. The entire unit should be augmented with the addition of extra maintenance technicians. This is important in that the greatest demands for maintaining equipment serviceability will usually occur at the outset of the operation.

Although the communications unit should most desirably be provided by one nation,* it may be useful to augment it with liaison personnel from other national contingents to anticipate and deal with the special problems that will arise in integrating different procedures or equipment. The communications squadron should be charged with establishing all the services required to serve the force headquarters and providing links from the headquarters to the subordinate units in the field. In this process, there will at least initially be a heavy reliance on radio facilities. The radio net should be supplemented by telephone as the situation progresses. The updating and improving of the facilities will necessarily be a continuing process throughout subsequent operations.

It is interesting to note that in some United Nations operations, e.g., in the Congo where the existing telephone circuits were limited, it did not prove possible or feasible to provide land line connections to all of the force elements. This may undoubtedly prove to be true again in some situations. In these circumstances, single side band radio transmission may have to be relied upon as the primary means available. On the other hand, there will be other situations, e.g., Cyprus, in which the existing telephone circuitry is fairly extensive

---

*Canada provided this unit for the UNEF and the ONUC and, at this date, by virtue of the actual field experience in such operations, is probably best qualified to field such a unit in the future.

and thus can provide a readily available asset for rapid communications. Where the telephone circuits are not adequate or are non-existent, and the distances involved are small, the force may decide to install its own land lines to key points. However, even when telephone circuits or other wire communications are available, there must always be a stand-by or back-up radio net readily available, and frequently exercised and tested, in the event that the telephone communications are interrupted for any reason.*

RELATIONSHIP OF UNITED NATIONS FORCE HEADQUARTERS WITH NATIONAL CONTINGENTS

In any United Nations field operation, there will be two lines of command, one from the United Nations Headquarters in New York to the force and thence to the lowest operational unit, and the other from each nation providing a contingent to its unit in the field. The first line is primarily for operational matters; the second for national administrative and support matters. At any time when more than one channel exists within a single enterprise, the possibilities of conflict are present. United Nations operations have proved to be no exception, and some complications have arisen during past operations. Although such instances have been frustrating to the commanders and personnel involved and at times detracted from the over-all efficiency of the operation, they have generally been resolved satisfactorily.

Because of these dual lines of authority, one guiding principle must be accepted--the United Nations Force Commander must have the final word on operational matters. This has been generally recognized and accepted. There is also widespread appreciation of the fact that the national commander has a responsibility to his own government. This responsibility is to insure that his unit is not used in a manner that would exceed the approved mandate

---

*The observations contained in this section and the next are based on interviews with officers who have served in one or more United Nations operations.

or would be inconsistent with the understanding of
his national authorities. He also has a responsibility to these authorities in personnel, administrative, and other non-operational matters of
exclusive national concern. Accordingly, it is
highly desirable that each contingent have a direct
communications tie to its parent national system.
Although this is sometimes possible, more frequently
it is not, in which case the contingent commander
must rely on alternate facilities--either the United
Nations, a commercial, or another national network.

SUMMARY

In summary, command and control for United
Nations forces, just as for any military force,
consists of the institutions, procedures, and
organization for insuring that the wishes of the
governing agency are expressed and fulfilled. In
the case of international forces, the problems
involved may of necessity be more extensive and
complex than those that might normally be expected
to exist within a single integral national system.
This is in the very nature of the international
operation. However, because of this, greater efforts
must be exerted to insure that the command and
control system is responsive to the needs. Special
attention must be given to insuring that the system
is as simple and uncomplicated as is consistent with
the requirements of the operation. Directives should
be as clear and direct as possible, and sufficient
facilities must be provided to both transmit the
directives and reflect the responses. Clarity of
direction, getting the directives to forces, and
supervision of execution thus become the essential
attributes of a workable and effective system.

NOTES

1.   An example of the items included within such regulations may be seen in the "Regulations for the United Nations Emergency Forces," published in a Secretary-General's Bulletin; see "Regulations for the United Nations Emergency Forces," U.N. Doc. ST/SGB/UNEF/1, February 20, 1957.

2.   U.N. Doc. S/5653, April 11, 1964.

3.   U.N. Doc. A/3943, October 9, 1958, par. 181.

4.   U.N. Doc. ST/SGB/UNEF/1, February 20, 1957, p. 3.

5.   For a review of the control arrangements for UNEF, see Gabriella Rosner, The United Nations Emergency Force (New York: Columbia University Press, 1963), pp. 131-36.

6.   This was evidenced on more than one occasion. For one such example, reflecting differing interpretations of the initial force mandate, see U.N. Security Council, Official Records, Fifteenth Year, 873rd Meeting (July 13 and 14, 1960), pp. 1-45.

7.   See King Gordon, The U.N. in the Congo: A Quest for Peace (New York: Harper, 1962), pp. 37ff and Lyman M. Tondel, Jr. (ed.), The Role of the United Nations in the Congo (New York: Oceana Publications for the Association of the Bar of the City of New York, 1963), pp. 17-23. For Dag Hammarskjold's views, set forth at Oxford University in 1961, on the sources of guidance available to assist the Secretary-General to resolve politically controversial questions when the directives are unclear and he is "confronted with mandates of a highly general character," see Wilder Foote (ed.), Servant of Peace: A Selection of the Speeches and Statements of Dag Hammarskjold (New York: Harper & Row, 1962), pp. 342-49.

8.   For a more complete account of this episode, see Gordon, op.cit., pp. 124-29. For a description by one of the participants, see Conor Cruise O'Brien, To Katanga and Back: A U.N. Case History (New York: Simon and Schuster, 1962), Ch. XV.

9.   Report by the Secretary-General on the
United Nations Operation in Cyprus, U.N. Doc. S/5950
September 10, 1964, par. 7 (a), p. 4.

10.   Report by the Secretary-General to the
Security Council on the operations of the UNFICYP,
U.N. Doc. S/5671, April 29, 1964, pars. 4 and 13.

PART **III**

PROBLEMS OF UNITED NATIONS
PEACE-KEEPING OPERATIONS

CHAPTER **9** PREVENTIVE DIPLOMACY:
POLITICAL, LEGAL AND
FINANCIAL PROBLEMS

In his summary study of the experience derived
from the establishment and operation of the UNEF,
Dag Hammarskjold stated that the force "was brought
into being to meet a particular situation" in which
a United Nations force could usefully serve the
interests of peace.[1] UNEF was the first sizable
operation in what has since been described as
preventive diplomacy. Another instance of preventive diplomacy in a particular situation took the
form of ONUC four years later, and UNFICYP provides
a further example. As we have seen, there are
elements of similarity as well as differences imposed
by the specific circumstances in each of these
"particular situations." Notwithstanding the
differences, each operation falls within the broad
category of actions that may be identified as
preventive diplomacy.

THE CONCEPT OF PREVENTIVE DIPLOMACY

The central concept underlying preventive
diplomacy is that the United Nations may be able,
through the employment of relatively modest forces,
to forestall the continued deterioration of a
situation that promises to threaten the international
peace. By prompt preventive action, it may be hoped
that a measure of stability can be introduced and
the conditions conducive to a more permanent
solution be promoted. This form of action has also
been described as an "international version of
containment,"[2] which in a sense is correct. Similarly, the term "preventive diplomacy" is an accurate
description because, despite the negative connotation
of the word "preventive" when used alone, the linking
of the two words together gives the expression
positive meaning. Preventive diplomacy represents

a constructive effort to take collective action on behalf of the international community to promote the cause of peace.

It is not surprising that this concept is associated with Dag Hammarskjold. In his capacity as Secretary-General in 1956 and again in 1960, he played a leading role in organizing and directing the UNEF and the ONUC, two history-making endeavors during which the concept took shape. In the interim period between these two events, he was the guiding force behind a number of other but less spectacular actions that lent force to the general notion of preventive diplomacy.* It was Dag Hammarskjold who, in his summary report, first set forth explicitly the essential characteristics of the measures that were to give form to the concept,[3] and it was he who gave it formal expression in what has been described as "his major exposition"[4] on the subject in the Annual Report to the General Assembly in 1960.[5]

Although UNEF has been described as the first instance of preventive diplomacy, it has also been described as a manifestation of the United Nations groping for a role. This groping reflects the organization's response to its members' concern that it should play a more positive role in keeping the peace. As this concern grew during the last ten years or so, several situations occurred in which the peace was threatened. Action by the United Nations appeared necessary and was taken. The results achieved justified the efforts initiated and, in retrospect, the actions were rationalized as a type of endeavor that might set a useful precedent for the future.

Some observers see preventive diplomacy as merely an ex post facto rationalization for the actions undertaken. Perhaps because the United Nations' record in maintaining peace since 1945 has been somewhat less than perfect, other viewers, who advocate a more effective United Nations role, were inclined to exaggerate the promise in this new form of endeavor. Some of these more enthusiastic

---

*For example, in helping to set up the UNOGIL in Lebanon (1958) and the United Nations presence in Jordan in the same year.

advocates have tended to overestimate the possibilities
contained in this new concept of peace-keeping.
However, despite certain inherent limitations, there
are constructive possibilities. How may these possibilities be expanded and the limitations be minimized?
What are some of the problems involved in such an
effort?

OBSTACLES TO SUCCESS

For convenience, the discussion of these
questions may be somewhat arbitrarily subdivided at
this point under the headings: political, legal,
financial, and military. The remainder of this
chapter will consider the first three, the following
chapter will, in somewhat more detail, review
military considerations.

The Role of Politics

If preventive diplomacy is to have useful
application for the future, there must be a willingness
by the principal states of the United Nations either
to give positive support to peace-keeping where the
circumstances warrant or, at a minimum, not to oppose
its application. The principal states must obviously
include the Great Powers and those other states
directly affected by or concerned with the operation.
In the Suez crisis, this would include Egypt and
Israel along with France and the United Kingdom; in
the Congo, both Belgium and the Republic of the Congo
were directly concerned. In addition, there must
also be a broad base of acceptance and support by a
substantial majority of the other states of the
world if the necessary forces are to be forthcoming
and if the action is to be truly international in
character. What are the various national attitudes
toward collective action to maintain peace?

Support for United Nations Peace-Keeping Role

Throughout history, appeals for peace and
security by members of the international community
have been frequently echoed. Is there real substance
behind these appeals? Are the states sincere in these
laudable goals? Or, are these statements merely
hollow expressions of a vague, pious hope?

On the 11th of December, 1964, during the
opening debates of the Nineteenth Session of the
General Assembly, P.M.C. Hasluck, the Minister for
External affairs of Australia, spoke at length on
"the problems of the maintenance and restoration of
international peace and security, including peace-
keeping in the sense in which we have come to use
the word in recent years" which he described as
"a vital issue."[6] Several days earlier, during the
same debates, Paul Martin, the Minister for External
Affairs of Canada, had stated:

> Canada attaches the highest importance to
> the concept of peace-keeping. We regard
> the evolution of the concept, as distinct
> from the concepts envisaged in Chapter VII
> of the Charter, as affording the most
> significant example of the vitality of
> this organization and its capacity for
> change in response to changing circumstances.
> Peace-keeping has evolved steadily from the
> designation of an observer group to assist
> India and Pakistan in avoiding further
> conflict in Kashmir to the dispatch of a
> United Nations Force to the island of Cyprus
> early this year, where Canadian soldiers
> have been helping to keep the peace. This
> is a period which is almost coterminous
> with the whole period of existence of the
> United Nations. Increasingly over this
> period there has been recourse to and
> reliance upon the United Nations presence
> to prevent unstable situations from
> erupting into open conflict.[7]

These statements are fairly typical of the views
of many nations. The record of the Nineteenth
General Assembly alone provides ample testimony of
the widespread support for United Nations peace-
keeping operations. The Nineteenth Session was unique
in several respects, one of which was the fact that
the principal concern of the entire session centered
on problems related to peace-keeping. However,
similar statements in previous and subsequent United
Nations forums, especially since the adoption of the
"Uniting for Peace" Resolution, suggest the common
interest in international peace-keeping in general
and support for the particular forms it has taken.

Unfortunately, these views have been expressed

most consistently in recent years by the representatives of Western, or Western-oriented, states. They
are not representative of the attitudes of all states,
particularly those of the Soviet bloc. The Soviet
bloc, France, and a few other countries have generally
been opposed to peace-keeping when conducted under
the auspices of the General Assembly and have been
unenthusiastic about the use of peace-keeping forces,
even under the direction of the Security Council,
when that direction did not involve immediate and
continuous supervision by the Security Council.
There are still other states which, although generally
favoring a greater United Nations role in preserving
peace, are sometimes less than ardent supporters
of the current forms of peace-keeping. This is true
of some members of the "non-committed" African and
Asian groups whose views are mixed. Their views
are influenced by a number of factors including, but
by no means limited to, (1) a desire to preserve the
international peace, (2) a heritage in many cases
of a recent colonial past, (3) the conduct of recent
peace-keeping operations, particularly that in the
Congo, and (4) a concern not to endorse or otherwise lend support to any actions that might lead to
an East-West confrontation and be disruptive to the
United Nations organization. This last factor has
tended to make even discussion of peace-keeping
procedures within the United Nations a consensus-type
affair--hardly an arrangement designed to promote
positive action. For these and other reasons, some
of which may not be governed by completely "rational"
assessments of how their own best interests might
be served, some of the Afro-Asian nations are not
presently as zealous in their support for peace-
keeping as might be expected. This attitude was
reflected, for example, in their views on the
financial problem.[8] Perhaps typical of one such
viewpoint was Cambodia's Huot Sambath's statement
that "the Cambodian delegation shares the French-
Soviet point of view on the illegal expenses which
the United States is trying to bring all Member
States of the Organization to pay. For its part,
Cambodia will refuse to contribute to the financing
of operations wherever the United Nations is involved
and forced to intervene in order to put an end to rule
(sic) or supposed aggression."[9]

    Despite such views, the record of General
Assembly debates since the adoption of the "Uniting
for Peace" Resolution shows that a great many states

have been concerned with bolstering the United Nations
peace-keeping capacity.* This belief has also been
demonstrated in the discussions within the more
specialized forums such as the Collective Measures
Committee which held an unproductive series of meetings
in the years following 1950.[10] Subsequently, the
launching of UNEF and the ONUC permitted the opponents
of these actions to question this form of enterprise.
At the same time, however, these activities lent
support to those who would increase the capacity of
the United Nations in this respect. In the year
immediately preceding the creation of UNFICYP, this
support was again widely affirmed. Several indications of this were especially noteworthy. For
example, Lester Pearson of Canada described to the
General Assembly the measures his country was taking
to be able to support United Nations operations.[11]
At the same time, the Scandinavian countries were
looking toward the earmarking of contingents for
possible future United Nations service and, in Oslo,
the Norwegian Institute of International Affairs
sponsored a non-official conference to explore
further this very subject.[12]

There is no need to review the complete record
of statements and actions on peace-keeping. By the
end of 1963, prior to the creation of UNFICYP, the
weight of evidence indicated a widespread interest
in suggestions for enhancing the United Nations
peace-keeping ability. The initiation of UNEF and
the approval of ONUC had substantiated the fact
that the oft-repeated declarations for peace contained
substance as well as hope. This was again demonstrated
with the creation of UNFICYP. The fact that these
operations were undertaken affirms the community
belief. The fact that they succeeded, to the extent
they did, provided precedents for the future.
However, whether similar actions can be taken in
future contingencies will depend on the political
issues existing at the particular time.

------

*At this point, it is again necessary to
distinguish between peace-keeping and enforcement
action. There are many states that will support a
United Nations peace-keeping operation of the UNEF
variety but would be reluctant or unwilling to approve
an enforcement venture similar to the Korean action.

The Intrusion of Political Factors

Obviously, the future of preventive diplomacy
will depend on the collective attitudes of the
member states, which shape the response and the
decisions of the United Nations organization as a
whole. Political factors are central in this process.
Although the philosophic predispositions of individual
states will help to mold their views, their actions
will in the final analysis be determined primarily
by hard political facts which their representatives
must assess in making their judgments. Once these
political decisions are made, military matters,
financial aspects, and legal questions may be
considered and, hopefully, be resolved or fall into
place.

Concepts of The Role of The United Nations. One
great difficulty lies in reaching agreement on the
proper role of the United Nations and that of its
various organs. Can there be a general acceptance
that the General Assembly has a part to play in peace-
keeping operations, or will some states continue to
maintain that this is exclusively within the
competence of the Security Council? Would the answer
to these questions be any different if we were to
re-emphasize that enforcement, as opposed to police,
action is not envisaged? What should be the proper
role of the Secretary-General? As long as such
questions remain unanswered in fact as well as in
form, the future prospects for initiating preventive
diplomacy will be tenuous at best. On the other
hand, if general agreement can be reached on the
answers to these questions, the differing views
on related matters such as the size and scope of a
particular operation, the financing, and the direction
of effort might then be reconciled. Accordingly, the
most pressing problem with respect to the future of
peace-keeping is to secure a genuine political
consensus on how the responsibilities of the United
Nations for maintaining peace will be exercised.

This is not an original observation. However,
even if it is not original, it is of profound
importance because in its answer lies the key to
the future of peace-keeping and perhaps the future
of the organization itself. This fact is widely
recognized. Much thought has been given to the
prospects for providing a satisfactory answer.
At the time of this writing, the Special Committee

on Peace-Keeping Operations (Committee of 33) is
continuing with its comprehensive review of the
"whole question of peace-keeping operations in all
their aspects" and is charged with reporting its
findings to the General Assembly. The initial
report was due "not later than 15 June 1965."[13]
That deadline came and passed with no significantly
new contribution being made. The mandate of the
Committee of 33 has been periodically renewed, but
to date it has been unable to arrive at a meaningful
consensus. However, there have been some indications
of possible future progress.

The Role of National Politics. We should also note
that "international" political questions are inextricably interrelated with "national" political considerations. Some of the interactions are quite obvious.
For example, the character and form that an international peace-keeping operation will take must
depend upon and affect the political decisions reached
by the individual states that vote the necessary
authority. Nevertheless, it is still possible and
useful to distinguish, if only in degree, between
those political aspects that have primarily national
implications and those, such as collective decisions
of the General Assembly, that might be categorized
as "international." On the "national" side, domestic
factors must be taken into account by leaders of the
various states when considering whether to support
or reject a specific proposal for peace-keeping.
Sometimes these internal pressures on the decision-
makers are greater than at other periods. What is
the impact of these internal pressures at a particular
moment? In addition to the domestic considerations,
what are the external factors bearing on a state's
decision? What are its international commitments,
its alignment in the Cold War, its views with respect
to the situation or dispute under consideration, and
its views on contributing forces? These are but a
few of the factors that have to be weighed separately
by each state in reaching a decision on its course
of action.*

---

*See Chapter 6 for a discussion of the political
factors involved in the creation of United Nations
forces.

In the case of some nations, such as Canada and the Scandinavian countries, an appraisal of the political considerations has permitted them to support preventive diplomacy to the extent of making advance preparations. Most other states have been unable or unwilling, either from apathy or opposition toward United Nations actions, to earmark forces.

The national decision on whether or not to support the initiation of joint action will set the framework for future state decisions concerning the degree and willingness with which it continues to support the action undertaken. It comes as no surprise that the attitudes of the various nations on this issue run along a continuum ranging from outright opposition or obstruction, to reluctant acquiescence, neutrality, acquiescence, or positive support. In the event that a state decides to provide direct support, this judgment must then be followed by subsequent determinations to fill in the details concerning contributions of manpower, money, facilities, and logistic support. These subsequent decisions, although still largely political, will be affected by non-political factors such as the economic and financial capacity of the state and the size and composition of its armed forces as well.

The Problem of Regional Obligations. Another question with political overtones relates to regional considerations. How does a state reconcile its regional obligations with its support or non-support of a United Nations operation? Are these two obligations always compatible? For example, what is the relationship between the Greek and Turkish NATO commitments and their position with reference to the UNFICYP and Cyprus? At one time, during the initial phase of the Suez crisis in 1956, there was a prospect, albeit remote, that the United States could become involved in action directed against two of its principal NATO allies. Despite the possibilities for conflict, regional commitments have been considered subordinate to and consistent with the basic obligations assumed under the Charter. This pattern was established and incorporated into the Charter at San Francisco in 1945.

If we accept the compatibility of regional obligations with those under the Charter of the

United Nations, is it desirable to develop capabilities that exploit the regional capacities for peace-
keeping? Will the development of capabilities on a
regional basis, whether under the aegis of a formal
regional organization or not, permit sufficient
flexibility so that these arrangements can still be
utilized for peace-keeping when one state within the
joint regional effort opposes a particular operation?
The political understandings surrounding the creation
of the Scandinavian Brigade might be enlightening in
this respect. Fortunately, this particular arrangement has incorporated within its structure the
flexibility to permit the use of the Brigade as a
whole or, if only certain of the members are willing
to provide contingents at any one time, the components
may be used separately on an individual basis. Can
this model provide a precedent for other regional
groupings of earmarked units--for example, by the
Organization of American States (OAS), by the Organization of African Unity (OAU), or, alternatively,
merely by combinations of like-minded neighboring
states? Would such developments be politically
desirable? Certainly there would be an immediate
military advantage in having forces located at
different places around the world for use in the
various regions.*

There could well be circumstances in which
regional forces, either earmarked for use directly
by the United Nations or indirectly under the
auspices of a regional association acting in
accordance with the provisions of the Charter, might
serve a politically useful purpose as will. In such
cases, the prompt availability of regional peace-
keeping forces might serve the broader purposes of
international peace. The OAS offers perhaps the
most promising possibility for utilizing regional
forces under an existing regional organization.[14]
This type of arrangement is obviously different from
regional earmarking on the nature of the Scandinavian
Brigade. However, both procedures offer possibilities
for the future.

---

*This observation has to be qualified with the
additional comment that a properly equipped and
trained unit can be airlifted from one point in the
world to another more distant location in certain
instances more quickly than a truck convoy of troops
can be moved between adjacent countries.

Legal Problems

The legal problems surrounding preventive diplomacy may also be viewed in either national or international terms. From the national standpoint, the legal questions center on those relating to the provision of national contingents, i.e., to the conditions under which contingents may be committed to serve outside the national territory and to matters connected with force administration and operations. The question of the use of national forces outside the home territory has already been covered (see Chapter 6). The legal implications concerning force administration will be covered in the following chapter along with a general consideration of military problems.

On the international side, what is the legal basis for using international military forces in a peace-keeping role? The answer to this question revolves around the interpretation of the provisions of the Charter setting forth the responsibilities of the principal organs. As we have seen, a sound legal argument can be presented to support the type of operation represented by the UNEF, the ONUC, and the UNFICYP. The validity of this interpretation has been affirmed by an advisory opinion of the International Court of Justice.[15] However, of even greater significance than the legal arguments to justify preventive diplomacy is the requirement to achieve a political consensus. In the final analysis, political agreement and not mere legal precedent is the essential requirement to be fulfilled if future actions are to be undertaken.

The Question of Finance

Unfortunately, no complete consideration of United Nations peace-keeping can ignore the perplexing and complicated question of financing. This subject has been much in the forefront of United Nations affairs during recent years, and it was moved directly to center stage during the crisis surrounding the Nineteenth General Assembly. Because of its central importance not only to peace-keeping but also to the continued health of the organization itself, the matter of financing has been addressed elsewhere at length. It is neither necessary nor

profitable to reproduce herein the whole analysis
of this problem.16   However, it will be useful to
mention two aspects as they affect this study: the
current deficit and the manner of paying for future
peace-keeping. The first has long-range implications
and, sooner or later, must be resolved if the
organization is to have continued vitality not only
in peace-keeping but in all other activities. The
manner and form in which this problem is ultimately
resolved will no doubt shape the future course of
the United Nations. A satisfactory resolution of
the second is essential if any future peace-keeping
project is to be undertaken.

With regard to the deficit of the United Nations,
the Secretary-General has indicated that "the current
situation, while not immediately critical, is precarious."17   Estimates on the precise size of the net
deficit vary considerably--depending on who makes
the estimate and what figures are included.18
Whichever figure is used, however, the total reflects
the unliquidated expenses of the organization, the
bulk of which represents obligations entailed in support of past peace-keeping operations. As long as
this deficit remains, the United Nations will be
faced with a problem of major proportions. The only
satisfactory answer will be general agreement on a
system which insures that the organization will be
assured sufficient revenues to meet its legitimate
expenses.

What about the more specific problem of how to
pay future peace-keeping costs? At the outset, we
should note that the financial problem involves more
than merely deciding how to raise funds to liquidate
past debts and then agreeing on a procedure for the
future. Underlying this problem are the basic political problems affecting every aspect of peace-keeping
It is difficult to see how the symptom of the
disease, poor financial health, can be effectively
cured without treating the cause, a political virus.
Accordingly, any resolution of the financial dilemma
must be accompanied by some form of political
agreement if peace-keeping in the form we are
addressing is to remain an option for the future.
As best, this would entail complete agreement on all
aspects of peace-keeping. However, lacking this,
it may be hoped that some sort of tacit agreement
short of a complete political settlement can be
reached that will preserve a role for the United

Nations in peace-keeping along the lines of the
Suez-Congo-Cyprus pattern.

The Pattern of Past Financing

In order to answer the question with reference
to future financing, it might be useful to review
briefly the methods under which such operations have
been underwritten to date. Several procedures have
been used. The initial method adopted to pay for
United Nations peace operations was the relatively
simple and direct procedure of including these
expenses in the regular United Nations budget. This
seemed to be a normal and natural way to share the
costs involved. It was the procedure followed in
paying the costs associated with the United Nations
operation in Indonesia (1947-48); in Greece for the
Special Committee on the Balkans (UNSCOB) (1947-1951);
in Palestine for the Truce Supervision Organization
(UNTSO) (1948 to date); in Kashmir for the U.N.
Commission (UNCIP) and the Military Observer Group
(UNMOGIP) (1948 to date); and in Lebanon for the
UNOGIL (1958). These and other "minor" peace-keeping
activities such as the establishment of United Nations
special presences and the dispatch of good-offices
missions have been paid for by the member states as
part of their regular assessments. Suez and the
UNEF witnessed the first change in this procedure.

Although the expenditures to support the UNEF
were considered to be regular expenses of the
organization by the Secretary-General[19] and by the
member states, it has become painfully apparent that
this is not a view shared by all. The expenses of
the UNEF were set forth in a Special Account to be
paid by the member states on a scale of assessments
similar to that used for the regular budget.
Unfortunately, the funds paid into the Special
Account in the first year were not sufficient to
cover all of the expenses of the UNEF; the additional
costs over and above those included in the Special
Account had to be made up by relying on voluntary
contributions.[20] However, there were objections on
the part of a number of states to paying their
assessed shares of the Special Account costs. Thus,
political objections to the financial procedure for
the UNEF were raised at an early date and, to some
extent, the accounting procedure of establishing a
Special Account instead of listing these expenses
in the regular budget was used as an argument to

support the case of those who denied that these costs
were regular expenses of the organization. The cost
of the UNEF operation to the United Nations through
the end of 1967 has been estimated at $217.1 million.*

    The pattern of financing UNEF, reflecting a com-
bination of assessments and voluntary contributions,
was again evidenced in the ONUC. However, in this
instance, the problem created by the lack of support
by certain members which either claimed financial
inability or were unwilling to acknowledge these
expenses as legitimate United Nations expenses was
even more critical because the expenses involved
were larger. Thus, greater difficulties were posed.
The magnitude of the Congo costs and the unwillingness
of certain states to bear their share of these and
the UNEF expenses, even in the face of an Advisory
Opinion by the International Court to the effect
that these constitute expenses of the organization
within the meaning of Article 17 of the Charter,[21]
presented a critical challenge to the organization.[22]
This challenge has been met in part by relying on
temporary and precarious expedients such as advance
payments by some member states against their future
annual assessments and the issuance of United Nations
bonds. However, pressing bills can only be delayed
so long; eventually they must be liquidated or the
integrity of the organization will be undermined.
The United Nations is faced with this unpleasant
prospect now.

    Another method of financing United Nations peace
operations, one antedating both the UNEF and ONUC,
was that used to finance the United Nations Command
in Korea. In this instance, the financing, like the
operation itself, bore a large U.S. imprint. The
costs were borne largely by the United States and
those countries providing national contingents. For
the United States, the cost of this operation for
the period from June, 1950, to June, 1953, totaled
$18 billion dollars. However, Korea was unique

————————————

    *The cost breakdown is roughly $197.9 million
plus $19.2 million to cover bond costs or a total
of $217.1 million through the end of 1967. These
figures are based on an official U.S. Government
estimate current as of 1969.

in the United Nations experience; its purpose was
different from the peace-keeping operations we are
presently considering, and the precise financial
arrangements adopted to underwrite that undertaking
have not been, and are not likely to be, repeated

Still another method of financing peace-keeping
operations was first utilized in West New Guinea and
subsequently in Yemen. On both of these occasions,
the participants directly concerned bore the costs.*
In West New Guinea, the total expense of the
UNTEA was more than $20 million but, of this sum, less
than one third represented the cost of the peace-
keeping force.[23] That expense was divided between
the Netherlands and Indonesia. A similar procedure
was adopted for financing the UNYOM in Yemen under
which the Saudi Arabian and United Arab Republic governments paid the principal expenses.

Thus, by the time the Cyprus question arose in
March of 1964, there were precedents for different
methods of financing. Even more important, however,
was the fact that by this point in time the difficulties flowing from the unpaid balance accruing
from past operations threatened the initiation of
any additional peace-keeping operations. When the
Cyprus question was handed over to the Security
Council, it soon became apparent that, because of
the Soviet and French objections (see Chapter 4),
no agreement could be reached to establish a United
Nations force if the costs of that force were to be
borne by the membership as a whole. The only
possibility for reaching agreement to establish a
United Nations peace force appeared to be to accept
the principle of voluntary financing by those states
willing to provide funds. This was the solution
adopted. Specifically, this solution provided:

----

*This bears some resemblance to the financing
scheme for the United Nations operation in Korea.
However, the essential difference is that the Korean
operation was financed by the states participating
in the United Nations effort which represented the
forces committed on only one side of the conflict.
In contrast, the UNTEA and the UNYOM were paid for
by the states that represented the opposing sides in
the dispute but which nevertheless joined together
in underwriting the expenses.

All costs pertaining to the [force] being
met in a manner to be agreed upon by them,
by the governments providing the contingents and by the Government of Cyprus. The
Secretary-General may also accept voluntary
contributions for that purpose.[24]

The quarterly costs of the UNFICYP initially ran
around $6 million but were subsequently reduced to
about $4 million and have been met by voluntary
contributions.[25] In addition to the maintenance of
the force, the United Nations and the specialized
agencies have had certain other expenses in connection
with the Cyprus situation. For example, a further
cost resulted from the establishment of a United
Nations mediator and his staff and, for this purpose,
the Security Council authorized the Secretary-General
to expend United Nations funds.[26]

Financing Proposals

     Despite the Soviet and French unwillingness to
contribute to the support of this undertaking, the
creation of UNFICYP, even on a tenuous financial
foundation, has been a plus factor in the cause of
promoting international peace. In the absence of
general agreement on how the organizational expenses
should be met, there have been a number of suggestions
regarding how and who should be responsible for
picking up the check for peace-keeping operations.
The U.S. position, supported by a substantial number
of those states supporting peace-keeping, has been
that such operations should be considered as an
appropriate charge against the organization and the
proper responsibility of the entire membership. This
position was supported by the decision of the International Court. However, even among these states,
there has been no consensus as to precisely how the
expenses should be apportioned among the membership.
Increasingly there has been much sympathy for establishing a special scale of assessments for peace-
keeping based on ability to pay.*

_____

     *The so-called Irish proposal, submitted to the
20th, 21st, and 22nd General Assemblies, reflects
this feeling. The Irish proposal would limit the
assessments on the less-developed countries to 5 per
cent of the first $100 million for any particular
peace-keeping operation.

Other states have suggested that not the United Nations but the states responsible for the difficulties be required to pay the costs. Thus, Egypt advocated that the British and French pay for UNEF. Still others, as indicated before, although perhaps sympathetic to a sharing formula, claim inability to pay. In some instances, this claim is understandable. However, formulae can be devised to take this objection into account and ease the payment problems for those states unable to pay their proportionate share. Procedurally, it should be no great problem to accomplish this, and there would appear to be a substantial political argument supporting such action.[27] Thus, the objection of financial inability to pay does not appear to offer great problems. It can be accommodated once the more basic political problem is resolved.

Perhaps the only immediate answer, until a better system may be agreed upon, is to continue to rely on voluntary contributions.* The experience in Cyprus indicates that such a method is better than the alternative of having no United Nations operation at all. Twenty million dollars a year is a relatively small sum for keeping the lid on a situation that otherwise would disrupt the international peace.

Cost Determination

So far we have been addressing the costs of the operation to the United Nations and chargeable to the membership as a whole. However, these are not the only expenses involved. In addition to the direct expense to the United Nations, the cost to the nations contributing contingents must be taken into account

----

*The other most likely alternative would be to agree on a system of special assessments. United Nations peace-keeping operations under the present circumstances are therefore limited by the financial restrictions imposed by relying on either (1) voluntary contributions, or (2) special assessments. The Article 19 crisis has demonstrated that, lacking a political consensus, any attempt to underwrite operations based on a system of mandatory regular budget assessments to support contingents volunteered by certain states in doomed to failure.

because, from the individual national standpoint, these sums can be substantial. In general, the ground rule that has evolved from the UNEF and ONUC experiences has been that the nation supplying a contingent would be responsible for the "normal" cost of maintaining a unit and be reimbursed by the United Nations solely for out-of-pocket expenses accruing from participation in a specific United Nations operation. As expressed by Dag Hammarskjold, "the underlying rule is that a contributing country . . . should not be subjected to financial sacrifices beyond those obligations which would be incurred if it were not contributing directly to the operation.[28]

This principle sounds rather simple and straight-forward. Accordingly, it would appear to be relatively easy to apply in practice. This has not always been the case, however, because some of the applications involved rather complex accounting procedures; difficult questions arise. Who will be responsible for the higher rate of depreciation, or the actual destruction, of unit equipment used during an operation? On what basis will the flying hour charges be figured for aircraft on United Nations missions? Will that charge cover only current operating expenses for fuel and oil, or will it cover costs for spare parts as well? Perhaps it should also take into account unusual maintenance costs and a higher air-craft depreciation factor. How will personnel costs, medical costs, and personnel equipment costs be apportioned in actual practice? Obviously, this list could become quite lengthy and, if the contributing nation and the United Nations were to take firm and unyielding positions, the problems to be resolved could be quite extensive. Fortunately, there has been a willingness on both sides to give and take. This might be expected if one considers the fact that the states involved in furnishing national contingents are voluntary participants.

Accordingly, the following procedures have gradually evolved from past experience. Many of the contributing nations provide all the pay and allowances plus the overseas allowances for their contingents.* Accommodations and rations, special

---

*This is not true in all instances, nor should it be considered fair in all cases. For example,

allowances, unusual depreciation of clothing and
personal equipment and such items as spare parts
for unit equipment, miscellaneous stores, transportation to the scene of action, and medical care
have generally been paid by the United Nations.
The practices in both the UNEF and the ONUC, and
the specific arrangements adopted between the United
Nations and individual countries, have necessarily
varied. For this reason, it is difficult to say
that a single precise formula for cost sharing now
exists. However, useful precedents have been
established, and the experiences gained in resolving
these issues should be of considerable value in the
future. Experience also suggests certain areas in
which standard procedures could be developed for
future operations.

     Other questions will arise in cost sharing if
continued reliance on the use of earmarked forces
is anticipated. If such forces are to be fully
responsive when required, certain readiness measures
should be initiated prior to the advent of an
emergency situation. For example, pre-emergency
training of earmarked forces involving joint training
exercises and the exchange of key personnel between
units to compare training techniques might be undertaken. These measures will be discussed in more
detail in the following chapter. However, in the
present context, it is sufficient to note that such
measures may well involve additional out-of-pocket
expenses for the countries concerned. In such an
event, would it not be both equitable and logical,
in order to encourage readiness preparations, for
the United Nations as an organization to assume
some portion of these added costs?

---

some of the contingents come from the regular national
defense structure (e.g., Canada). In this case, that
country would be paying the salaries and allowances--
but not necessarily an overseas allowance--whether
the unit were on home duty or in United Nations
service. However, in other cases (e.g., Sweden),
the contingent in United Nations service does not
come from the active force. In this instance, an
out-of-pocket expense is involved in mobilizing a
unit for United Nations duty.

In addition, the financial arrangements consummated by member states with the organization
have in many instances provided a bonus to the
United Nations. Many of the troop-contributing
countries have gone beyond the "out-of-pocket"
formula in underwriting the collective effort. This
has materially reduced the amounts the Secretary-
General has had to solicit in the form of financial
contributions from the membership at large. Thus,
at the outset Canada agreed to accept all of the
costs of its contingent in Cyprus. Similarly,
Ireland agreed initially to bear the costs of pay,
overseas allowances, supplies, and equipment sent
from Ireland; the United Kingdom indicated its
willingness to pay all the costs of its contingent;
and the United States airlifted 8,500 troops without
cost to the United Nations.[29] The impact of these
and other voluntary gestures reduced considerably the
amount the United Nations has had to raise to underwrite particular operations.

However, such actions place an unequal burden
on the contributing states, some of which may not be
able to go on indefinately accepting the additional
financial burdens. In the specific instance of
UNFICYP, how long will the troop contributors be
willing to bear the additional financial load and
continue to participate? For the six-month period
ending in December, 1967, the total cost for the
United Nations was approximately $10 million; the
additional costs to the troop contributors exceeded
$3 million. In recommending the fourth three-month
force extension, U Thant stated that it was becoming
"increasingly difficult to maintain UNFICYP because
of the special burdens of those [countries] providing
contingents."[30] That statement, made in 1965,
continues to be true today with no end in sight.

NOTES

1. "Report of the Secretary-General," U.N. Doc. A/3943, October 9, 1958, par. 149.

2. Inis L. Claude, Jr., Swords into Plowshares (3rd ed.; New York: Random House, 1964), p. 286.

3. U.N. Doc. A/3943, October, 9, 1958.

4. Claude, op. cit., p. 286.

5. U.N. General Assembly, Official Records, Fifteenth Session, 1960, Suppl. No. 1A (A/4390/add 1).

6. U.N. General Assembly, Official Records, Nineteenth Session, 1964, 1299th Meeting (December 11, 1964), pp. 17-21.

7. U.N. General Assembly, Official Records, Nineteenth Session, 1964, 1294th Meeting (December 8, 1964), pp. 6-10. A more recent statement made by the newly elected Prime Minister, Pierre Trudeau, in a press conference in Ottawa, April 7, 1968, indicated that the Canadian role in peace-keeping was being reassessed in connection with an over-all review of foreign policy. That review has now been completed and, although there is an indication that Canada may look more critically at its particular role in a specific peace-keeping operation in the future, Canadian support for peace-keeping in general has been reaffirmed.

8. The lack of support by some of the smaller states for the U.S. position on the financing of peace-keeping operations led the late U.S. Representative to the United Nations Adlai E. Stevenson to compare this neutrality on the financial deadlock "collision course" with the attitude of the Arkansas farm boy who applied for a job on a railroad. Reportedly, the station master, by way of a test, asked the youngster what he would do if he saw two trains approaching each other on a collision course on the same track, each going sixty miles an hour. The boy allegedly replied that he would run to get his brother who had never seen a train wreck either. Address by Adlai E. Stevenson to the American Bankers Association, New York City, February 10, 1965, USUN Press Release 4499.

9. U.N. General Assembly, Official Records, Nineteenth Session, 1964, 1299th Meeting (December 11, 1964), pp. 1-7.

10. See particularly the Yearbook of the United Nations for the years 1951 through 1954 for summaries of the history of this committee's efforts. It should be noted that the Collective Measures Committee was concerned to a large extent with enforcement action.

11. Statement to the General Assembly, U.N. General Assembly, Official Records, Eighteenth Session 1963, 1208th Meeting (September 19, 1963), pp. 8-12.

12. For a record of the conference, see Per Frydenberg, Peace-Keeping Experience and Evaluation-The Oslo Papers (Oslo: Norwegian Institute of International Affairs, 1964).

13. General Assembly Resolution 2006 (XIX), March 2, 1965.

14. For a discussion on the possibilities of regional peace-keeping by the OAS and other regional organizations, see Arthur M. Cox, Prospects for Peacekeeping (Washington, D.C.: The Brookings Institution, 1967), pp. 57-72. Although Cox discusses the OAS peace-keeping experience in the Dominican Republic in 1965-66, a more detailed analysis of this episode should provide further insights into the relationship of United Nations and regional peace-keeping.

15. International Court of Justice, Reports of Judgments, Advisory Opinions and Orders, 1962, "Certain Expenses of the United Nations (Article 17, par. 2 of the Charter) Advisory Opinion as of July 20, 1962," pp. 151ff.

16. This has already been done. See John G. Stoessinger and Associates, Financing the United Nations System (Washington, D.C.: The Brookings Institution, 1964). See also, "Issues Before the Nineteenth General Assembly," International Conciliation, No. 550 (November 1964), pp. 9-18; "Political Influences in the General Assembly," International Conciliation, No. 557 (March, 1966); and Ruth Russell, "United Nations Financing and 'The Law of the Charter,' "The Columbia Journal of Transnational Law, Vol. 5, No. 1 (1966), pp. 68-95.

17.   "Budget Estimates for the Financial Year 1968," Statement by the Secretary-General to the Fifth Committee, U.N. Doc. A/C.5/1127, October 18, 1967, p. 1.

18.   The estimates vary from $36.5 to $38.5 million as the amount "of new voluntary contributions" "as the minimum needed to restore solvency," to $67 1 million which represents the amount of unpaid assessed contributions as of September 30, 1967. Ibid., p. 2.

19.   U.N. Doc. A/3943, October 9, 1958, par. 189.

20.   Gabriella Rosner, The United Nations Emergency Force (New York: Columbia University Press, 1963), pp. 158ff.

21.   International Court of Justice, Reports, 1962, pp. 151ff.

22.   See the Annual Report of the Secretary-General on the Work of the Organization for the years ending June, 1957, through June, 1970, for a summary of the continuous story of the unpaid UNEF and ONUC assessments. Running throuh these reports is a prevailing and plaintive plea to the membership to take some effective steps to resolve this bothersome problem.

23.   Stoessinger, op. cit., pp. 104-5.

24.   U.N. Doc. S/5575, March 4, 1964.

25.   Letter dated June 24, 1969, from the Secretary-General to Governments Appealing for Contributions. U.N. Doc. S/9287, June 30, 1969. The estimated cost of UNFICYP to June 15, 1969, was $102,865,000. Report of the Secretary-General on UNFICYP, U.N. Doc. S/9233, June 3, 1969.

26.   U.N. Doc. S/5575, March 4, 1964.

27.   See Stoessinger, op. cit., pp. 302ff., for several possibilities in this vein.

28.   U.N. Doc. A/3943, October 9, 1958, par. 188.

29.   "Report of the Secretary-General on the UNFICYP," U.N. Doc. S/6228, March 11, 1965, p. 71.

The initial offer of Ireland has been subject to some later modifications as a result of negotiations conducted with the Secretary-General.

30. Ibid., p. 73.

CHAPTER **10** MILITARY READINESS

Having reviewed some of the political, legal, and economic considerations that may be expected to influence the course of peace-keeping operations, it remains to consider the military implications in somewhat more detail. It appears that this is one area in which there may be some immediate promise of improving the United Nations peace-keeping capabilities to respond to at least limited emergencies. It is also in this area that this writer, both as a professional military observer and as a student of peace-keeping, believes he may be able to set forth some modest but perhaps useful suggestions.

What military measures might be anticipated or adopted before a crisis arises? Here we may make some specific proposals. Obviously there are many things that might be done now to enhance future capabilities. A number of suggestions along this line have been advanced in the past few years; their volume, which has been increasing, is a testimonial to a growing concern. Unfortunately, few of these suggestions have been given full consideration and fewer still have been put into practice. Some are politically infeasible. Others, however, are not and should be given a fair test.

One of the first steps that might be taken, or more properly speaking continued, would be to encourage more actively the earmarking of national force contingents for peace-keeping service. In the pattern of peace-keeping activity that has evolved, relying as it does on a United Nations force composed of voluntary contributions of national units, the immediate availability of qualified national contingents is a source of continuing concern. As we have already noted, precedents have been established for earmarking of such forces and several additional states have

evidenced an interest in earmarking.* This trend
must be fostered if forces are to be readily available,
if the confusion of soliciting force contributions
during the early stages of a crisis is to be avoided,
and if United Nations operations are to be initiated
promptly.

The question then arises, what about the readiness of these earmarked forces? Readiness of military
forces is not a static condition; it is dynamic and
continuous. There are several things that could be
done to assist in developing and maintaining a ready
posture for earmarked forces. For ease in reviewing
these suggestions, they will be grouped in accordance
with the traditional military categories: command,
personnel and administration, intelligence, plans
and operation, supply and logistics, and communications.

From a strictly military standpoint, the most
important factor is command. Next in consequence are
those matters relating to operations and training
followed closely by logistics, communications, and
intelligence considerations. Finally, in this arbitrary hierarchy, we will consider the areas of
personnel and administration. However, it should be
borne in mind that any effective military operation
must be an integrated whole. Thus, the problem and
the measures listed under these various headings

---

*It might perhaps be useful, when considering
the general subject of earmarking of national forces,
to make some distinctions according to the degree to
which the national commitment has been implemented.
The first category might include such countries as
Canada, the Netherlands, and the Nordic countries
which have actually designated units or forces for
future use. The second group might include countries
that have taken steps to provide the legislative and
constitutional authority to earmark units (e.g.,
Austria) or provide forces on occasion (Ireland).
Another group of states have indicated their willingness to provide logistic support sufficient to
support a specific force structure (United Kingdom)
or in more general terms (United States). Still
other states have indicated their willingness to
earmark forces but have not yet specified a specific
unit (Iran, New Zealand, Malta) or have advised the
Secretary-General that they are willing to provide
military observers (Italy).

should not be considered in isolation. They are
interrelated. For example, poor personnel procedures
will sooner or later have an adverse impact on operational effectiveness. It should also be noted that,
although the inclusion of individual items within a
specific category will generally be consistent with
normal military usage, there may be some exceptions.
This arises from the fact that certain subjects might
properly be included under more than one general
heading. For example, morale, herein included under
personnel and administration, might just as logically
be considered under command. With these preliminary
qualifications, let us review some of the problems
to see what solutions might be offered.

COMMAND

Selection of Force Commander and Staff

It is a military axiom that no operation can be
better than its command, and for this reason, as
previously noted, the selection of a Force Commander
is a matter of utmost importance. The choice of a
capable and competent commander may well spell the
difference between a successful and an unsuccessful
operation. Obviously political considerations will
be taken into account in the selection of the commander but, apart from these considerations, it is
imperative that the personal and professional qualifications of the individual selected be of the highest
quality. It is likewise essential that the designation of this individual not be delayed as a crisis
unfolds and United Nations action becomes necessary.
This is one area in which it would be relatively easy
to prepare for crisis action by maintaining a list
of potential, qualified, individuals within the
Secretariat from which to select a commander. This
could eliminate some of the uncertainties and guess-
work that otherwise might arise during a crisis.
Fortunately, the United Nations' experience in past
operations provides both a valuable guide to qualifications required in the selection of a Force Commander
and a list of potential prospects.

It would not be difficult to review the roster
of key officers who participated in those past efforts
and tentatively determine those best qualified to
command future actions. However, this tentative list

should not be restricted to those officers who had
previously served with United Nations field forces.
Although such experience is highly desirable, the
selection list could be broadened to provide a wider
basis of choice. It is conceivable that the requirements in a specific future emergency might be such
as to rule out, for political reasons, many of the
officers who had served in earlier operations. A
"new face" might be required, and the search for this
new figure would be facilitated by the existence of
a pre-screened roster of potential candidates.
Furthermore, this "list" need not, and probably should
not, be established as a formal roster subject to
Security Council or General Assembly approval. Instead, a less formal procedure designed only to insure
that advance thought is given to the selection of a
Force Commander would probably be politically more
acceptable and therefore better serve the United
Nations purposes. This could be accomplished within
the Secretariat. It can only be assumed that the
logic of this very obvious proposal is apparent to
those concerned within the Secretariat.

The observations concerning the selection of a
field commander may, in large measure, properly be
extended to the process of choosing key staff officers
for the field headquarters as well. Rosters of qualified personnel from the countries either participating
in past operations or evidencing an interest in earmarking units could likewise be maintained. Here
again, a sizable nucleus of experienced personnel already exists in the list of officers from the different nations who served in prior operations.

Is it feasible for a multi-national secretariat
to maintain a roster of efficient and available force
commanders and key staff officers? This question may
be answered affirmatively. The names of those who
have served in previous operations are already available. This list might be supplemented by requesting
member states to submit the names of those they consider to be qualified for future undertakings in much
the same manner that certain member nations now provide the names of military experts to the Secretary-
General for the panel of military experts established
under the "Uniting for Peace" Resolution. Whether
or not all of the individuals named are fully qualified from a professional military viewpoint and
whether they would be politically acceptable for a
particular operation would necessarily be subject to

review by the Secretary-General if and when he was
directed to create a new force. However, the immediate availability of such a listing would be a step
in the right direction.

The Secretary-General's Military Staff

As we have noted in our review of command and
control, the command line originates at the United
Nations headquarters. What can be done at this level
to assist in developing a more effective command support capacity? One suggestion frequently discussed
is to strengthen the military staff within the Office
of the Secretary-General in order to enhance the capability (1) to prepare plans for future contingencies;
and (2) to provide the Secretary-General with the
military advice he needs during actual operations.*
The Secretary-General has assumed an increasingly
important and central role in the direction of peace-
keeping operations. To assist him in discharging
this function, at present he has an experienced and
highly professional political staff but, as we have
already seen, there is no military adviser. This
office had previously been manned by not more than
four officers during the Congo operation. Following
the initiation of that operation, Brigadier, now
Major General, I. J. Rikhye was appointed Military
Adviser and given a small staff of officers to assist
him. This staff rendered great assistance to the
Secretary-General in his direction of both the Congo
and the Cyprus operations. At the time the Cyprus
undertaking was initiated, that staff consisted of
three officers in addition to General Rikhye. Subsequently, General Rikhye was assigned as Commander of
the UNEF, and two of the three assistant advisers
departed without being replaced. The sole remaining
incumbent has now been reassigned to other duties.[1]

Despite the fact that the Military Adviser's
office has been manned by highly skilled and dedicated
officers, it did not have sufficient depth to

---

*This assumes, of course, the continuation of
the pattern of peace-keeping evidenced in recent
United Nations operations in which the Secretary-
General has provided the executive direction for the
international force.

undertake comprehensively the task of advance planning
For this reason, it was even taxed in merely providing
assistance to the Secretary-General in discharging
his responsibilities for day-to-day supervision of,
and support for, the current operations in which the
United Nations has been engaged. Accordingly, there
is a pressing requirement to reconstitute this office,
and this brings us to the question of size.

It is difficult to suggest a precise size.
Certainly, at a minimum and as a modest start, the
military staff of the Secretary-General should be
provided with three or four officers immediately,
given increased responsibilities for future planning,
and authorized to request additional personnel as
the fulfillment of this responsibility dictates the
need for additional personnel. The initial task for
this expanded office would be to outline a comprehensive and systematic program for increasing the future
United Nations peace-keeping capabilities.

Most commentaries on the subject of strengthening
the military capabilities for peace-keeping agree
with the need for augmenting the staff of the Military
Adviser. This is probably to be expected because this
is one area in which the shortcomings are readily apparent and a modest proposal can provide a corrective.
However, one caveat should be noted--the permanent
staff should not be increased indiscriminately. The
military forces engaged in peace-keeping operations
are not, by present-day force-level standards, large.
The size of the staff charged with the planning for
these forces should be kept proportionate. It is not
necessary to attempt to duplicate the Pentagon or to
create a small model of the Soviet General Staff.
In practice, the creation of an unduly large staff
might actually prove to be counterproductive. Accordingly, both in keeping with the purposes and objectives of recent peace-keeping operations and from
the standpoint of efficiency, the staff should be kept
"lean" and relatively austere. Second only to the
earmarking of additional force contingents, an increase in the Military Adviser's staff is the priority
task if the United Nations peace-keeping capabilities
along the lines reflected in recent operations are to
be enhanced. Most of the other suggestions for increasing the United Nations capacities flow from, and
are dependent upon, this initial step.

The Military Staff Committee

Before looking at these further suggestions,
however, we might properly consider the role of the
Military Staff Committee. Although the Military
Staff Committee was originally designed as the agency
to provide military advice to the Security Council,
it must be acknowledged that it has neither been
called upon frequently to perform this service nor,
in the one instance that it was, has its record been
impressive. However, assuming that some kind of
basic understanding regarding the constitutional and
financial aspects of peace-keeping might be forthcoming in the future, the Security Council and the
Military Staff Committee will continue to have responsibilities in the areas of control and direction
of military operations of an enforcement nature.
Certainly it is possible that agreement and resolution
of the problems concerning non-enforcement peace-
keeping operations could be compatible with, and
might even facilitate, further agreements and understanding in the enforcement area. If such understandings could be reached, the United Nations
capacity for preserving the peace would be greatly
enhanced. Many of the proposals herein discussed
with relation to the Secretary-General's staff could
apply in some degree to the Military Staff Committee.
This could be a positive step forward because the
Military Staff Committee, consisting as it does of
military representatives of the permanent members,
has the inherent potential of furnishing highly
professional staff support. Even short of the
Security Council assuming full responsibility for
the complete control and direction of future peace
operations and assuming, alternatively, that the
Secretary-General continues to play a part in the
immediate supervision of certain United Nations
forces under the over-all direction of the Security
Council, e.g., as reflected in UNFICYP, it is not
inconceivable that some useful services might be
extracted from the Military Staff Committee. Possibly
some arrangement could be developed under which the
potential of this group, as expert military advisers,
could be made available to assist the Secretary-
General in his task. The basic prerequisite for such
a development would obviously be an agreement, perhaps
informal in nature, among the major powers. Although
it might be difficult to secure such an agreement,
this idea has some merit and should not be discarded
too abruptly. It might also have a measure of appeal
to the permanent members of the Security Council.

OPERATIONS

There are three logical subdivisions within the operations area: training, operations, and plans. Let us consider each in turn.

Training

United Nations forces, by their very nature, require highly trained and effective personnel. Normally, the force organized for a particular operation will be of the minimum size consistent with the requirements of the specific situation. For this reason, each individual should be thoroughly trained in the task to be accomplished and his role in contributing toward that end. The Secretary-General has acknowledged the importance of individual training:

> Many incidents which could easily escalate
> if not dealt with promptly can be sorted
> out by a junior officer on the spot. An
> armed man, for instance, crosses the cease-
> fire line and the opposite side threatens
> to shoot if he does not go back; a United
> Nations non-commissioned officer will
> escort the man to safety and explain to
> the other side that he did not know the
> exact position of the line. A shot is
> heard and one side starts manning its
> fire positions in anticipation of an
> attack; an UNFICYP officer investigates
> and finds that it was an accidental dis-
> charge, and what might have been a
> perilous situation has been brought under
> control.[2]

In each of these situations, it was important that the "junior officer on the spot," the "UNited Nations non-commissioned officer," or the "UNFICYP officer" was trained in operations of a somewhat different character from what might be expected in "normal" military operations.

Training is one of the areas in which the prospects for improving United Nations capabilities are the brightest and in which the promise of considerable gain with only modest efforts appears possible. Several of the countries that have already earmarked

forces for possible future use have, not unnaturally,
either taken steps or are considering measures in
this general direction. However, much more can be
done on a wider and a more coordinated basis.

Standard Operating Procedures

     How can this be accomplished? First, a training
officer (or section) could be designated on the staff
of the Military Adviser to the Secretary-General.
Under the direction of the Military Adviser, the
training officer could be charged with the preparation
of standardized training guides, or Standard Operating
Procedures (SOP).[3] These could be progessively developed from outlines into a more comprehensive series
of training regulations covering the various subject
areas in which earmarked troops could be trained.
These guides should then be made available to those
nations with earmarked forces and to any other nation
that, although unwilling to earmark a unit in advance,
might be willing to prepare certain elements of its
national forces for possible United Nations service
depending on the conditions and circumstances.*

Higher Training Standards

     Second, the training officer (or section) could
actively assist in promoting higher training

----

     *Some of the non-aligned underdeveloped countries
might be willing to receive training guides and, perhaps, other forms of United Nations assistance in the
training of their national forces. These forces could
then become more effective in an internal security
role within their own national area. These forces
would also, depending on the state of training
achieved, be qualified for United Nations service.
The very fact of working with the United Nations in
the training of their national forces, in addition
to insuring uniform standards of training oriented
along the lines of international police actions,
might serve to make the countries so involved more
willing to provide forces to the United Nations.
However, it must be acknowledged that the sword cuts
both ways and there is always the danger that the
creation of additional military capacities would
create capabilities that might be used for purposes
other than maintaining internal stability or policing
an emergency situation.

standards. This could be achieved through the medium
of periodic staff visits during which advice and suggestions could be provided to the country concerned.
Ideally, the training officer, in coordination with
his operations staff counterparts, should be able to
prescribe and conduct readiness inspections to check
the state of readiness of national units. This would
provide the Secretary-General's staff with detailed
information on the relative capacity of various units.
At this point in time, formal readiness inspections
of national forces by representatives of an international agency would probably be considered too great
an infringement on national sovereignty. But this
objective could probably be achieved in the near
future by less formal procedures, perhaps by conducting personal visits. For the long term, and
with a carefully developed approach, more comprehensive inspections might well be accepted by those
countries willing to cooperate with the United
Nations.

Content of Training

What kind of training should be given? In the
first instance, earmarked units should be thoroughly
trained in their basic branch specialities. For
example, an infantry battalion from "X" country
should be composed of well-trained, disciplined
officers and men fully qualified in infantry tactics
and organized and supplied as an integrated and self-
sufficient unit. This is a national responsibility,
and the United Nations staff should not be directly
involved at this level of training. However, to
better prepare such units for peace-keeping duties,
additional training is desirable. It is in this area
that the staff might furnish guidance and coordinate
training activities.

What are these special fields of training?
First and foremost, earmarked forces should be provided with a fundamental knowledge of the United
Nations, its purposes and aims, its role in peace-
keeping, and the character of United Nations operations with military forces.* Other subjects in which

---

*For this, as well as for other subject areas
on this open-ended list, the level of knowledge
required will obviously be different in the case of

such forces should receive special training are (1)
the rules of conduct for United Nations forces including the rights and privileges that may be normally
expected; (2) internal security operations including
establishing check points and observation posts,
patrolling, controlling unlawful assemblies, riot
control, the use of riot control equipment such as
tear gas, and assisting civilian authorities in
maintaining law and order; (3) limited military
operations including buffer force activities, controlling specific areas, and sweep-ambushes; and (4)
familiarization with standard operating procedures
in communications, logistics, supply, and in all
other areas in which standardized procedures can be
prepared in advance. In addition, earmarked forces
should be fully trained for air movement. They should
also be given generalized area orientation training
covering the environmental factors in the different
geographic areas in which they may be required to
operate. This list could be extended almost indefinitely. It would then have to be refined and
priorities established in order to insure that the
most important elements were covered first. This is
a task better left in the hands of the future training
officer to be provided on the staff of the Military
Adviser. However, it should be noted that the
practical advantages to be gained through the adoption
of such measures are readily apparent when the record
of past United Nations operations, particularly the
early stages of the United Nations experience in the
Congo, is reviewed.[4]

Techniques

What techniques can be utilized to assist in the
accomplishment of this training? Here again, there
are a number of useful devices that could be of
assistance. Two have already been mentioned: standardized training guides and staff visits. In
addition, visits by key officers and selected non-
commissioned officers between national earmarked
forces to exchange information and share training
techniques should be encouraged. Officers and non-
commissioned officers who have previously served in

---

officers and key non-commissioned officers than for
the ordinary ranks, and the training guidance should
be designed accordingly.

international operations would be particularly helpful
in this process. In addition to assisting in furthering the training mission, these visits might have
a bonus effect in creating a better common understanding and a joint esprit among the key unit personnel who might in the future be called upon to serve
together. If such a by-product effect could be
achieved, it would considerably enhance future
operations.

    Another technique that should prove helpful would
be the use of Mobile Training Teams.* Mobile Training
Teams might conceivably be made available from
countries that had previously provided national
contingents to United Nations operations, e.g.,
Canada, or even from the permanent members of the
Security Council, the United States, the United
Kingdom, and perhaps the Soviet Union.** This could
be considered under the heading of providing "logistic
support" to peace-keeping, an area in which some of
the permanent members have not been inhibited from
participating in the past. These Mobile Training
Teams might demonstrate specific techniques such as
riot control and assist in establishing uniform
standards. These activities should be coordinated
through the Secretary-General's staff.

----

    *Mobile Training Teams are, as the name implies,
completely mobile units. They are manned by qualified
instructors, equipped with training aids, and designed
to provide instructions in a particular subject.
They can be moved easily and quickly from place to
place, hence they are "mobile." As an aid in training
in subject areas, Mobile Training Teams are usually
cheaper, and sometimes more effective, than sending
selected personnel or an entire unit to a central
training site or school. They should be admirably
suited for United Nations military training purposes.

    **Canada, by virtue of its wealth of field
experience in providing support to the United Nations
in technical areas, would be well qualified to provide
Mobile Training Teams or qualified instructors in
communications, logistics procedures, military police
activities, postal services, etc.

Still another technique peculiarly suitable and applicable for the training of United Nations forces is the Command Post Exercise. The Command Post Exercise provides a procedure to exercise and test the commander and his staff elements during a simulated operation. Normally, no tactical units, or at most very few, participate. For this reason, this type of exercise is fairly economical to conduct and, at the same time, it gives the command and staff elements practice and training under simulated conditions. In this manner, deficiencies may be spotted and corrected and the commander and his staff may become more cognizant of the type of problems they may expect to encounter during the actual operation. Again, this type of exercise could be initiated and supervised by the Military Adviser and his staff. It could be conducted if necessary on a quiet and discreet basis without fanfare. The exercise could also be so modified to insure the minimum travel of the elements and personnel participating. On an austere basis, portions of the exercise could be conducted by correspondence.

A Central Training Area?

Suggestions have been advanced that a central training area be established for the training of United Nations forces.[5] Although such suggestions are worthy of future consideration and the door should be kept open for possibilities to move in this direction, proposals for an island base, a North African base, or some other central base for the training of United Nations troops appear to be premature at this time. Such proposals should be carefully filed for consideration at a future date when the atmosphere is more receptive. In the meantime, we should devote our energies to something more modest, and something that may be achieved in the reasonably near future. One thing that can be accomplished within this time restriction is the coordination and standardization of training for future forces.

The Need for Specialized Technicians

A special comment should be made regarding the availability and training of certain specialized technicians whose services are required in United Nations operations. Although it is true that the well-trained infantryman forms the backbone of any operation, qualified specialists are needed as well

to make the operation run smoothly, and it has been
in the recruitment of such specialists that the
United Nations has been faced with many frustrations.
It is impossible to train a helicopter pilot, a light
aircraft mechanic, a communications technician, or
a vehicle repairman overnight. On many occasions
during the life of ONUC or more recently in Cyprus,
the United Nations force has been confronted with a
shortage of fully trained technicians and these
shortages, until alleviated, may critically affect
a particular aspect of the current operations.
Accordingly, as an additional readiness measure, the
staff of the Military Adviser should identify and
categorize the specialist skills required to support
particular undertakings and encourage those countries
with earmarked forces to train and include such
technicians within their national contingents. In
addition, uniform training standards might be suggested to cover certain skill areas.

Operations

     In the pre-deployment stage, operations and
training go hand in hand and training is oriented
along operational lines. After deployment, operations
become dominant and training is secondary (with
training, to the extent possible, continuing even
during the operational phase). There are many operational problems unique to peace-keeping as opposed
to "normal" military operations. For example, civil-
military relationships, which may differ radically
from one situation to another, will always be of unusual importance in a United Nations operation.*
Liaison with civil authorities, assisting or augmenting civilian police, and activities of a civic
action nature will have a direct influence on the
operations of the force. On the military side,
limited military operations such as those occurring
in the Congo may be required. Such operations pose
difficult problems. How can operations of this nature
be conducted within the prescribed limits of a minimum

----

     *The word "civil" is used to refer to the local
civilian authority of the state on whose territory
the operation occurs. It is not intended to refer
to the civilian portion of the United Nations organizational structure.

use of force? Minimum use of force is not consistent
with the normal military practice of using sufficient
force to assure that the job is done. These unique
characteristics of peace-keeping can be anticipated
to some extent and accommodated by proper advance
training, and such training will to a large measure
determine the capacity of the United Nations force
to discharge its mission.[6] Furthermore, operational
manuals outlining the procedures to be utilized in
such situations can be developed in advance and be
available for the guidance of the force contingent
commanders during actual operations.

One "peace-time" task of the operations officer
on the military advisers staff should be to maintain
the troop lists of earmarked units. This would constitute the inventory of potential forces.[7] The
troop lists should contain detailed information, by
contingent, on the strength of each unit and its
basic equipment, the special problems concerning
equipment or resupply, the length of availability
for continuous operations, the state of training,
the state of readiness, and the length of time
required to prepare the unit for shipment.

Plans

The chances of success of any military operation
will be materially enhanced if it is executed in
accordance with a soundly conceived and well-developed
plan. Conversely, without such a plan the risks of
failure, or of achieving only limited success, will
be high. Ad hoc arrangements are not a satisfactory
substitute. They will neither assure a successful
mission nor provide the insurance to preclude failure.
Proper planning, then, and the existence of contingency
plans are the key to the success of any military
venture. This is true also for peace-keeping operations, and this is an area in which much can be done
now to improve future prospects.*

---

*As indicated in Chapter 1, there are two dis-
tinguishable ways in which the United Nations readiness to respond may be enhanced: (1) by taking the
necessary steps which lie within what is politically
feasible to enhance the institutional arrangements
for peace-keeping; or (2) by attempting to identify

At the outset of this review, it should be noted
that planning encompasses every aspect of military
activity. A complete plan is not limited merely to
an enumeration of the basic underlying concepts and
a listing of the operational tasks. Even for a
comparatively limited operation, the primary plan
should include an intelligence annex, a logistics
and supply annex, and such other annexes as required
to cover all essential aspects. Thus, a complete
plan will necessarily cover the full range of
military activity: personnel, intelligence, logistics
and supply, and communications, as well as operations
It is in this sense that the planning capability for
United Nations military operations will be reviewed.

The first step to improve that capability is
clearly to provide for an adequate planning staff.
After this has been done, what should be the tasks
for this planning staff? Here the possibilities are
almost unlimited because, as indicated, planning is
an all-encompassing activity. However, certainly
near the head of the list of priority tasks is the
requirement to develop a series of contingency plans
for future operations. These contingency plans should
cover the various types of peace-keeping operations
that could be initiated. For example, basic plans
could be developed covering several different types
of operations (observation, force supervision,
maintenance of law and order) and for different size
forces (small observer force, Suez-type force, ONUC-
type force). Alternative plans could be developed
for different geographic regions taking into account
climate, terrain, logistics capabilities, and other
peculiar regional factors.

Each plan developed should be as complete and
inclusive as possible. It should contain all of the
normal annexes: communications, intelligence (or
information), logistics, and personnel. In this
manner, the communications annex, for example, for
a particular plan would provide a guide for the

---

and anticipate future crisis situations in which an
international response would be appropriate. It is
doubtful whether much can be done along the second
line of action within the present political environment. Accordingly, the proposals contained herein
will fall within the first category.

communications needed as well as the communications
available and in like manner the logistics annex
would outline the logistics requirements and
responsibilities. In the development of force tabs,
i.e., the personnel and units required, estimates
would have to be made to anticipate what forces might
be available; in this task, the operations personnel
responsible for maintaining the troop lists could be
of considerable assistance.

   The process of developing a comprehensive array
of plans will not be easy but neither will it be as
difficult as it may sound. Almost any plan is better
than no plan at all. For this reason, brief outline
plans may be developed initially and subsequently
expanded to be more inclusive with additional review.
The essential requirement is to prepare a family of
plans promptly so that whenever an operation is
initiated, an appropriate guide for action is available. If this is accomplished, the personnel concerned and charged with conducting the operation will
be fully acquainted with the general mission and
their particular responsibilities, thus insuring a
coordinated effort. In developing a family of plans,
priorities should be established to insure the
preparation of those more likely to be required first.
Only after this has been done should the other less
likely contingencies be considered. The possibilities
of enhancing the United Nations capacities through
sound advance planning are substantial and this action
could be initiated as soon as a planning staff is
made available.

   In addition to preparing contingency plans, the
planning section in the Military Adviser's office
should monitor the preparation of standing operating
procedures covering other fields of activity. These
standing operating procedures are required to provide
essential guidance in different areas of activity, and
they should be developed by the staff section primarily
responsible for the particular activity, e.g., the
standing operating procedure on supply should be
prepared within the logistic staff section. All of
these procedures should be designed with the objective
of standardizing the particular practices covered.
To insure the compatibility of all of the standing
operating procedures prepared, each should be
coordinated closely with the plans section. In
addition, certain of the standing operating procedures, e.g., those covering air movement, overflight

clearances, and deployments, will fall strictly
within the plans and operations area of primary
responsibility and, in these cases, the planners
should prepare the basic procedural guides in the
first instance.

As a final word, it must emphasized that planning
is a continuous process. The blueprints for possible
future action must be reviewed and updated at regular
and frequent intervals. An outdated plan not only
may be useless but also may be counterproductive or
imperil the operation it is designed to promote.
The requirement for periodic review, of course, means
that the plans section must be staffed in sufficient
depth to accomplish this continuing task.

SUPPLY AND LOGISTICS

The UNEF and ONUC operations have provided a
wealth of experience on the supply and logistics
problem that might be expected in field operations.
Cyprus is currently furnishing a similar experience
factor. Based on this field experience, there appears
to be a number of advance actions that can be taken
profitably in the logistics area. These actions cover
the entire range of activities from the pre-packaging
of equipment for air movement and the preparation of
loading tables to the planning for en route support
and the anticipation of supply problems that may be
expected to arise during operations.

Standard Operating Procedures

The primary requirement in this area is first
to develop adequate standard operating procedures
based on field experiences, and then to initiate the
preliminary action in advance of crisis calls as
suggested by those procedures. This task should be
undertaken by a logistics officer (or section) on
the Military Adviser's staff. The problems are
numerous and include such matters as the standardization of equipment; the development of uniform, or
as nearly uniform as possible, ration scales;* the

----

*It has been reported that at one stage during
the early days of the UNEF operation there were nine

development of standard accommodations requirements,
postal facilities, and military arrangements, to
mention just a few.

Procedures should be established covering (1)
the preliminary steps to be taken before an emergency;
(2) the measure to be adopted during the deployment
phase; and (3) the logistics actions to be implemented
during subsequent operations. Among the items to
be considered prior to an emergency should be the
standardization of equipment and the preparation of
equipment lists, the development of supply levels,
and the preparation of equipment for overseas air
or sea shipment. For the deployment phase, guidance
should be prepared with regard to troop and equipment
movements, en route support requirements during
deployment, and the supply and logistics procedures
to be established initially during the operational
phase. Finally, procedures should be developed
governing the follow-on resupply and maintenance
and the establishment of lines of communications.
The guidelines and standard procedures prepared
should have the common aim of contributing toward
better operational capacity.

Supply Availability Survey

A number of other measures could be effected in
the logistics area prior to an operation. For

---

different ration scales in existence; seven for
national forces, one for indigenous employees of the
UNEF, and one for UNEF guard dogs. Not much imagina-
tion is required to see how this would complicate a
ration supply officer's life. The provision of even
one standard ration, including as it does all of the
items that go to make up the diet for one soldier for
one day, is a continuous and complex task. When this
chore is complicated not only by multiplying the one
standard ration by the number of troops involved but
by introducing a number of other and, on occasion,
entirely different ration scales, the task becomes
even more complex. By standardizing the use of
certain items within the seven different national
ration scales, at the same time making allowance for
essential national dietary differences, the supply
officer's existence could be made happier (and the
dogs could still enjoy their special diets).

example, the logistic staff officer might conduct a
survey to determine at which locations around the
world it would be possible to arrange for United
Nations military forces to draw on national supply
depots for support. Preliminary stand-by arrangements
could be consummated. Thus, it might be possible to
anticipate and prepare for such situations as occurred
when the UNEF drew upon United States overseas supply
sources in Italy during the initial stages of the UNEF
operation. At the present time, the UNFICYP units
rely heavily on United Kingdom national supply
facilities in Cyprus. A survey of facilities for
possible future use would not be very difficult.
Tentative arrangements might be made to define the
levels of supply that might be available for use by
the United Nations, the reimbursement procedures, and
related matters. The immediate availability of such
information, collected and collated on a regional
basis, would be invaluable during the early critical
stages of mounting a police operation. Similarly,
coordinated procedures could be worked out with the
Field Operations Service covering the other aspects
of logistics and supply. To a substantial extent,
this has already been done. However, as in other
programs of advance preparation, further refinements
are possible. One such refinement might be in arranging for regional stockpiles for special items of
United Nations equipment. The stockpile might consist
of either critical items of operational equipment or
the items peculiar to the United Nations, such as
berets, armbands, and flags.

Provisions for Movement of Forces

Almost every aspect in mounting an operation has
a particular significance, but certainly the movement
of forces to the scene of operations is of primary
importance. In the past, this has been accomplished
by a process that included frantic phone calls, hurried consultations, and other improvised ad hoc
techniques. Perhaps some, but not all, of this
confusion surrounding the movement of forces might
be avoided by (1) determining the requirements for
airlift to support each contingency plan; (2)
surveying the potential sources of airlift, both
military and civilian; and (3) outlining tentative
procedures to be followed at the time of a crisis
to match the requirements with the airlift available.
The determination of the United Nations requirements

could be effected by a review of contemporary plans.
The survey of military airlift available would also
be comparatively easy. Only a relatively few nations
have the airlift capacities required; and, unfortunately, fewer still have demonstrated the willingness
to make such airlift available. However, military
resources do not exhaust the list of potential airlift. Civilian charter aircraft have in the past
and might again in the future be utilized during an
emergency. Up to this time, this use has been on a
limited basis. Perhaps stand-by arrangements with
civil air carriers might be negotiated to provide
for a minimum amount of such aircraft to be made
available to the United Nations on short notice.
The United States has negotiated arrangements with
a number of air carriers under the Civil Reserve Air
Fleet plan which would call upon the civil carriers
under certain national emergency conditions to
supplement the Military Airlift Command in fulfilling
national needs. The United Nations might negotiate
similar arrangements and, for some operations, it
might even be preferable to rely on civil aircraft
rather than upon the military airlift of a permanent
member.

        Another suggestion offered has been to make each
nation providing forces responsible for the movement
of its personnel to the scene of action. This
suggestion has both merit and limitations. From the
standpoint of the United Nations' staff, such
decentralization would pass a knotty problem on to
the national authorities concerned. It might also
have the advantage of insuring, at least in certain
cases, that the forces could be moved more expe-
ditiously. Objections by the countries concerned
to the added cost accruing to them could be met by
specifying that such costs would be reimbursed by
the United Nations. However, despite the initial
appeal this suggestion offers, there are some
fundamental objections. First, the individual
movement scheme could prove to be unreliable in
practice. Individual arrangements might in practice
be tenuous and subject to delay in getting units to
the scene of the crisis. This fact, and the
decentralized control inherent in such a concept,
could result in operational difficulties and impede
the initiation of a prompt and coordinated operation.
Finally, the adoption of such a procedure might
discourage individual countries from earmarking
forces in the future, a process that should be encouraged and facilitated, not discouraged.

However, maybe the answer is not always an either/or proposition. Perhaps, as was done in the movement of forces to Cyprus, a combination of national and United Nations efforts to provide the required airlift might be the solution. In this event, the United Nations' staff would be responsible for coordinating and/or arranging all of the transportation required. Thus, as in the Cyprus situation, a nation such as Canada which possessed an integral airlift capability might use that capacity to move its own forces. At the same time, the United Nations' staff might assist, as it did in the creation of the UNFICYP, in arranging for the airlift of the other units from countries that did not have the necessary military or civilian airlift resources to move their own units. This combination of techniques would be of particular importance if, in the future, contingents of the permanent members who could transport their own units to the scene were to serve side by side with contingents from smaller nations that would expect the United Nations' staff to arrange for their airlift.

COMMUNICATIONS

The problems that may be expected to arise in communications during actual operations and certain suggestions for their resolution have been reviewed in Chapter 8. Here it is only necessary to re-emphasize that communications are the right arm of command and that many of the problems in past operations may be anticipated in advance. To insure that this is done, standard operating procedures should be developed to set forth standardized communications procedures; standards for equipment capability; criteria for the types and amount of equipment and for maintenance and resupply of communications items. In addition, a communications plan (or annex) should be developed as an essential and integral part of each basic contingency plan.

INFORMATION

In a strictly military discussion, this section would normally be headed with the title "Intelligence. However, the word "intelligence" has unfortunate connotations that make it of questionable usefulness when referring to United Nations activities.

Accordingly, "information" will instead be used in
this discussion and will refer to the process of
gathering facts and data in contrast to "public
information," which is concerned with the dissemination of information. Furthermore, it is very
appropriate to use the word "information" when referring to United Nations activities because the word,
within its most common meaning, very precisely
defines the need to be fulfilled.

     The acquisition of adequate and complete informa-
tion is one of the prerequisites in developing plans.
What area is involved and what are the pertinent
characteristics, the geographic setting, the climate,
the port facilities, the airfields, the supply sources
for food, petroleum, and other products, and the
facilities for maintenance of vehicles and other
items of equipment? What is the status, size, and
capability of the local security forces? What are
the routes of access to that region, the en route airfields, the facilities available at the en route
airfields, the en route commercial communications?
These are but a few of the questions for which
answers are required during an operation. To the
extent that such information is readily available
before an operation, the chances of success will be
enhanced.

     At this point, a word of caution should be
introduced. An extensive information collecting and
disseminating service in the Office of the Military
Adviser is not required. What is required is an
information officer (or section) who should be
directed to review the information requirements to
support United Nations operations and then to set
up an austere and minimum-size information collection
center. Most of the information required is readily
available and need not be reproduced or consolidated
within the Military Adviser's office. For example,
detailed data on airfields on a world-wide basis are
available in International Civil Aviation Organization, national aviation authorities, and commercial
publications; information regarding regional geography
is readily available in atlases, gazettes, and travel
books; the specific information on ports and harbors
is available in navigation charts and shipping direc-
tories. However, the information officer should be
charged with the responsibility of knowing where such
information can be secured and for providing the
required data to support contingency plans as they

are developed. He should also be ready to prepare
and provide information packages to national contingents as they deploy for a specific mission. The
information officer should also develop a standard
operating procedure for the subsequent handling of
information activities during actual operations.*
Admittedly, the suggestions set forth herein concerning information activities are sketchy. However,
they should be sufficient to indicate the nature of
the task and to demonstrate that substantial
opportunities exist for advance preparation.

PERSONNEL AND ADMINISTRATION

With respect to personnel, two observations
should be made. First, the selection of personnel
is an essential consideration in assembling a United
Nations force. In the case of earmarked forces, this
consideration may and should be taken into account
before the unit is committed. Second, the functional
area that includes personnel procedures and policies
is one that does not lend itself to standardization
as readily as some of the areas already surveyed.
Many personnel matters are peculiarly national in
character; a number of personnel policies and procedures are rooted in national tradition or law and
therefore do not lend themselves to uniform international standards. Furthermore, certain personnel
matters such as promotion and pay and allowances must
remain uniform within a national defense system
despite the fact that a contingent or a portion of
the force might be on international service. Otherwise inequities could arise within a national service
between those units retained in the national force
structure and those units serving with the United
Nations.

However, there are some aspects of administration
that can be standardized within the United Nations
force, e.g., Status of Forces arrangements. Status

---

*The actual field operations in the Congo and
in Cyprus very vividly reinforce the need for information. Time after time, it was demonstrated that
the effectiveness of operations could be greatly
enhanced and the chances of failure minimized by the
receipt of timely, adequate, and complete information.

of Forces arrangements are, by their very nature, complicated and can involve complex and tedious negotiations between the host government and the state sending forces. These arrangements necessarily cover a variety of items. For example, the Status of Forces agreement for the UNFICYP defines the international status of the force and its members; entry and exit requirements; civil and criminal jurisdiction responsibilities; the use of the U.N. flag; authority to carry arms; privileges and immunities of force; taxation and customs responsibilities; freedom of movement; the use of roads, waterways, port facilities, and airfields; and the settlement of disputes and claims.[8]

An administrative standing operating procedure could also usefully be developed setting forth the accounting procedures between the United Nations and the individual states for supplies and items of equipment expended during operations. Other procedures might well be developed covering recreation and welfare activities, special services, and morale considerations. Here again is a task for the Military Adviser's staff.

CONCLUSIONS

From the foregoing, two conclusions may be drawn. First, there are many things that can be done within the realm of the politically possible to improve the readiness posture of military forces earmarked for possible United Nations use and to insure that field operations, when and if undertaken by these forces, have a greater chance for success. Second, one key to getting most of these actions under way, to the coordination of the efforts of the states earmarking forces, to the preparation of troop lists and plans for action, and to the development of a variety of standard procedures is to augment the staff of the Military Adviser to the Secretary-General and authorize him and his staff to initiate steps along these suggested lines.

NOTES

1. For a detailed discussion on the subject of
a Military Staff for the Secretary-General, see Lt.
Col. L. M. K. Skern, Military Staffing at U.N. Head-
quarters for Peace-keeping Operations--A Proposal
(Monograph No. 3; Paris: International Information
Center on Peace-Keeping Operations, July 3, 1967).

2. Report of the Secretary-General on the
United Nations Operation in Cyprus, U.N. Doc. S/6228,
March 11, 1965, pp. 30-31.

3. Standard Operating Procedures (SOP) has been
defined: "A set of instructions covering those features of operations which lend themselves to a
definite or standardized procedure without loss of
effectiveness. The procedure is applicable unless
prescribed otherwise in a particular case. Thus,
the flexibility necessary in special situations is
retained." Dictionary of U.S. Military Terms for
Joint Usage (Washington, D.C.: Joint Chiefs of Staff,
1960), pp. 136-37.

4. See, for example, King Gordon, The U.N. in
the Congo: A Quest for Peace (New York: Harper, 1962);
Ernest Lefever, Crisis in the Congo (Washington, D.C.:
The Brookings Institution, 1965); and Conor Cruise
O'Brien, To Katanga and Back: A U.N. Case History
(New York: Simon and Schuster, 1962).

5. For several such suggestions see Lincoln P.
Bloomfield, International Military Forces (Boston:
Little, Brown and Co., 1964), pp. 77 and 161-67; and
Per Frydenberg, Peace-Keeping Experience and
Evaluation--The Oslo Papers (Oslo: Norwegian Institute
of International Affairs, 1964), p. 177.

6. However, it must be acknowledged that advance
training can not anticipate every circumstance, and
difficult situations will arise in the future to con-
front United Nations forces just as they have in the
past. For one illustrative past instance, see Lefever,
op.cit., pp. 34-37, which describes the circumstances
arising from an unfortunate confrontation between the
Ghanaian contingent commanded by Major General H. T.
Alexander, the British commander, and the local
Congolese army. General Alexander, reflecting a
prevailing military review, believed that force

should be used to extent necessary to insure pacification even to the extent of disarming the
Congolese army.

    7.   The troop list should include also any
auxiliary or supporting civilian units such as
civilian police which would be used along with the
military forces. The civilian police utilized in
the UNFICYP have served the force purposes as well
by providing a special link in the Cypriot police.
There are many occasions in which the use of a
civilian unit or personnel may serve a useful purpose in supplementing the activities of the United
Nations force. One such occasion in the recent
history of UNFICYP, and one which is perhaps typical,
occurred when the civil police were called in to
investigate an explosion in a Turkish coffee shop.
Immediately following this incident, shots were
exchanged by the opposing Greek and Turkish Cypriot
forces and the situation became tense. A UNFICYP
patrol was sent to the scene, interposed itself
between the two sides, and established an uneasy
temporary truce. In the meantime, the United Nations
civil police were called in to investigate and, in
an apparently professional and unobtrusive manner,
determined that some Greek Cypriots who were having
a brandy party about fifty yards from the Turkish
cafe had lighted a home-made bomb which had gone off.
Both communities reacted by assuming that the other
side had attacked them and wild firing ensued. The
UNFICYP police investigation was able to determine
the facts and order was restored. See Report by the
Secretary-General, U.N. Doc. S/6228, March 11, 1965,
pp. 28-29.

    8.   See Report of the Secretary-General on the
Organization and Operation of the UNFICYP, U.N. Doc.
S/5634, March 31, 1964. Fortunately, the precedents
and the agreements adopted in the UNEF, the ONUC,
and the UNFICYP operations provide useful models for
future use.

PART IV

THE FUTURE OF UNITED NATIONS
PEACE-KEEPING

CHAPTER **11** IMPLICATIONS FOR
THE FUTURE

The pattern for maintaining and preserving
international peace today is not the same as that
initially envisaged by the framers of the Charter
in San Francisco at the end of World War II. In
practice, the entire role of the United Nations in
maintaining peace is quite different from that
foreseen in 1945. But the world itself is also
quite different from the world of 1945. The manner
in which the responsibilities of the principal
organs involved--the Security Council, the General
Assembly, and the Secretary-General--have changed
and the fact that the actual pattern of peace-
keeping operations that has evolved is not the same
as originally anticipated should not be startling.
It is both a tribute to those who drafted the
Charter and a reflection of the flexibility and
willingness of the majority of the membership that
it has been possible to make adjustments to fit
actual political circumstances. These adjustments
have been effected, not without posing some difficult
political problems, because there is a substantial
desire on the part of many states to preserve international peace. In attempting to realize this
desire, there is a natural inclination to utilize
the instrumentalities that may be available. The
United Nations is in existence, it can serve a useful
function, and there are many members who are
unwilling to abandon the effort to fulfill the
initially stated purposes--"to maintain international
peace and security and to that end: to take
effective collective measures" (Article 1 [1]).

What has been the success of the organization
in contributing toward this goal? The record is
mixed. Observation forces have assisted in resolving
troublesome situations in Greece and Indonesia. An
observer mission is continuing to keep the lid on
a potential source of difficulty in the Kashmir,

United Nations military observers are engaged in the Middle East, and peace-keeping forces are continuing to discharge their responsibilities in Cyprus. The record in other areas, Lebanon, Yemen, and the Congo, has been more ambiguous. Yet the over-all record does show some pluses. It would appear that this record, which documents the continuing attempts to act positively to promote peace, presents a substantial argument for the continuation of such efforts in the future. Despite the Article 19 crisis and the subsequent difficulties faced in the Nineteenth General Assembly in attempting to resolve some of the pressing problems concerning the future of peace-keeping, there is nothing to indicate that the majority of member states are ready to abandon the thought that the United Nations should continue to play a useful, even though limited, role in peace-keeping. The very existence of the Special Committee on Peace-Keeping Operations which emerged from the Article 19 impasse and the nature of its mandate, envisaging as it does a comprehensive review of "the whole question of peace-keeping operations in all their aspects," supports this view.[1]

In reviewing the recent history of peace-keeping by the United Nations, several trends are apparent. As we have witnessed, the role of the General Assembly in the period immediately following 1950 was greatly enhanced. Likewise, the Secretary-General assumed a significant role in the direction of peace-keeping operations. At the same time, there was at least a temporary down-swing in reliance on, and the role played by, the Security Council. With respect to individual operations, a new pattern emerged with the initiation of the UNEF. Relatively sizable, though still modest, forces were used in the Suez crisis, in the Congo, and now in Cyprus. Still more modest forces were used in West New Guinea and in Yemen. These forces have, in each instance, operated with the consent of the states involved and on whose territories the operations have been conducted. The forces acted under limited mandates. They have, as a general rule, not engaged in military operations of a combat nature, and the use of force itself has been limited to self-defense. They have provided a stabilizing presence and attempted to create the conditions under which the basic issues of the controversy might be resolved. In view of this record and of

manifest desire of many of the members to continue
to search for procedures that will permit the conduct
of similar activities in the future, it is entirely
appropriate to assume that the United Nations is
not dead in this respect and that peace-keeping
will continue to play a role in the United Nations
scheme of activities, and to inquire into what that
role should be. At this point, it is appropriate
to return to the original two questions providing
the focus for this study. What can be done to
improve and institutionalize United Nations peace-
keeping capabilities? And what are the likely
prospects for the future?

RESPONSIBILITIES OF THE
PRINCIPAL ORGANS OF THE UNITED NATIONS

First, what will be the future role of the
principal organs?

The General Assembly

Although, as we have seen, the General Assembly
quite properly has a "residual" responsibility for
maintaining international peace and security which
is substantiated by specific charter provisions, the
General Assembly came to play a more important role
in peace-keeping than originally intended and
possibly a more important role than justified by
political realities. The passage of the "Uniting
for Peace" Resolution in 1950, the utilization of
the provisions of that resolution in the Suez crisis
in 1956, and the speculations and afterthoughts on
the contribution of UNEF to world peace lent
encouragement to those who hoped to revitalize the
United Nations as a preserver of the peace. During
this period, the role of the General Assembly as a
peace-keeper reached its zenith.

Subsequently, there have been second thoughts
concerning the proper function of the General
Assembly as it has become increasingly apparent
that peace-keeping operations of the UNEF and ONUC
variety, if they are not going to pose major
problems, will depend largely upon a political
consensus that includes the Great Powers. At this
point in time, it is difficult to conceive of a very
successful, or in fact any, peace-keeping operation

being launched if either the United States or the
Soviet Union were strongly opposed to the effort
because, in addition to the direct influence they
could bring to bear, they could rely on a number of
states willing to support their respective views.*
It is even more difficult to envisage an operation
in which both opposed the action. Yet, theoretically
but hardly likely in practice, under the present
"Uniting for Peace" procedures, the General Assembly
could authorize an operation to which all five
permanent members of the Security Council objected.
Although it is doubtful that the General Assembly
would go to such lengths, it is even more incompre-
hensible that an operation so authorized could ever
be effectively pursued.

How did this situation come about? It may be
remembered that when the "Uniting for Peace"
Resolution was adopted, the General Assembly consisted of 60 members. Since that time, the Assembly
has grown with the addition of 66 new states; the
twenty-fourth General Assembly included the representatives of 126 states. Many of the new member
states, although "sovereign equals" within the
meaning of Article 2 of the Charter, are not in a
position to make substantial contributions of either
finances or forces to peace-keeping. Because their
votes carry equal weight, it would conceivably be
possible to secure a two-thirds affirmative vote in
the General Assembly authorizing a peace operation
in which the states comprising the two-thirds
majority could contribute very little to the joint
effort. Such a situation is neither equitable nor
consistent with political reality. Accordingly,
some new institutional arrangements might be
desirable.[2]

The Security Council

If 1956 and the UNEF operation marked the
high point in the influence of the General Assembly
in peace-keeping, the period since that time has
witnessed a swing back toward the Security Council.

---

*Although it must be acknowledged that the
hard core on each side no longer appears to be as
"hard" and "dependable" as in former years.

Although the "Uniting for Peace" Resolution clearly
prescribes an initial appeal to the Security Council
and reference to the General Assembly only when the
Security Council is unable to discharge its responsibilities, and although the General Assembly has
continued to be in the center of the financial
question, the Congo action was authorized initially
by the Security Council and subsequently the Yemen
and Cyprus operations were approved by the Security
Council.* At the present time, the Security Council
is the organ of competence providing direction to
the Secretary-General in Cyprus, and it is significant
to remember that the UNFICYP was authorized by a
vote of the Security Council in which all of the
permanent members concurred. Subsequently, the
United Nations experience with respect to Kashmir
in 1965 and in the Middle East in 1967 again re-empha-
sized the importance of the role of the Security
Council.

The Secretary-General

As the relationships and responsibilities of
the General Assembly and the Security Council have
been changed somewhat in the process of evolution,
so has the role of the Secretary-General been altered.
The Secretary-General has come to play a leading and
very useful role in the peace-keeping process.[3]
He has been able to provide needed leadership and
executive direction, under the mandate from the
Security Council or the General Assembly, for the
day-to-day operation of the United Nations force.
In this process, he has been assisted on two
occasions, e.g., UNEF and ONUC, by an Advisory
Committee composed of the representatives from some
of the principal countries contributing to the
particular operation. These Advisory Committees, in
assisting the Secretary-General to interpret his
mandate and translate it to a program of action,
have proven to be useful devices. They have not in
practice served to limit the Secretary-General's

---

*However, during this same period the
Secretary-General and the General Assembly both were
involved in the establishment and direction of the
UNTEA in West Irian, with the Secretary-General
assuming the major responsibility.

capacity to act. However, in order to enhance
further his capacity to provide direction to future
operations, we have seen where there is a pressing
requirement to augment his military staff. This can
be accomplished by reconstituting the staff of the
Secretary-General's Military Adviser. At the same
time, it is not inconceivable that some use can be
made of the inherent capacities within the Military
Staff Committee for providing some such assistance.

There is widespread agreement that the Military
Staff Committee would have a major role to play in
the unlikely event that Article 43 negotiations were
resumed or if enforcement actions were initiated.
However, it might be possible to devise some
arrangements whereby the Military Staff Committee
could be of use in providing military advice and
support for peace operations short of enforcement
situations and not involving Article 43 forces.
Perhaps some sort of formal or informal arrangements
could be agreed upon for furnishing professional
military advice, as required, to the Secretary-
General for operations with which he is charged under
the Security Council. If such procedures could be
established, they would serve the dual purpose of
providing the Secretary-General with additional
professional assistance in the discharge of his
responsibilities and of insuring that the Security
Council, through an agency responsive to it, has a
continuing supervisory or consultative role.

READINESS OF NATIONAL FORCE CONTINGENTS

In every peace-keeping, or peace-observation
mission,* the personnel comprising the force have
been made available in the final instance on a
voluntary basis by the member states. It has not
proven feasible to constitute a peace-keeping force
by any other means. This was true in the instances
with which we have been primarily concerned, the
UNEF, the ONUC, and the UNFICYP, and in these
instances the number of the states willing to
support such actions has been reassuring. Other
recent endeavors, for example, in Yemen and in

---

*The distinction between a peace-keeping and a
peace-observation force has frequently been blurred.

West New Guinea, reflect the same pattern of
voluntary force contributions. It appears that
future operations will continue to depend upon the
availability of national contingents provided on a
voluntary basis. For this reason, it is highly
desirable that forces be earmarked in advance for
possible United Nations use. At the time of an
operation, the speed of deployment may be of utmost
importance. The fact that Canadian forces were
ready to deploy promptly in March, 1964, permitted
the leading elements of Canadian troops to reach
Cyprus within 24 hours after they had been given
the "go" order and the entire contingent, consisting
of 881 personnel and supported by 170 vehicles and
52 tons of stores, to complete the initial movement
within seven days. This was a fitting demonstration
of the effectiveness of advance planning and an
example of the degree of readiness that may be
attained. This, and the examples set by the
Scandinavian countries and the Netherlands, might
well be emulated by other nations.

     If the efforts of these states can be matched
by efforts of other states, the United Nations
could be provided with a broad base or "shopping
list" from which to select forces politically
acceptable for use in a particular situation. The
very existence of such a list should encourage
those who see the need for maintaining and developing

The distinction has been confused both in terms of
function and of size. The functions of a peace-
observation force may overlap with those associated
with a peace-keeping force. Both will have observation responsibilities. In general, however, the
duties of a peace-keeping force will be more comprehensive than those of an observer group. For
this reason, peace-keeping forces have generally
been organized more along "military" lines, i.e.,
composing the force by assembling integral military
units, and have generally been larger than peace-
observer groups. However, in one study, a peace-
observation force of up to 1,002 personnel was
envisaged. For the purpose of the present discussion,
the UNEF, the ONUC, and the UNFICYP are considered
peace-keeping forces. Forces such as those used in
Yemen, although peace-keeping in a broad sense,
are considered to be primarily observer missions.

the United Nations capacity to respond to threats
to the peace. Possibly at some later date, a small
nucleus for a permanent force can be created.
However, until more modest efforts in the realm of
voluntary commitments can be developed on a wider
scale, it is futile to think of establishing such a
permanent force.

SOURCE OF NATIONAL CONTINGENTS

     The national contingents made available to the
United Nations, with the exception of the United
Kingdom forces serving in UNFICYP, have been made
available from the middle and smaller powers,* but
must this always be the case? In a sense, the central
problem to date has been how best to fuse the funds
and logistics of the larger states with (1) the troops
that are acceptable to and made available by other
states, and (2) whatever funds other states may be
willing to contribute. There has been substantial
support for the idea that the proper role of the
Great Powers should be limited to furnishing
logistic support to United Nations forces and that
they should not be required to furnish national
contingents. This view was given support initially
by Dag Hammarskjold[4] and subsequently endorsed by U
Thant.[5] The concept behind these views, that of
limiting the possibilities of introducing the Cold
War into United Nations operations, has merit.
However, this need not be a hard and fast rule. In
cases where the permanent members agree that a
dispute threatens the peace of the world and should
be contained, it is quite possible that contributions
of military forces from the Great Powers might
assist in achieving that goal. Certainly the Great
Powers have the resources to commit; their military
forces could provide highly effective contingents.
Such contributions could be particularly useful in
instances where a fundamental political agreement
on the merits of the operation might be achieved.
In such circumstances, it is possible to conceive
of units of U.S. and Soviet military forces working
side by side to preserve the peace. This possibility
will obviously be a more likely contingency if the
general international environment improves.

----

     *There was a small U.S. Air Force detachment
in the West Irian operation.

ALTERNATIVE PEACE-KEEPING PROPOSALS

Are there any other possibilities for securing international forces? Both the U.S. and Soviet disarmament proposals tabled in Geneva anticipate the advent of a permanent police force. The U.S. plan envisages such police forces as being gradually and progressively created, given additional responsibilities as the disarming of national forces proceeds. The Soviet plan would delay the institution of an international police force until the disarmament process had been completed. Neither view is likely to be accepted by the opposing side in the immediate future and it is, therefore, not probable that we may expect to have these forces available for United Nations peace-keeping.

A number of other proposals, however, have been put forth that also look toward some form of a permanent force, in being and available to the United Nations. The forces proposed vary from modest to awesome. Granville Clark and Louis Sohn suggest a rather comprehensive army of from 200,000 to 600,000 backed up by a substantial reserve force of 600,000 to 1,200,000.[6] More modest proposals have been advanced by Frye (5,000 to 50,000),[7] the Commission to Study the Organization of Peace (2,000),[8] Lincoln Bloomfield (25,000),[9] Trygvie Lie (1,000 to 5,000),[10] and others. Although it is difficult to argue against the intrinsic value of having a permanently constituted force available to the United Nations for police actions, none of these proposals appears likely to be accepted within the reasonable future.[11] This is particularly true for proposals that envisage large-scale organization. Accordingly, we should concentrate our efforts on attempting to achieve something in the realm of possibility. Earmarking of forces may be within that realm.

However, in addition to the unlikelihood of setting up a permanent international police force, there is perhaps a distinct danger in pushing such measures at too early a date. Besides diverting attention from the more limited measures likely to be achieved, such far-reaching proposals, if they were tried and did not prove successful, could destroy sound precepts already built up and accepted and lead to disillusionment.[12] Thus the cause of peace would be served in a negative fashion.

In a more positive vein, if we assume that
nations are willing to designate or set aside forces
to be available for peace-keeping, it is entirely
logical to look forward to the adoption of measures
that will encourage and foster the maximum readiness
of such forces. Likewise, it is logical to institute
procedures in anticipation of future action. We
have seen that there are a number of politically
feasible steps to take--although some may be more
acceptable than others. They range from proposals
for standardizing equipment and logistics procedures
to the coordination and standardization of training.
They include the development of plans and procedures
that would assist in the initiation and subsequent
conduct of actual operations. We have noted that
this is a largely untapped field. It is in these
areas that practical steps can be taken now to
enhance the capacity for maintaining peace.

CONSENSUS,
THE CRITICAL FACTOR, AND PROSPECTS

The United Nations forces we have been reviewing have all been dispatched with the consent of
the state or states directly concerned, and each of
the forces has operated within a comparatively
limited mission directive regarding the use of
force to achieve its objectives. The primary
mission has been to provide a stabilizing presence
pending the resolution of the more basic underlying
political problems by negotiation, mediation, or
other comparable procedures. Will this be the
pattern for the future? What kind of missions will
United Nations forces be likely to be given?

The objectives of past peace-keeping operations
have been fairly limited--to observe and report, to
monitor a cease-fire or truce line, to provide an
interposition force, or to maintain local law and
order. Whether it will be possible to undertake
more comprehensive tasks in the future will depend
on several factors: first, the development of a
fundamental agreement on the future role of the
United Nations in peace-keeping including the
definitions of the types of missions that may be
presently undertaken and the modus operandi to be
followed in such operations; second, the securing
of a political consensus in a particular instance;
and third, on the willingness of the member states

to furnish units, facilities, and financial and other support for such operations. If future missions of a more comprehensive nature are to be undertaken by the United Nations, they would very probably have to be considered within the scope of Chapter VII of the Charter and therefore come under the competence of the Security Council. Although it does not appear likely that the immediate future will witness any expansion of activity in this direction, the possibility should not be ruled out. If the Security Council could agree on the need for international action as in the interests of both the members of the Security Council and the international community at large, and if certain states, perhaps including some of the permanent members, would agree to furnish forces, such actions could be taken with or without the consent of the state whose territory was involved.

Is such an eventuality likely? It is certainly conceivable, especially if some forward momentum can be engendered in progressively strengthening the United Nations' peace-preserving capacities. One way to do this would be to seek additional opportunities for positive United Nations action in the containment and resolution of conflict. For example, if the Soviet Union were to decide that the continuation of the present situation in South Viet Nam was not in their best interests, might not an approach through the United Nations be appropriate in searching for an acceptable alternative? Perhaps a United Nations peace-keeping force might be a useful ingredient in the search for an end to this conflict. [13]

There are other areas and circumstances in which a United Nations force might prove useful. There are also possibilities for broadened mandates to include the dispatch of a force to a peace-threatened area in which the host country consent is ambiguous or not forthcoming. For example, if another Congo were to arise in Africa and the Security Council could agree on the need to restore order, action by that organ might be initiated in accordance with its Charter responsibilities. In such an instance, the Security Council would be resuming the role originally foreseen but never fulfilled. Although operations of this nature appear unlikely at present, this does not mean that they must be ruled out for all of the future. The

circumstances could arise and the United Nations
should be ready to move in this direction.

Short of anticipating United Nations action in
the enforcement area, is the continuation of the
limited type of activity represented by the UNEF,
the ONUC, and the UNFICYP worthwhile? The answer
to this question can only be yes. Even these
limited actions have achieved some success.
Although they may not provide a guarantee to preserve
peace under all circumstances, they can contribute
toward that goal in containing some troubled
situations that could escalate, under unfavorable
conditions, into major threats resulting in an
East-West confrontation. This would be in the
interests of neither the East nor the West, and
there are numerous indications confirming that both
sides recognize this danger. The United Nations'
contribution to world peace as herein reviewed is
at the lower end of the war spectrum. In a sense,
this type of peace-keeping complements the role
played by the strategic forces of the Great Powers
at the higher end of the spectrum in deterring
general war.

The danger of general war and the threat
contained therein is widely recognized. It has led
to the creation of large-scale national strategic
deterrent forces. Unfortunately, no such comprehensive deterrent capabilities have been achieved
in the area of limited war and other lesser threats
to the peace with the inherent capacity for
escalating into more ominous situations. To the
extent that the peace-keeping capabilities of the
United Nations, on the pattern of the Suez and
Cyprus endeavors or on a more expanded scale, can
assist in pacifying or eliminating such potentially
dangerous situations at this lower level, the
efforts are well worthwhile. The possibilities for
enhancing the United Nations' capabilities in this
respect progressively and surely are present.
Just as the architects of strategic weapons systems
see new deterrent systems within "the state of the
art" technically, so should improved United Nations
peace-keeping abilities of a reasonable and modest
nature be within "the state of the art" politically.

It has frequently been stated that the Suez-
Congo-Cyprus type of operations were made possible
by the peculiar circumstances existing at the time

each of these operations was initiated. It has
also been stated that, because of the developments
that led to the Article 19 crisis and as an aftermath
of that crisis, no further operations of this type
will be approved. It is therefore alleged that
attempting to plan for or anticipate similar United
Nations undertakings in the future is a futile and
useless exercise.

Nothing could be further from the truth.
Although it may be true that the future may witness
no additional endeavors in the nature of past
peace-keeping operations, this does not automatically
follow from the fact that past operations have led
to controversy and occasioned some heated debates.
Whether future operations of the UNEF-ONUC-UNFICYP
type will be approved will depend in the future,
just as in the past, on the political circumstances
prevailing. If the political circumstances warrant,
and a United Nations peace-keeping operation will
serve the purposes of the powers concerned, it is
quite likely that they will concert to initiate
such a venture. Such a convergence of interests
may occur in the future just as it did on occasion
in the past. So long as this possibility exists,
it is in the common interest to do everything
possible to anticipate and improve the prospects
for a successful operation.

NOTES

1.   Resolution by the General Assembly,
A/Res./2006 (XIX) Rev. 1, March 2, 1965.

2.   One suggestion along this line deserving
careful consideration would be to establish a
"Permanent" Special Committee of 15, 21, or some
other appropriate number within the General Assembly.
The United States has been among those who have
advanced such a proposal. See U.N. General Assembly,
Official Records, Nineteenth Session, 1964-5,
Annex No. 21 (A/5739), pp. 17-18. This committee,
although constituted within the General Assembly,
might include in its membership all the permanent
members of the Security Council and be heavily
weighted with representatives from both the middle
powers that have provided forces to past United
Nations operations and those countries that might
be expected to carry a significant portion of the

financial burden. Matters concerning the initiation and financing, or financing alone, of a peace-keeping operation might then be referred to this committee for recommendation when the Security Council or the General Assembly is contemplating peace-keeping action. The Committee might recommend on the basis of a two-thirds majority, thus insuring a large measure of support for any particular operation by the states that would bear a heavy proportionate responsibility for supporting any subsequent action.

3. See Elmore Jackson, "The Developing Role of the Secretary-General," International Organization XI (Summer, 1957), 431-50; Richard N. Swift, Annual Review of the United Nations 1960-61 (New York: Oceana Publications, 1962, pp. 1-14; and Mark W. Zacher, "The Secretary-General and the United Nations' Function of Peaceful Settlement," International Organization, XX (Autumn, 1966), 724-49.

4. Summary Report on the UNEF, U.N. Doc. A/3943, October 9, 1958, par. 160.

5. Speech by U Thant, "Strengthening of the United Nations," given at the University of Denver, April 3, 1964.

6. Granville Clark and Louis B. Sohn, World Peace Through World Law. (Cambridge, Mass.: Harvard University Press, 1958).

7. William R. Frye, A United Nations Peace Force (New York: Oceana Publications for Carnegie Endownment for International Peace, 1957), pp. 74ff.

8. Strengthening the United Nations (New York: Harper, 1957).

9. Lincoln P. Bloomfield, International Military Forces (Boston: Little, Brown and Co., 1961), pp. 79ff.

10. "Annual Report of the Secretary-General on the Work of the Organization, 1 July, 1947-- 30 June 1948," U.N. General Assembly, Official Records, Third Session, 1948-49 (Suppl. No. 1).

11.   Despite the difficulty in arguing against
the intrinsic merits of an international police,
there are many who oppose such a force within the
present political environment on solid, practical
grounds.   See Dag Hammarskjold's views contained in
his Summary Report on the Operation of the UNEF,
U.N. Doc. A/3943, October 9, 1958, pp. 27-28; and
Lt. Gen. E.L.M. Burns, Between Arab and Israeli
(New York: Ivan Obelansky, Inc., 1962), p. 281.

12.   I am indebted for this thought to John W.
Holmes, "The Political and Philosophical Aspects
of U.N. Security Forces," International Journal,
Vol. XIX, No. 3 (Summer 1964), pp. 292-307.

13.   At the time the first drafts of this
study were being prepared, the view that Viet Nam
might be an appropriate locale for United Nations
peace-keeping activity was not widely held.
Gradually, during the period that this study was
in preparation, such an idea has gained ground.
This idea has been consistent with U.S. policy,
which has favored any reasonable solution and has
indicated a willingness to look toward the United
Nations to promote such a settlement.   See, for
example, the Remarks of the President of the United
States delivered at the United Nations Twentieth
Anniversary Commemorative Session, San Francisco,
California, June 25, 1965.

APPENDIX

SELECTED SECURITY COUNCIL AND
GENERAL ASSEMBLY RESOLUTIONS
ON THE MIDDLE EAST, CONGO, AND
CYPRUS PEACE-KEEPING OPERATIONS

I. United Nations Emergency Force - Middle East

    A. General Assembly, Resolution 997 (ES-1),
       November 2, 1956.

       [adopted by a vote of 64 to 5, with 6
       abstentions]

       Noting the disregard on many occasions by
parties to the Israel-Arab armistice agreements of
1949 of the terms of such agreements, and that the
armed forces of Israel have penetrated deeply into
Egyptian territory in violation of the General
Armistice Agreement between Egypt and Israel of 24
February 1949,

       Noting that armed forces of France and
the United Kingdom of Great Britain and Northern
Ireland are conducting military operations against
Egyptian territory,

       Noting that traffic through the Suez Canal
is now interrupted to the serious prejudice of many
nations,

       Expressing its grave concern over these
developments,

       1. Urges as a matter of priority that
all parties now involved in hostilities in the area
agree to an immediate cease-fire and, as part
thereof, halt the movement of military forces and
arms into the area;

2. Urges the parties to the armistice agreements promptly to withdraw all forces behind the armistice lines, to desist from raids across the armistice lines into neighbouring territory, and to observe scrupulously the provisions of the armistice agreements;

3. Recommends that all Member States refrain from introducing military goods in the area of hostilities and in general refrain from any acts which would delay or prevent the implementation of the present resolution;

4. Urges that, upon the cease fire being effective, steps be taken to reopen the Suez Canal and restore secure freedom of navigation;

5. Requests the Secretary-General to observe and report promptly on the compliance with the present resolution to the Security Council and to the General Assembly, for such further action as they may deem appropriate in accordance with the Charter;

6. Decides to remain in emergency session pending compliance with the present resolution.

B. General Assembly, Resolution 998 (ES-2), November 4, 1956.

[adopted by a vote of 57 to None, with 19 abstentions including all nine members of the Soviet Bloc and Egypt]

Bearing in mind the urgent necessity of facilitating compliance with its resolution 997 (ES-1) of 2 November 1956,

Requests, as a matter of priority, the Secretary-General to submit to it within forty-eight hours a plan for the setting up, with the consent of the nations concerned, of an emergency international United Nations Force to secure and supervise the cessation of hostilities in accordance with all the terms of the aforementioned resolution.

C. General Assembly, Resolution 1000 (ES-2), November 5, 1956.

[vote same as for Resolution 998 (ES-2)]

Having requested the Secretary-General, in its resolution 998 (ES-1) of 4 November 1956, to submit to it a plan for an emergency international United Nations Force, for the purposes stated,

Noting with satisfaction the first report of the Secretary-General on the plan, and having in mind particularly paragraph 4 of that report,

1. Establishes a United Nations Command for an emergency international Force to secure and supervise the cessation of hostilities in accordance with all the terms of General Assembly resolution 997 (ES-1) of 2 November 1956;

2. Appoints, on an emergency basis, the Chief of Staff of the United Nations Truce Supervision Organization, Major-General E. L. M. Burns, as Chief of the Command;

3. Authorizes the Chief of the Command immediately to recruit, from the observer corps of the United Nations Truce Supervision Organization, a limited number of officers who shall be nationals of countries other than those having permanent membership in the Security Council, and further authorizes him, in consultation with the Secretary-General, to undertake the recruitment directly, from various Member States other than the permanent members of the Security Council, of the additional number of officers needed;

4. Invites the Secretary-General to take such administrative measures as may be necessary for the prompt execution of the actions envisaged in the present resolution.

II. Operation des Nations Unies au Congo

   A. Security Council, Resolution 4387, July 14, 1960

      [adopted by 8 votes--Argentina, Ceylon, Ecuador, Italy, Poland, Tunisia, the U.S.S.R., and the United States--to 0, with 3 abstentions--China, France, and the United Kingdom.]

Considering the report of the Secretary-General on a request for United Nations action in relation to the Republic of the Congo,

Considering the request for military assistance addressed to the Secretary-General by the President and the Prime Minister of the Republic of the Congo (document S/4382),

1. Calls upon the Government of Belgium to withdraw their troops from the territory of the Republic of the Congo;

2. Decides to authorize the Secretary-General to take the necessary steps, in consultation with the Government of the Republic of the Congo, to provide the Government with such military assistance as may be necessary, until, through the efforts of the Congolese Government with the technical assistance of the United Nations, the national security forces may be able, in the opinion of the Government, to meet fully their tasks;

3. Requests the Secretary-General to report to the Security Council as appropriate.

B. Security Council, Resolution S/4405, July 22, 1960

[adopted unanimously]

Having considered the first report by the Secretary-General on the implementation of Security Council resolution S/4387 of 14 July 1960 (document S/4389),

Appreciating the work of the Secretary-General and the support so readily and so speedily given to him by all Member States invited by him to give assistance,

Noting that as stated by the Secretary-General the arrival of the troops of the United Nations force in Leopoldville has already had a salutary effect,

Recognizing that an urgent need still exists to continue and to increase such efforts,

Considering that the complete restoration
of law and order in the Republic of the Congo would
effectively contribute to the maintenance of international peace and security,

Recognizing that the Security Council
recommended the admission of the Republic of the
Congo to membership in the United Nations as a unit,

1. Calls upon the Government of Belgium
to implement speedily the Security Council resolution
of 14 July 1960, on the withdrawal of their troops,
and authorizes the Secretary-General to take all
necessary action to this effect;

2. Requests all States to refrain from
any action which might tend to impede the restoration
of law and order and the exercise by the Government
of the Congo of its authority and also to refrain
from any action which might undermine the territorial
integrity and the political independence of the
Republic of the Congo;

3. Commends the Secretary-General for the
prompt action he has taken to carry out resolution
S/4387 of the Security Council and his first report;

4. Invites the specialized agencies of the
United Nations to render to the Secretary-General
such assistance as he may require;

5. Requests the Secretary-General to
report further to the Security Council as appropriate.

    C. Security Council, Resolution S/4426, August
        9, 1960

        [adopted by 9 votes to 0, with 2 absten-
         tions--France and Italy]

Recalling its resolution of 22 July 1960
(S/4405) inter alia, calling upon the Government of
Belgium to implement speedily the Security Council
resolution of 14 July (S/4387) on the withdrawal of
their troops, and authorizing the Secretary-General
to take all necessary action to this effect,

Having noted the second report by the

Secretary-General on the implementation of the
aforesaid two resolutions and his statement before
the Council,

Having considered the statements made by
the representatives of Belgium and the Republic of
the Congo to this Council at this meeting,

Noting with satisfaction the progress made
by the United Nations in carrying out the Security
Council resolution in respect of the territory of
the Republic of the Congo other than the Province
of Katanga,

Noting however that the United Nations had
been prevented from implementing the aforesaid
resolutions in the Province of Katanga although it
was ready, and in fact attempted, to do so,

Recognizing that the withdrawal of Belgium
troops from the Province of Katanga will be a positive
contribution to and essential for the proper implementation of the Security Council resolutions,

1. Confirms the authority given to the
Secretary-General by the Security Council resolutions
of 14 July and 22 July 1960 and requests him to
continue to carry out the responsibility placed on
him thereby;

2. Calls upon the Government of Belgium
to withdraw immediately its troops from the Province
of Katanga under speedy modalities determined by the
Secretary-General and to assist in every possible
way the implementation of the Council's resolutions;

3. Declares that the entry of the United
Nations force into the Province of Katanga is
necessary for the full implementation of this resolution;

4. Reaffirms that the United Nations
force in the Congo will not be a party to or in any
way intervene in or be used to influence the outcome
of any internal conflict, constitutional or otherwise;

5. Calls upon all Member States, in
accordance with Articles 25 and 49 of the Charter,
to accept and carry out the decisions of the Security
Council and to afford mutual assistance in carrying
out measures decided upon by the Security Council;

6. <u>Requests</u> the Secretary-General to implement this resolution and to report further to the Security Council as appropriate.

III.   United Nations Peace-Keeping Force in Cyprus

A.   Security Council, Resolution S/5575, March 4, 1964

[Paragraph 4 was voted separately and adopted by 8 votes to 0, with 3 abstentions--Czechoslovakia, France and the U.S.S.R. The resolution as whole was adopted unanimously.]

<u>Noting</u> that the present situation with regard to Cyprus is likely to threaten international peace and security and may further deteriorate unless additional measures are promptly taken to maintain peace and to seek out a durable solution,

<u>Considering</u> the positions taken by the parties in relation to the Treaties signed at Nicosia on August 16, 1960,

<u>Having in mind</u> the relevant provisions of the Charter of the United Nations and its Article 2, paragraph 4, which reads: "All Members shall refrain in their international relations from the threat or use of force against the territorial integrity or political independence of any State, or in any other manner inconsistent with the Purposes of the United Nations,"

1. <u>Calls upon</u> all Member States, in conformity with their obligations under the Charter of the United Nations, to refrain from any action or threat of action likely to worsen the situation in the sovereign Republic of Cyprus, or to endanger international peace;

2. <u>Asks</u> the Government of Cyprus, which has the responsibility for the maintenance and restoration of law and order, to take all additional measures necessary to stop violence and bloodshed in Cyprus;

3. <u>Calls upon</u> the communities in Cyprus and their leaders to act with the utmost restraint;

4.   Recommends the creation, with the consent of the Government of Cyprus, of a United Nations peace-keeping force in Cyrus. The composition and size of the force shall be established by the Secretary-General, in consultation with the Governments of Cyprus, Greece, Turkey and the United Kingdom. The commander of the force shall be appointed by the Secretary-General and report to him. The Secretary-General, who shall keep the governments providing the force fully informed, shall report periodically to the Security Council on its operation;

5.   Recommends that the function of the force should be, in the interest of preserving international peace and security, to use its best efforts to prevent a recurrence of fighting and, as necessary, to contribute to the maintenance and restoration of law and order and a return to normal conditions;

6.   Recommends that the stationing of the force shall be for a period of three months, all costs pertaining to it being met, in a manner to be agreed upon by them, by the governments providing the contingents and by the Government of Cyprus. The Secretary-General may also accept voluntary contributions for that purpose;

7.   Recommends further that the Secretary-General designate, in agreement with the Government of Cyprus and the Governments of Greece, Turkey and the United Kingdom, a mediator, who shall use his best endeavors with the representatives of the communities and also with the aforesaid four Governments, for the purpose of promoting a peaceful solution and an agreed settlement of the problem confronting Cyprus, in accordance with the Charter of the United Nations having in mind the well-being of the people of Cyprus as a whole and the preservation of international peace and security. The mediator shall report periodically to the Secretary-General on his efforts;

8.   Requests the Secretary-General to provide, from funds of the United Nations, as appropriate, for the remuneration and expenses of the mediator and his staff.

B.   Security Council, Resolution S/5603, March
     13, 1964

     [adopted unanimously]

          Having heard the statements of the repre-
sentatives of the Republic of Cyprus, Greece and
Turkey,

          Reaffirming its resolution of 4 March 1964
[S/5575],

          Being deeply concerned over developments
in the area,

          Noting the assurance from the Secretary-
General that the United Nations Peace-keeping Force
in Cyprus envisaged in the Council's resolution of
4 March 1964 is about to be established, and that
advance elements of that Force are already en route
to Cyprus.

          1.   Reaffirms its call upon all Member
States, in conformity with their obligations under
the Charter of the United Nations, to refrain from
any action or threat of action likely to worsen the
situation in the sovereign Republic of Cyprus, or
to endanger international peace;

          2.   Requests the Secretary-General to
press on with his efforts to implement the Security
Council resolution of 4 March 1964 and requests
Member States to cooperate with the Secretary-General
to that end.

BIBLIOGRAPHY

BIBLIOGRAPHY

PUBLIC DOCUMENTS

International Court of Justice. Reports of Judge-
    ments, Advisory Opinions and Orders, 1962.
    "Certain Expenses of the United Nations (Article
    17, par. 2 of the Charter) Advisory Opinion as
    of July 20, 1962." 151ff.

Republic of Egypt, Ministry of Foreign Affairs.
    White Paper on the Nationalization of the Suez
    Maritime Canal Company. Cairo: Government Press,
    1956.

United Nations. Annual Report of the Secretary
    General on the Work of the Organization, 1946
    (and subsequent years). New York: United
    Nations, 1947.

United Nations. General Assembly Official Records
    1946 (and subsequent years). New York: United
    Nations, 1947.

United Nations. Security Council Official Records
    1946 (and subsequent years). New York; United
    Nations, 1947.

United Nations. Yearbook of the United Nations.
    1946-47 (and subsequent years). New York:
    Columbia University Press in cooperation with
    the United Nations.

United Nations Office of Public Information.
    Everyman's United Nations (7th ed.). New York:
    United Nations, 1964.

United Nations Office of Public Information. UN
    Monthly Chronicle, commencing with Vol. 1, No. 1
    (May, 1964).

United Nations Office of Public Information. United Nations Review, commencing with Vol. 1, No. 1 (January, 1954) through Vol. 11, No. 4 (April, 1964).

United Nations Office of Public Information. The United Nations in West New Guinea. New York: United Nations, 1963.

U.S. Department of State. American Foreign Policy, Current Documents, 1959. Department of State Publ. 7492, 1963.

U.S. Department of State. Bulletin. Washington, D.C: Government Printing Office.

U.S. Department of State. "Congo Realities and United States Policy," Foreign Affairs Outline, No. 14., Department of State Publ. 7892, June, 1965.

U.S. Department of State. United States Policy in the Middle East. September 1956 - June 1957. Documents. Department of State Publ. 6505, August, 1957.

U.S. House of Representatives. Committee on Foreign Affairs. Staff Memorandum on the Republic of the Congo, 86th Cong., 2nd Sess., 1960.

BOOKS

Annual Review of the United Nations. New York: Oceana Publications, 1962 and subsequent years.

Bloomfield, Lincoln P. International Military Forces. Boston, Mass.: Little, Brown and Co., 1964.

_____. The United Nations and U.S.Foreign Policy. Boston: Little, Brown and Co., 1961.

_____. A World Effectively Controlled by the United Nations. Washington, D.C.: Institute for Defense Analysis, Study Memorandum 7, 1962.

Bowett, D. W. United Nations Forces: A Legal Study. New York: Frederick A. Praeger, 1964.

Burns, Arthur Lee, and Heathcote, Nina. Peacekeeping by U.N.Forces. New York: Frederick A. Praeger, 1963.

Burns, Lt. Gen. E. L. M. Between Arab and Israeli. New York: Ivan Obelansky, Inc., 1962.

Clark, Granville, and Sohn, Louis B. World Peace Through World Law. 2nd ed. rev.; Cambridge, Mass.: Harvard University Press, 1962.

Claude, Inis L., Jr. Swords into Plowshares. 3rd ed.; New York: Random House, 1964.

Cox, Arthur M. Prospects for Peacekeeping. Washington, D.C.: The Brookings Institution, 1967.

Davies, David. The Problem of the Twentieth Century. London: Ernest Benn Ltd., 1930.

Frydenberg, Per. Peace-Keeping Experience and Evaluation--The Oslo Papers. Oslo: Norwegian Institute of International Affairs, 1964.

Frye, William R. A United Nations Peace Force. New York: Oceana Publications for Carnegie Endowment for International Peace, 1957.

Gardner, Richard N. Blueprint for Peace. New York: McGraw-Hill Book Co., 1966.

_____. In Pursuit of World Order. New York: Frederick A. Praeger, 1964.

Goodrich, Leland M. Korea: A Study of U.S.Policy in the United Nations. New York: Council on Foreign Relations, 1956.

_____, and Hambro, Edvard. Charter of the United Nations Commentary and Documents Rev. ed.; Boston: World Peace Foundation, 1949.

_____, and Simons, Anne P. The United Nations and the Maintenance of International Peace and Security. Washington, D.C.: The Brookings Institution, 1955.

Gordon, King. The U.N. in the Congo: A Quest for Peace. New York: Harper, 1962.

Gross, Ernest A. The United Nations: Structure for Peace. New York: Harper, 1962.

Hoskyns, Catherine. The Congo Since Independence: January 1960 - December 1961. London: Oxford University Press, 1965.

Kelsen, Hans. The Law of the United Nations. London: Stevens & Sons, 1950.

Larus, Joel. From Collective Security to Preventive Diplomacy. New York: John Wiley and Sons, Inc., 1965.

Lash, Joseph P. Dag Hammarskjold: Custodian of the Brushfire Peace. Garden City, N.Y.: Doubleday and Co., 1961.

Lefever, Ernest W. Crisis in the Congo. Washington, D.C.: The Brookings Institution, 1965.

Lie, Trygve. In the Cause of Peace. New York: Macmillan, 1954.

O'Brien, Conor Cruise. To Katanga and Back: A U.N. Case History. New York: Simon and Schuster, 1962.

Report of the Commission to Study the Organization of Peace. Strengthening the United Nations. New York: Harper, 1957.

Rosner, Gabriella. The United Nations Emergency Force. New York: Columbia University Press, 1963.

Russell, Ruth B. United Nations Experience with Military Forces: Political and Legal Aspects. Washington, D.C.: Institute for Defense Analysis, 1963.

Stoessinger, John G. and Associates. Financing the United Nations System. Washington, D.C.: The Brookings Institution, 1964.

Tondel, Lyman M., Jr. (ed.). The Role of the United Nations in the Congo. New York: Oceana Publications for the Association of the Bar of the City of New York, 1963.

Wainhouse, David W., and Associates. International Peace Observation. Baltimore, Md.: The Johns Hopkins Press, 1966.

Walters, Francis P. A History of the League of Nations. 2 vols. London: Oxford University Press, 1952

Wolfers, Arnold (ed.). <u>Alliance Policy in the Cold War</u>. Baltimore, Md.: The John Hopkins Press, 1959.

World Veterans Federation. <u>The Functioning of Ad Hoc United Nations Emergency Forces</u>. Helsinki: The Finnish National Committee of the World Veterans Foundation, 1963.

ARTICLES AND PERIODICALS

Adams, T. W., and Cottrell, Alvin J. "The Cyprus Conflict," <u>Orbis</u>, VIII (Spring, 1964), 66-83.

Bloomfield, Lincoln P. "Peace-Keeping and Peace-Making," <u>Foreign Affairs</u>, XLIV (July, 1966), 671-83.

Boyd, James M. "Cyprus: Espisode in Peace-keeping," <u>International Organization</u>, XX (Winter, 1966), 1-18.

Claude, Inis L., Jr. "The United Nations and the Use of Force," <u>International Conciliation</u>, No. 532, March, 1961, pp. 325-81.

Cordier, Andrew W. "The Role of the Secretary General," in <u>Annual Review of the United Nations 1960-61</u>, ed. Richard N. Swift (New York: Oceana Publications, 1962).

"Cypriot Complaint Against Turkey," <u>International Organization</u>, XVIII (Spring, 1964), 478-85.

Goodrich, Leland M. "The Maintenance of International Peace and Security," <u>International Organization</u>, XIX (Summer, 1965), 429-44.

Gordon, King. "The U.N. in Cyprus," <u>International Journal</u>, XIX (Summer, 1964), 326-47.

Haas, Ernest B. "Types of Collective Security: An Examination of Operational Concepts," <u>American Political Science Review</u>, March, 1955, pp. 40-62.
;
Halderman, John W. "Legal Bases for United Nations Armed Forces," American Journal of International Law, Vol. 56, No. 4 (October, 1962), pp. 971-96.

Hoffman, Stanley. "In Search of a Thread: The U.N. in the Congo Labyrinth," International Organization, XVI (Spring, 1962), 331-61.

_____. "Sisyphus and the Avalanche: The United Nations, Egypt, and Hungary," International Organization, XI (Summer, 1957), 446-69.

Holmes, John W. "The Political and Philosophical Aspects of U.N. Security Forces," International Journal, Vol. XIX, No. 3 (Summer, 1964), pp. 292-307.

"Issues before the Nineteenth General Assembly," International Conciliation, No. 550, November, 1964, pp. 9-18.

Jackson, Elmore. "The Developing Role of the Secretary-General," International Organization, XI (Summer, 1957), 431-45.

Kotani, Hidejiro. "Peacekeeping: Problems for Smaller Countries," International Journal, XIX (Summer, 1964), 308-22.

Lefever, Ernest W. "The U.N. as a Foreign Policy Instrument: The Congo Crisis," in Foreign Policy in the Sixties: The Issues and the Instruments, ed. Roger Hilsman and Robert C. Good (Baltimore, Md.: The Johns Hopkins Press, 1965).

Martin, Paul. "Peace Keeping and the United Nations-- The Broader View," International Affairs, XL (April, 1964), 191-204.

Mezerik, A. G., (ed.). "The United Nations Emergency Force (UNEF)," International Review Service, III, No. 33 (May, 1957).

Miller, E. M. "Legal Aspects of the United Nations Action in the Congo," American Journal of International Law, LV (January, 1961), 1-28.

The New York Times. 1964-1968.

Nicholas, H. G. "Financing the U.N.: Pressures and Principles," The Reporter, Vol. XXXI, No. 12 (December 31, 1964), pp. 17-18.

Osgood, Robert E. An International Military Force
     in a Disarming and Disarmed World. Washington,
     D.C.: Institute for Defense Analysis (Research
     Paper P-2), 1963.

Pearson, Lester B. "Force for the U.N.," Foreign
     Affairs, XXXV (April, 1957), 395-404.

Rikhye, Major General I. J., Preparation and Training
     of United Nations Peace-Keeping Forces.   ("Adelphi
     Papers," No. 9.) London: Institute for Strategic
     Studies, April, 1964.

_____. United Nations Peace-Keeping Operations--
     Higher Conduct. International Information
     Center on Peace-keeping Operation Monograph No.
     1, May, 1967.

Russell, Ruth B. "Changing Patterns of Constitutional
     Development," International Organization, XIX
     (Summer, 1965), 410-25.

_____. "Development by the United Nations of
     Rules Relating to Peace-keeping," Proceedings
     of the Annual Meeting, American Society of
     International Law, April, 1965, 53-60.

_____. "United Nations Financing and 'The Law
     of the Charter,'" The Columbia Journal of
     Transnational Law, Vol. 5, No. 1 (1966), pp.
     68-95.

Schachter, Oscar. "Legal Issues," in Annual Review
     of the United Nations 1960-61, ed. Richard N.
     Swift (New York: Oceana Publications, 1962).

Skern, Lt. Col. L. M. K. Military Staffing at U.N.
     Headquarters for Peace-keeping Operations--A
     Proposal. Monograph No. 3; Paris: International
     Information Center on Peace-keeping Operations,
     July 3, 1967.

Stenqvist, Colonel Nils. The Swedish U.N. Stand-by
     Force and Experience. Monograph No. 4; Paris:
     International Information Center on Peace-keeping
     Operations August, 1967.

Sterling, Claire. "Cyprus: The Archbishop Can't
     Lose," The Reporter, Vol. XXX, No. 12 (June 4,
     1964), pp. 12-16.

Waern, Col. Jonas. "Diary of a U.N. Peacekeeper," _Saturday Review_,L (November 18, 1967), pp. 19-21, 55-56.

Wall, Michael. "Cyprus Problem = Makarios Problem," _The New York Times Magazine_, October, 18, 1964 pp. 38, 108-10.

Watkins, Brig. Gen. Tarleton H. "The Congo Airlift," _Air University Quarterly Review_,Summer, 1961, pp. 19-33.

Windsor, Philip. _NATO and the Cyprus Crisis_. ("Adelphi Papers," No. 14.) London: Institute for Strategic Studies, November, 1964.

Yost, Charles W. "The United Nations: Crisis of Confidence and Will," _Foreign Affairs_, VL, (October, 1966), 19-35.

Zacher, Mark W. "The Secretary-General and the United Nations' Function of Peaceful Settlement," _International Organization_, XX (Autumn, 1966), 724-49.

UNPUBLISHED MATERIAL

Ottawa Conference on Peace-keeping Operations. Unpublished working papers. Ottawa, 1964. (Mimeographed.)

Stegenga, James A. _The United Nations Force in Cyprus_. Ph.D. dissertation, University of California at Los Angeles, 1966, published by Ohio State University Press as a Mershon Program Publication, 1968.

INDEX

Congo, 54n, 105, 163, 216,
   background to U.N. action,
      20-22, 27-33, 41-44, 94
Congo, Republic of, 20-22, 28,
   31, 42, 43, 59-61, 62-63,
   85, 119, 163
   appeal to the U.N., 59-60,
      109
Conwell-Evans, T.P., 14n
Cordier, Andrew, 115n
Cottrell, Alvin J., 34n
Covenant, League. See League
   of Nations.
Cox, Arthur M., 14n, 182n
Cyprus (see also Greece; Greek
   Cypriot; Turkey; Turkish
   Cypriot; United Kingdom),
   3, 39, 54, 169, 216
   appeal to U.N., 47, 51, 64
   background to U.N. action,
      22-26, 27-33, 44-50, 62,
      63-64, 105-07
   guarantor powers, 24-25, 45-
      51, 63, 65, 101
   joint peace force, 46-50, 51,
      65, 101
   London Conference, 1964, 47-
      48, 50, 51, 65;
      mediation, 48, 91
   Security Council considera-
      tion, 47, 64-68, 92, 105,
      175
Cyprus, Government of, 31, 44-
   46, 47-49, 50, 64-66, 68,
   105
   appeal to U.N., 47, 64-65
Czechoslovakia, 68, 108
   arms to Egypt, 17, 21
Davies, Lord David, 74n
Dean, Sir Patrick, 53n
Denmark (see also Nordic
   countries), 104-05, 107, 108
   110, 123, 124
Disarmament, 12, 223
Eden, Sir Anthony, 19n, 52n
Egypt. See United Arab Re-
   public.
Eisenhower, Dwight D., 43
Elizabethville, 147
Enosis, 24, 46, 49
Ethiopia, 108, 109n, 109, 110
Field Operations Service, U.N.,
   129, 131, 135, 204
Financing. See Peace-keeping.
Finland (see also Nordic Count-
   ries), 105-07, 108, 110, 145
Foote, Wilder, 156n
France
   Middle East crisis of 1956,
      17-20, 29, 36-37, 38-40,
      41, 56-57, 163, 177

France (cont'd)
   position on peace-keeping,
      55-56, 68, 74, 165, 175-76
Frydenberg, Per, 182n, 210n
Frye, William R., 54n, 74n,
   115n, 223, 228n
General Assembly: Congo, 64,
   69;
   maintenance of peace, 8-9,
      55-59, 69-70, 71-74, 104,
      140-41, 165, 167-68, 188,
      215, 216-19
   Middle East crisis of 1956,
      57-59, 107-08, 119, 127,
      129, 145
Ghana, 109-10
Good, Robert C., 53n
Goodrich, Leland M., 13n, 14n,
   75n, 76n
Gordon, King, 75n, 98n, 115-
   16n, 156n, 210n
Great Powers
   Congo, 42-43, 63
   Cyprus, 50, 51, 65;
   Middle East crisis of 1956,
      17, 20, 39-41, 56-57
   role in maintenance of
      peace, 6, 7-8, 10, 70, 103,
      225
   role in peace-keeping oper-
      ations, 96, 110-11, 112,
      163, 217-18, 222-23
Greece (see also Cyprus), 6,
   54n, 93
   contingent in Cyprus, 47, 49,
      64, 105
   U.N. action in Cyprus, 22-
      26, 28, 47-50, 64-66, 104-05,
      169
Greek Cypriot, position in
   Cyprus dispute, 23-26, 28,
   45-47, 49-50
Grivas, George, 24
Guarantor powers. See Cyprus;
   Greece; Turkey, United King-
   dom.
Guinea, 109, 109n
Gyani, Lieutenant General P. S.,
   47, 105, 149
Halderman, John W., 76n
Hambro, Edvard, 76n
Hammarskjold, Dag, 60, 63, 96,
   109, 116n, 120, 145, 147,
   161-62, 178, 222, 229n
Hasluck, Paul, 164
Heathcote, Nina, 75n
Hilsman, Roger, 53n
Holmes, John W., 229n
Hungary, 18, 20, 40
Ignatieff, George, 99n

256

India (see also UNMOGIP;
  UNIPOM), 108, 109, 110, 114,
  145
Indonesia (see also West Irian;
  UNTEA), 6, 33, 54n, 81, 85-
  86, 93, 108, 173, 175, 215
International Court of Justice
  (ICJ), 69-70, 171, 174, 176
International Information
  Center on Peace-Keeping
  Operations, 13, 137n
International police force, 5,
  12, 54, 223
Iran, 108, 110, 186n
Ireland, 102-03, 105-07, 109,
  110, 123-24, 133n, 180, 186n
  proposal on financing, 117n
Israel (see also Middle East),
  16-20, 29, 36-37, 38, 41,
  56, 163
Italy, 109, 186n, 204
Jackson, Elmore, 228n
Johnson, Lyndon B., 51
Jordan, 30, 55n
Kashmir (see also UNMOGIP;
  UNIPOM), 6, 54n, 81, 87, 97,
  173, 215, 219
Katanga, 42, 61, 119, 147
Koho, Lieutenant Colonel Lauri,
  142
Korea, 6, 7, 12, 54n, 55n, 70,
  81, 82, 95, 96, 174-75
Kotani, Hidejaro, 115n
Kuznetsov, V.V., 69
Laos, 30, 55n, 108
League of Nations, 3, 6-7, 54
Lebanon (see also UNOGIL), 6,
  30, 54n, 83-84, 93, 94-95,
  96, 97, 216
Lefever, Ernest W., 13n, 53n,
  210n
Liberia, 109n, 109-10
Libya, 29, 109n
Lie, Trygve, 104, 223
Linner, Sture, 89
London Conference of 1964.
  See Cyprus.
London-Zurich Agreements. See
  Zurich Agreements.
Lumumba, Patrice, 109
Makarios, Archbishop, 25, 47,
  48, 49-50, 51
Malaysia, 110, 123-24
Mali, 110
Malta, 186n
Martin, Paul, 10, 14n, 164
Martola, General A.E., 149
Middle East, 13n, 302; back-
  ground for U.N. action, 16-
  20, 27-33

Middle East, (cont'd)
  crisis of 1956, 5-6, 16-20,
    36-41, 58-59, 163, 169, 217
  crisis of 1967, 37n, 55n, 87,
    219
Military Adviser to the Sec-
  retary-General, 141-42, 145,
  189-90, 193, 195, 197, 198,
  201, 202, 207, 209, 220
Military Airlift Command (MAC),
  205
Military Staff Committee, 140,
  142, 191, 309
Miller, E.M., 75n
Mixed Armistice Commission
  (MAC), 17
Morocco, 109n, 109-10
Nasser, Gamal Abdel, 17, 19n,
  20, 29, 40, 41
National Citizens Commission,
  White House Conference on
  Peace-Keeping, 10, 14n
Netherlands, 33, 85, 175;
  earmarking, 101-02, 110, 113,
  186n, 221
New Zealand, 108, 186n
Nigeria, 110
Nordic countries, 101, 103,
  113, 166, 169, 170, 186n, 221
North Atlantic Treaty Organ-
  ization (NATO), 41, 47, 49-
  51, 169
Norway (see also Nordic coun-
  tries), 104-05, 108, 110, 145
Norwegian Institute of Inter-
  national Affairs, 166
O'Brien, Conor Cruise, 147,
  156n, 210n
ONUC. See U.N. Force in Congo.
Organization of African States
  (OAU), 170
Organization of American
  States (OAS), 170
Ottawa Conference on Peace-
  Keeping, 1964, 122n
Pakistan (see also UNMOGIP;
  UNIPOM), 85, 108, 110, 145
Palestine (see also Middle
  East), 29, 54n
Peace-keeping (see also spec-
  ific operations, e.g., U.N.
  Force in Cyprus; Special
  Committee on Peace-Keeping
  Operations): advance plan-
  ning, 5n, 27-28, 33, 95,
  112-13, 169, 185-86, 189-90,
  199-202, 221, 224 advisory
  committee, 141, 145, 219;
  authorization, 55-56, 71, 74
  characteristics, 93-98

Secretary-General (cont'd)
  peace-keeping role, 9, 55-56,
    69, 70-71, 72-74, 85-87,
    96, 100-01, 136, 140-43,
    147-48, 161-62, 167-68,
    188-89, 191, 215, 216,
    218-20
Security Council:
  Congo, 28, 59-62, 64, 84, 88,
    108-09, 120-21, 147;
  Cyprus, 3, 47, 48, 59, 64-
    71, 90, 92, 99n, 105-06,
    175-76
  enforcement role, 6, 62, 66-
    67, 69, 103-04, 224-25
  maintenance of peace, 6-8, 9,
    54-55n, 55-57, 58, 61-64,
    70-73, 103-04, 140-41,
    164-65, 167-68, 188, 191,
    215, 216, 218-20, 225
  Middle East crisis of 1956,
    56-57, 59
Senegal, 110
Sierra Leone, 110
Simons, Anne P., 75n, 76n
Sinai, 17, 18, 36, 37
Skern, Lieutenant Colonel
  L.M.K., 210n
Sohn, Louis B., 223
Soviet Union, 7, 196, 218,
  223, 225;
  Congo, 43, 63, 69, 109;
  Cyprus, 23, 65, 68-71, 175-
    76
  Middle East crisis of 1956,
    17, 18, 20, 40-41, 57, 69
  position on peace-keeping
    55-56, 68-71, 74, 164-65,
    175-76
Special Committee on Peace-
  Keeping Operations (Com-
  mittee of 33), 74, 167-68,
  216
Stegenga, James A., 13n
Stenqvist, Col. Nils, 137n
Stevenson, Adlai, 181n
Stoessinger, John G., 182n,
  183n
Sweden (see also Nordic
  countries), 105-08, 109,
  110
Swift, Richard N., 228n
Sudan, 109n
Suez. See Middle East; Suez
  Canal.
Suez Canal (see also Middle
  East), 17, 19n, 20, 31, 37n,
  37-38, 39, 87
Taksim, 46, 50
Thailand, 55n, 104-05

Thant, U., 90, 96, 100, 105,
  148, 180, 222
Tondel, Lyman M. Jr., 53n,
  116n, 156n
Treaty of Alliance (Cyprus).
  See Zurich Agreements.
Treaty of Guarantee (Cyprus).
  See Zurich Agreements.
Treaty of Lausanne, 23
Trieste, 55n
Trudeau, Pierre, 181n
Tunisia, 109-10
Turkey (see also Cyprus):
  contingent in Cyprus, 47,
    49, 64, 101;
  U.N. action in Cyprus, 22-
    26, 28, 47-50, 64-66, 101,
    105, 169
Turkish Cypriot, position in
  Cyprus dispute, 23-26, 28,
  45, 46-47, 49-50
Union of Soviet Socialist
  Republics. See Soviet Union.
United Arab Republic (UAR):
  Congo, 109n, 110
  Cyprus, 23, 24
  Middle East crisis of 1956,
    16-20, 29, 31, 36-41, 163,
    177
United Kingdon (see also Cyp-
  rus), 196;
  Congo, 109;
  Cyprus, 3, 23-25, 46-49, 65,
    96, 101, 105-07, 110, 133,
    149, 180, 204, 311;
  Middle East crisis of 1956,
    17-20, 29, 36-37, 38-40,
    41, 56-57, 163, 177
  position on peace-keeping,
    110, 186n
United Nations (see also Char-
  ter; General Assembly; Sec-
  retariat; Secretary-General;
  Security Council):
  Congo, 42, 43, 44, 59-64;
  Cyprus, 44, 45, 47, 48-50,
    51-52, 62-71, 101, 105
  Field Service, 104
  Guard Force, 104
  maintenance of peace, 5n, 6-
    10, 16, 30, 32-33, 36, 52,
    54-56, 94, 95-96, 103-04,
    118, 140-44, 162-63, 167-
    68, 215-17, 220-21, 224-
    25, 226-28
  Middle East crisis of 1956,
    38, 40-41, 56-59
U.N. Emergency Force (UNEF),
  4, 5n, 9, 13n, 54, 94, 166,
  202-03n, 217, 218, 220, 226,
  227

ABOUT THE AUTHOR

    James M. Boyd served as Deputy U.S. Air Force
Representative and Chief of Staff, U.N. Military
Staff Committee, from 1965-69. Colonel Boyd's Air
Force background includes positions as Representative
at the State Department Senior Seminar in Foreign
Policy, 1963-64; Deputy Assistant Director of Plans,
and Division Chief of Plans, Policy Division. He
was U.S. Air Attache in Cairo, 1956-59.

    Colonel Boyd is a graduate of the Air War College,
and was Research Associate at the Institute of War
and Peace Studies at Columbia University prior to
assuming his positions at the U.N. He holds a Ph.D.
in Political Science from Columbia.